IMAGES
of America

SEBRING
OHIO

IMAGES
of America

SEBRING
OHIO

Craig S. Bara

ARCADIA
PUBLISHING

ISBN 978-0-7385-0180-2

Published by Arcadia Publishing
Charleston, South Carolina

Printed in the United States of America

Library of Congress Control Number: 2007938737

For all general information, please contact Arcadia Publishing:
Telephone 843-853-2070
Fax 843-853-0044
E-mail sales@arcadiapublishing.com
For customer service and orders:
Toll-Free 1-888-313-2665

Visit us on the Internet at www.arcadiapublishing.com

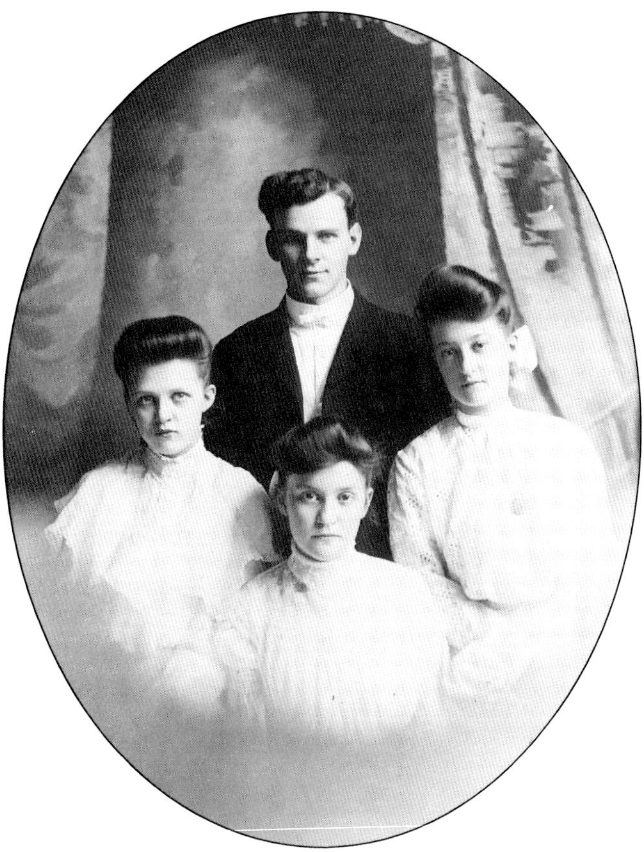

The first graduating class (1904) at the Ohio Avenue School is shown in this photograph. Earl McIntosh is represented along with (left to right) Gertrude Beggs, Gladys Lamborn Barkley, and Ella B. Larkins.

Contents

ACKNOWLEDGMENTS

My interest in Sebring's history began when I was very young. I attended the Faith United Presbyterian Church and could not help but notice the big, white Sebring mansion across the street. I was awestruck. I was intrigued by its grandeur and yearned to know about the people who lived within its walls. That childhood intrigue was a spark that ignited a blaze, which ultimately led to this book. Over the years, there have been many people whose life experiences and memories helped lay the foundation for my interest in Sebring. My Uncle Charles and Aunt Hazel Strain, and my Grandfather Ruskin M. Strain were great contributors of factual information and guided my quest as I delved into the rich history of this fine community. My friend Betty Turkle Donaldson, age 92, also contributed greatly to my research, thanks to her marvelous memory. Her lifelong friendship with members of the Sebring family adds tremendous flavor to this book.

I want to express my sincere gratitude to Mayor Daphne Cannell for her years of work as president of the Sebring Historical Society. Through her leadership, many photographs and relevant historic materials have been preserved for future generations. She was a tremendous help to me during the development of this book. My thanks to two very talented people, Phillip Gehm and Jennifer Mastroianni, for their hours of proofreading and creative suggestions.

The Sebring Historical Society is grateful to the many people who have donated pictures and materials to the Society over the years. I would like to thank the following individuals who loaned photographs and reference material for this book: Frank Barrett, Grace Woods Kuniewicz, Vaunda Gorby, Sebring United Methodist Church, Irene and Stanley Sams, Winifred Bryarly, Jane Zang, Paul and Edith Hetrick, R. Brent Johnston, Roger and Marilyn Johnston, Ethel Preston, and Max "Meether." Finally, sincere appreciation to my parents June and Joseph Bara and my brother Brian Bara for their help.

INTRODUCTION

The Sebring family relocated from the Netherlands to Pennsylvania. George E. and his wife Elizabeth Larkins Sebring eventually settled in East Liverpool where they ran a grocery business. They had ten children: Oliver Howard 1857–1929, George Eugene 1859–1927, Ellsworth Henry 1861–1937, Joseph 1862–1890, Eva 1865–1956 and Frank Albert 1865–1936 (twins), Frederick E. 1868–1925, William Henry 1870–1904, and Emma 1872–1957 and Charles 1872–1877 (twins).

The Sebring family decided to find property to build a pottery town, as they had been involved in potteries in East Liverpool and East Palestine. They settled on 200 acres of farmland near the Mahoning River with the railroad running through the property. After much work of starting a new town, the Articles of Incorporation were filed in 1899, and a clause in the deed forbade the sale of intoxicating beverages. The streets were numbered and the avenues bore the names of the States of the Union. Potteries and homes were built, and Sebring became a flourishing town, which at one time was considered the pottery center of the world.

This pictorial history is not in a specific chronological order but structured more as to content as titled in each chapter. The purpose of this book is to show a visual history of the different aspects of Sebring's growth as we celebrate 100 years, 1899–1999. We hope this book strikes a memory or a thought long forgotten as you enjoy its pictures and the commentary. This book is not intended to give a full or complete history, for it is of early events and people, rather than current times. We must understand the past to connect us with the current as well as the future.

Daphne Cannell
Mayor—Sebring, Ohio
President—Sebring Historical Society

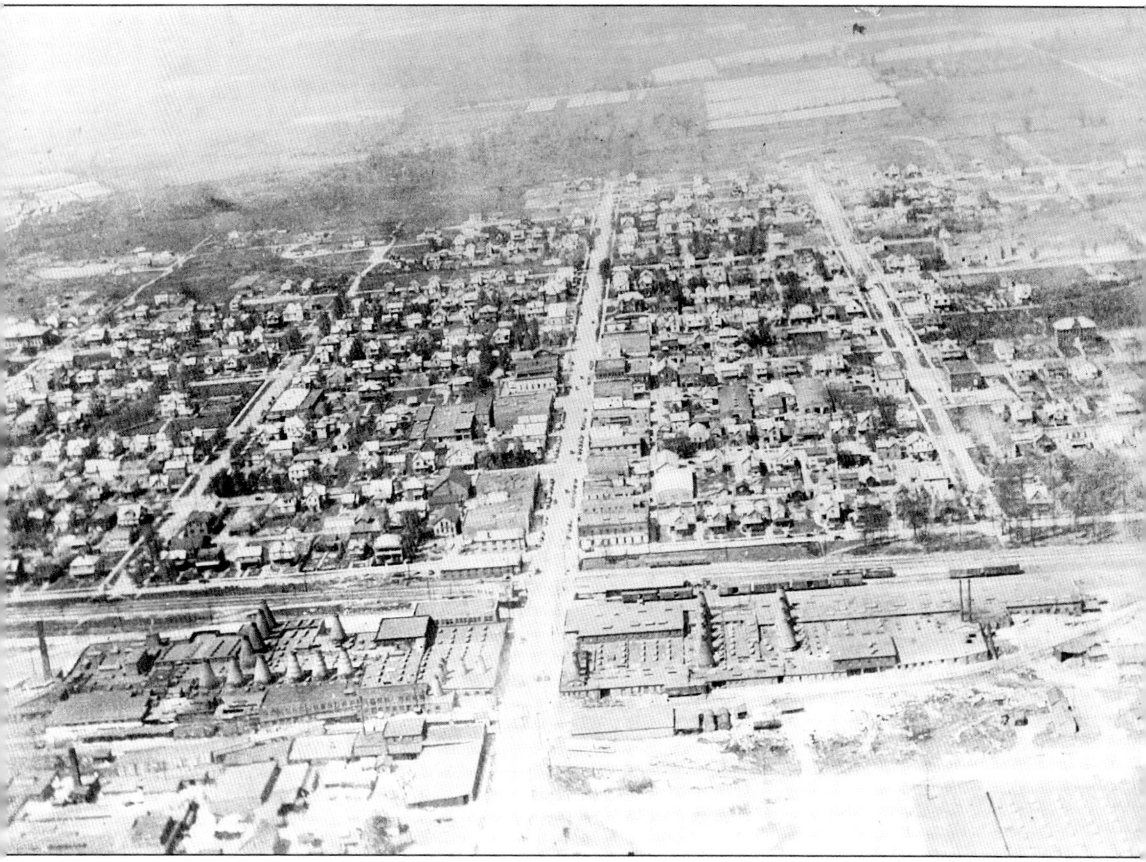

Shown here is an aerial view of Sebring, Ohio, in the 1920s. The focal point of the picture is Fifteenth Street. The lower portion of this image shows South Fifteenth Street along with the Sebring Pottery Company and the E.H. Sebring Pottery Company. The photograph extends from North Seventeenth Street (Lincoln School), at the extreme left, to North Fourteenth Street on the right, where the Ohio Avenue School is visible. When this photograph was taken, the community was at the peak of success in the pottery industry.

One

Molding a Community

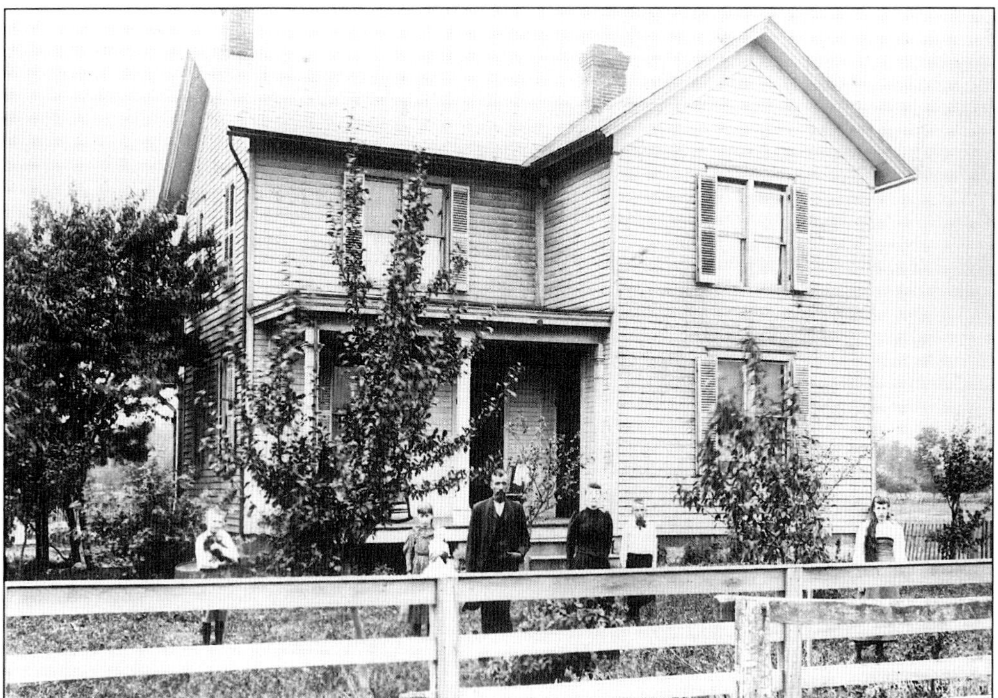

Stephen and Lizzie Gray and family stand in front of their home in the late 1890s on what is now West Ohio Avenue. Numerous farms were located on what became the thriving community of Sebring. In April 1898, the Sebring Land Company was incorporated for $50,000. Within a few days, much of the land that also included the farmland of Jacob and Margaret Biery, William and Sarah Johnson, and I.B. and Alfretta Heacock was purchased at $50 an acre. The Sebring family felt this location fit the criteria (railroad, interurban, and water supply) necessary to build their industry and the community. The story that clay was the reason this site was selected is a myth. The Alliance Review announced on May 9, 1898, that the new community east of Alliance would be named Sebring.

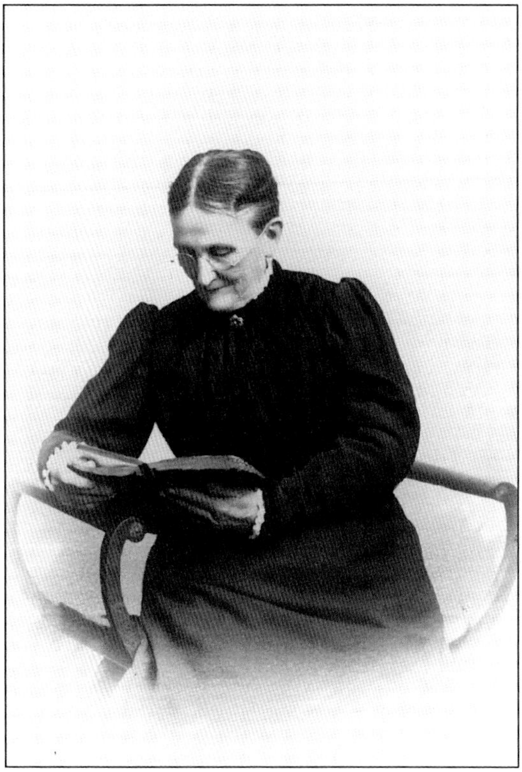

Sebring, Ohio, certainly proves that a community can have a mother and father. George E. (1834–1915) and Elizabeth Larkins (1836–1910) Sebring Sr. were the spirit and drive behind their sons' and daughters' success in the pottery business as well as the development of our village. They endured a move in the winter of their lives to a new and uncertain future, but deep down they had confidence that their children and grandchildren would succeed.

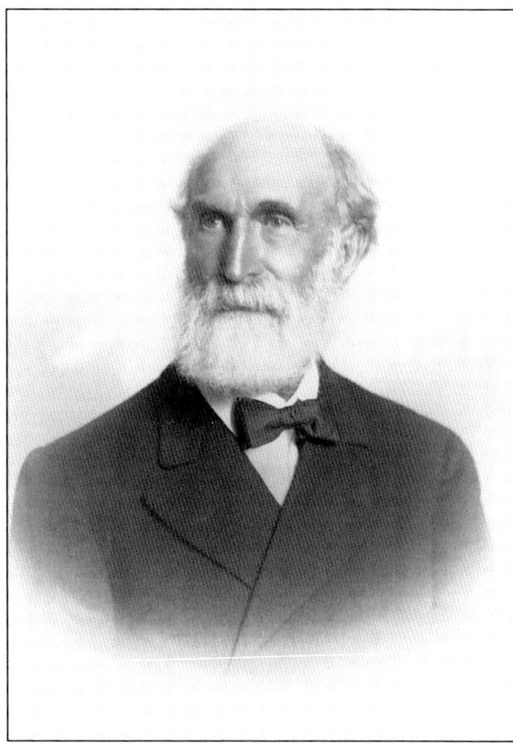

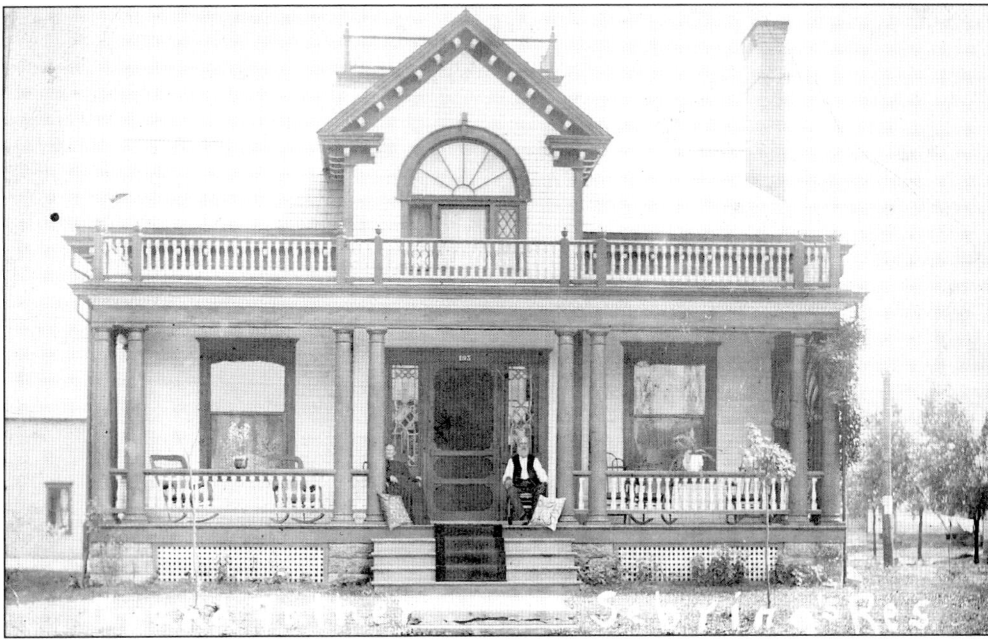

Built by the Sebring children for their parents, George E. and Elizabeth Larkins Sebring Sr. (seated on the porch), this lovely home stood on the southeast corner of West Ohio Avenue and Sixteenth Street. The post-Victorian- (Edwardian) style house is an eclectic style of architecture, which became prevalent in this small community. The back of this photo postcard is postmarked September 24, 1910. The note to Mrs. Clara Merrick Faloon of Hanoverton reads: "Dear Clara, this picture was taken the day grandma Sebring took sick. She died such a sweet death." Today, the Sebring Public Library is located on this site.

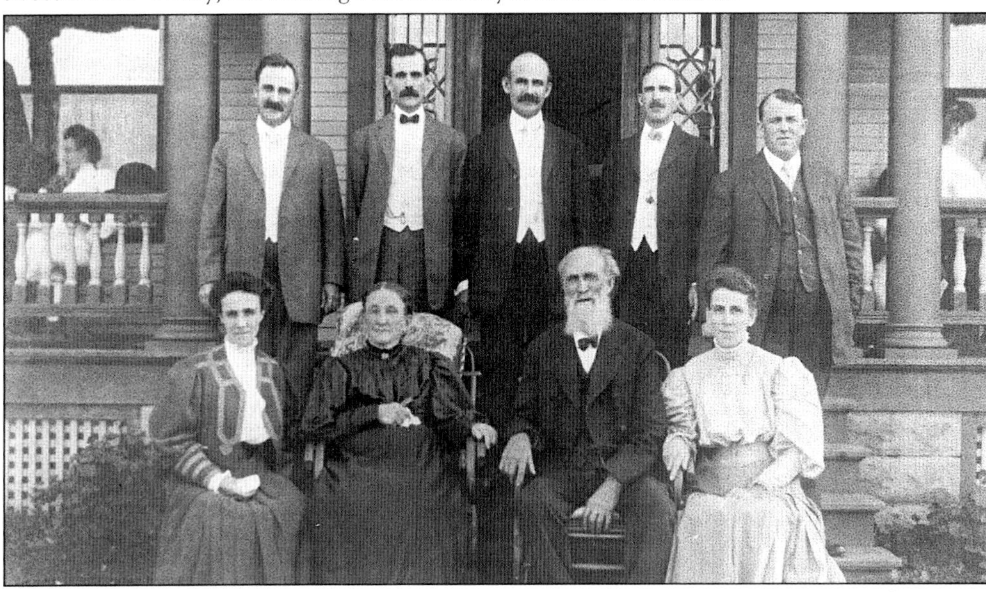

The Sebring family pose in front of George and Elizabeth's home *c.* 1905. Shown in this image, from left to right, are as follows: (seated) Mrs. Emma Sebring Albright Barclay, Elizabeth Larkins Sebring, George E. Sebring Sr., and Mrs Eva Sebring Norris; (standing) Frank A. Sebring, Oliver H. Sebring, George E. Sebring Jr., Ellswoth H. Sebring, and Fred Sebring.

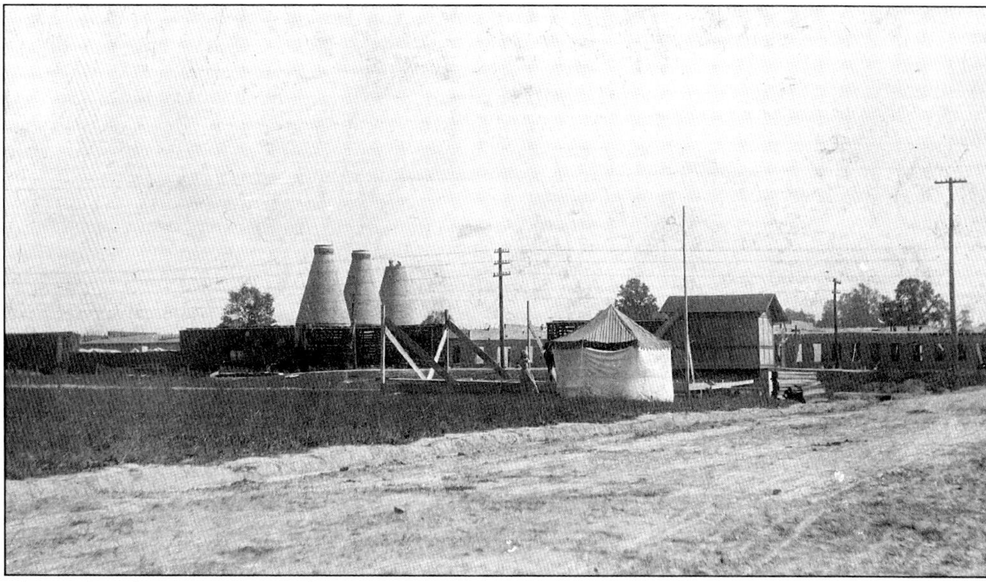

The earliest known picture of a pottery plant in the Sebring Historical Society archives depicts the construction of the Oliver China Company. This photograph was taken by Nesbitt Studios of Alliance, Ohio, in August 1899. Named in honor of Oliver Sebring, the plant was the first to be built in the community and became the site of the Royal China Company in the 1930s.

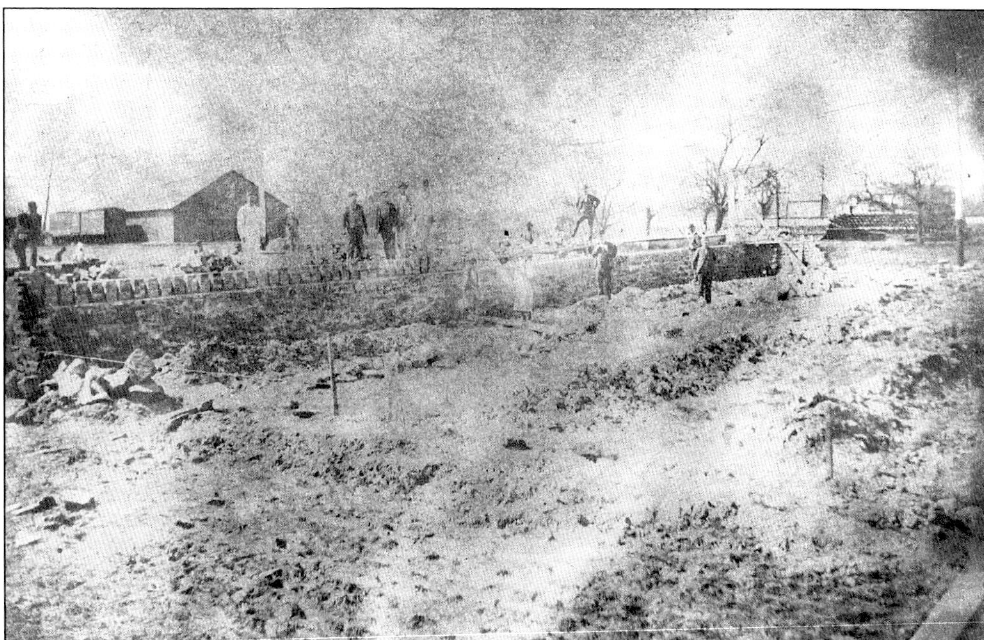

This poorly developed, but historically significant, photograph shows the first bricks being laid for the Sebring Pottery Company on April 19, 1900. The frame building in the background, on the left, is the Biery Brothers Livery and Transfer.

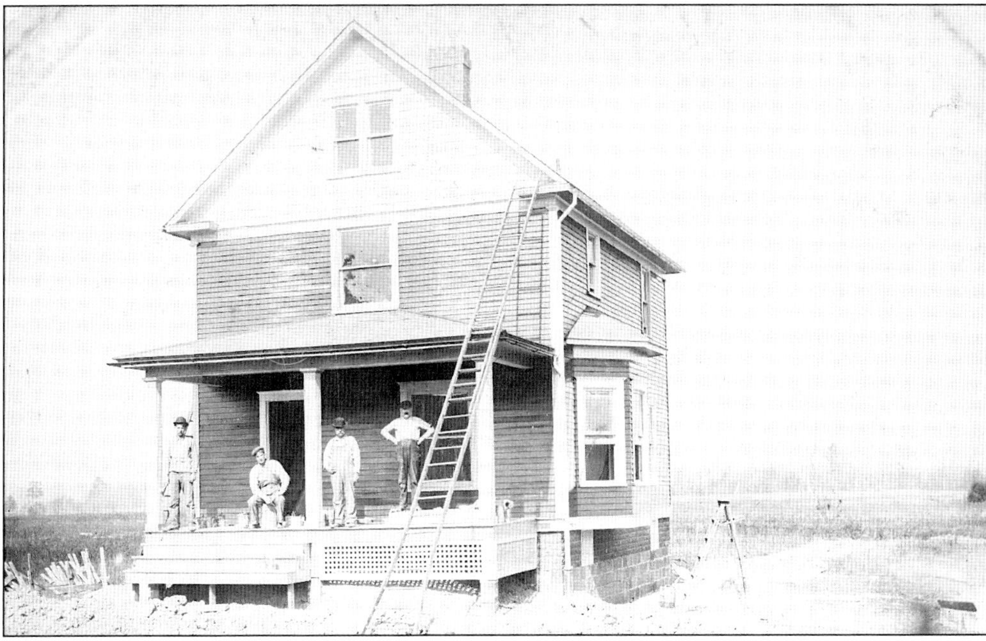

Various advertisements by local builders in the early development of the village offered homes from $500 to $5,000. Some of the early builders were W.F. Scott, Wetzel and Leiner, and John Gamble. The exact location of the home pictured here is unknown. This picture postcard is addressed to Miss Ruth Scott of East Palestine, from R.S. of Sebring in October 1909.

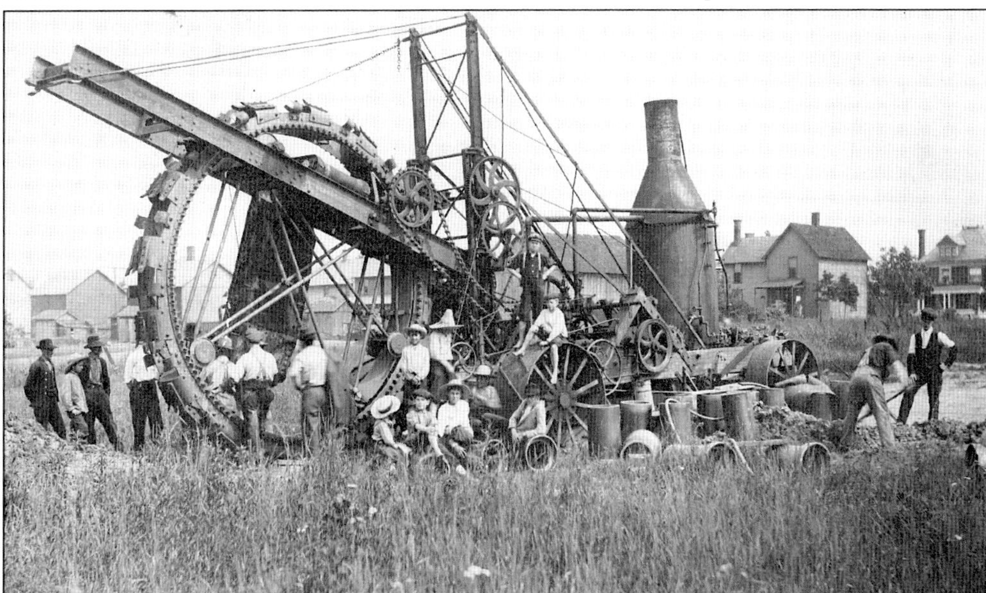

Because Sebring was developed on low and flat ground, drainage was a considerable problem during the early years. The trencher, which was powered by steam, was a tremendous help in the lying of drainage tile. This photograph was taken in the vicinity of what was later Maryland Avenue, between Eighteenth and Nineteenth Streets. Ohio Avenue is in the background. The large home, on the far right, is the W.L Murphy residence, between Seventeenth and Eighteenth Streets.

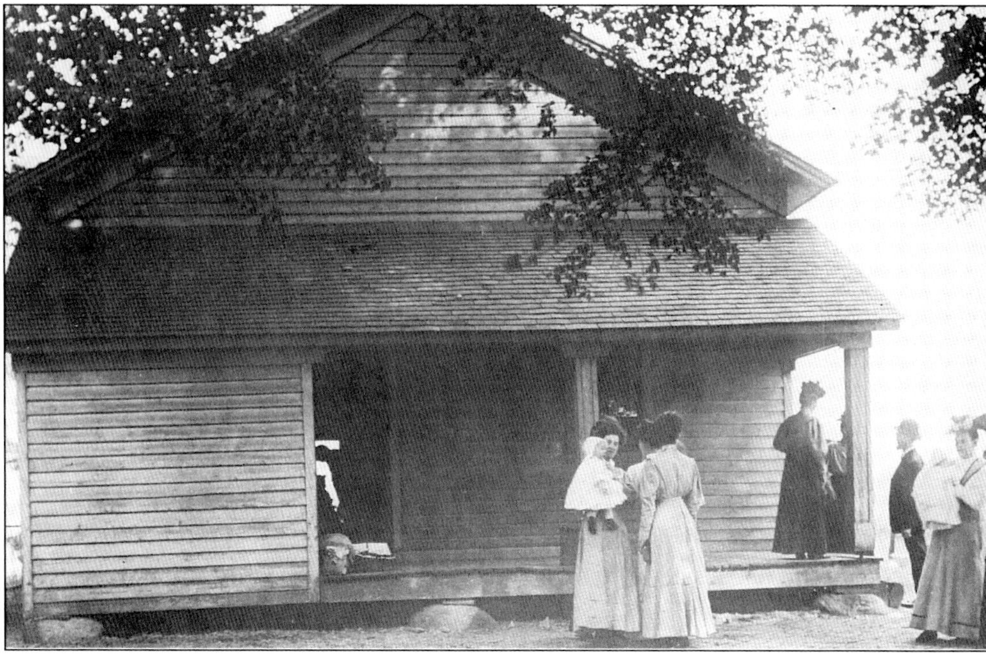

Many years before Sebring existed, a small group of people settled in the forest near the Maple Ridge School and developed the land for farming. On a hill nearby, the settlers built a small frame structure for worship. The Friends' Meeting House on "Quaker Hill," shown in this 1890s photograph, still stands today next to the Quaker burial ground.

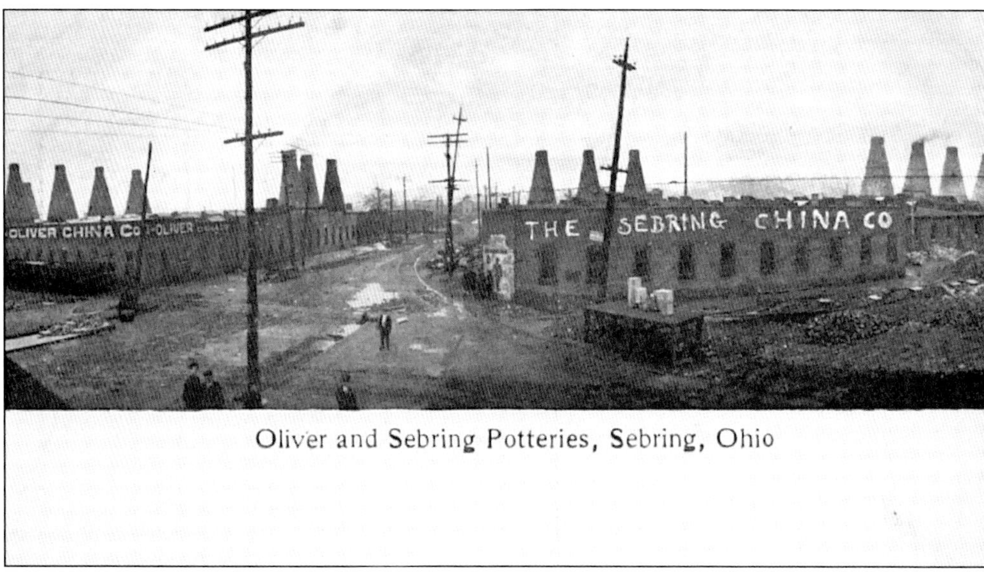

This postcard shows the Oliver China Company and the Sebring Pottery Company, with its hastily painted sign, shortly after their completion. The Sebrings knew the importance of advertising. The potteries were built close to the railroad tracks not only for the convenience of shipping and receiving, but also for the viewing of the hundreds of passengers who traveled on one of the nation's busiest rail lines. If you look carefully you can see Stark Electric's interurban rail tracks making the bend around the east side of the Sebring Pottery building.

Two

SMOKING BEEHIVES

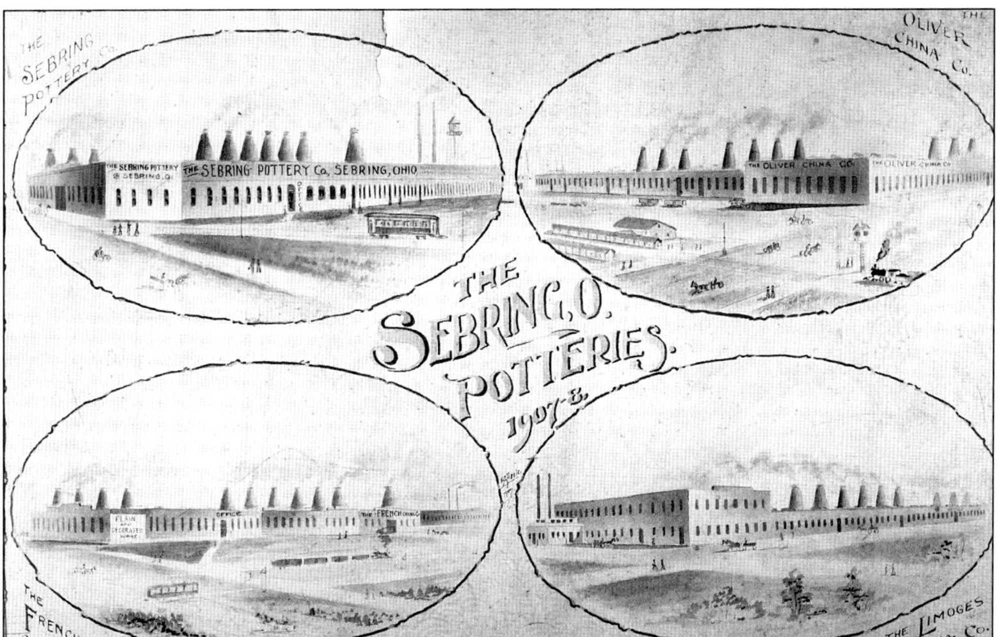

Shown here is an artist's conception of the four major potteries in Sebring, Ohio, between 1907 and 1908. By this time, the community had already established a reputation throughout the nation for its high-grade premium china. Most tables in homes, hotels, and churches east of the Mississippi were set with the European touch of American Limoges or the gold-trimmed lace of a French China plate.

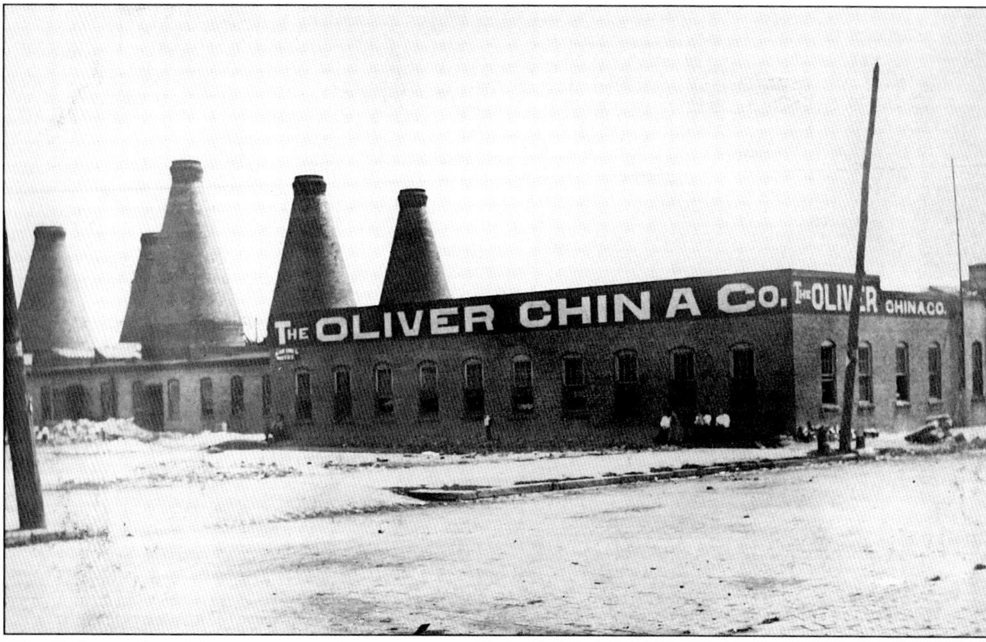

The Sebring family's success in the pottery trade can be traced back to East Liverpool, Ohio, in the late 1880s. By the 1890s, this modest business grew into three major plants. George soon ventured off to East Palestine, Ohio, to operate the East Palestine Pottery Company. His success enabled the community to raise funds to build the Ohio China Company. It was through this investment that the Sebrings were able to erect the Oliver China Company in 1899, in Sebring, Ohio, with O.H. Sebring as its owner, thus establishing a new community. Soon afterward, O.H.'s brother George E. took over the plant placing his son Orval in the position of manager. By 1908, George E. was planning out a new community in Florida, and he sold the plant to his brother Ellsworth, who changed the name to The E.H. Sebring China Company, which operated until the crash of 1929. In 1934, the plant was purchased for $30,000, through a Youngstown bank, by Beatrice L. Miller, John Briggs, and William Habenstreit. The new enterprise opened as The Royal China Company.

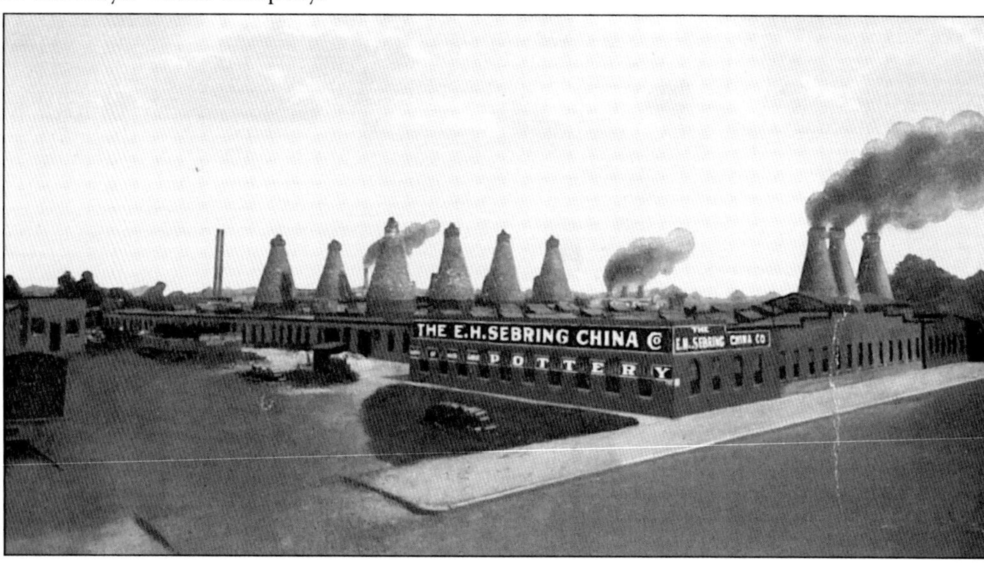

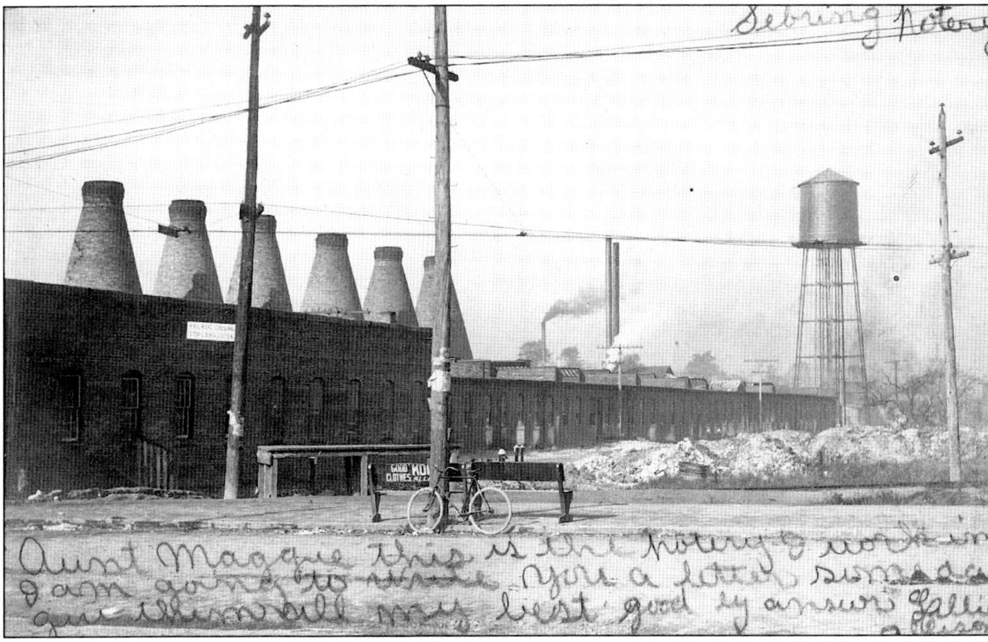

In 1887, the Sebring Pottery Company began operation in East Liverpool, Ohio, in the old Agner & Gaston plant. The six brothers and two sisters were involved in all aspects of the business. After a successful decade, the family moved the business to their new plant in the recently formed community that bore their name. The company operated under the direction of Frank A. Sebring. This plant, which was located on the corner of Fifteenth Street and California Avenue, remained in operation until the late 1920s or early 1930s. The building was purchased by J. Harrison Keller, who rented a portion of the building to the Stanford Pottery Company in the mid-1940s. The Sebring Container Company also occupied space in the building. Because the building was hastily and poorly constructed, part of the building was torn down; however, the entire structure was destroyed by fire in 1960.

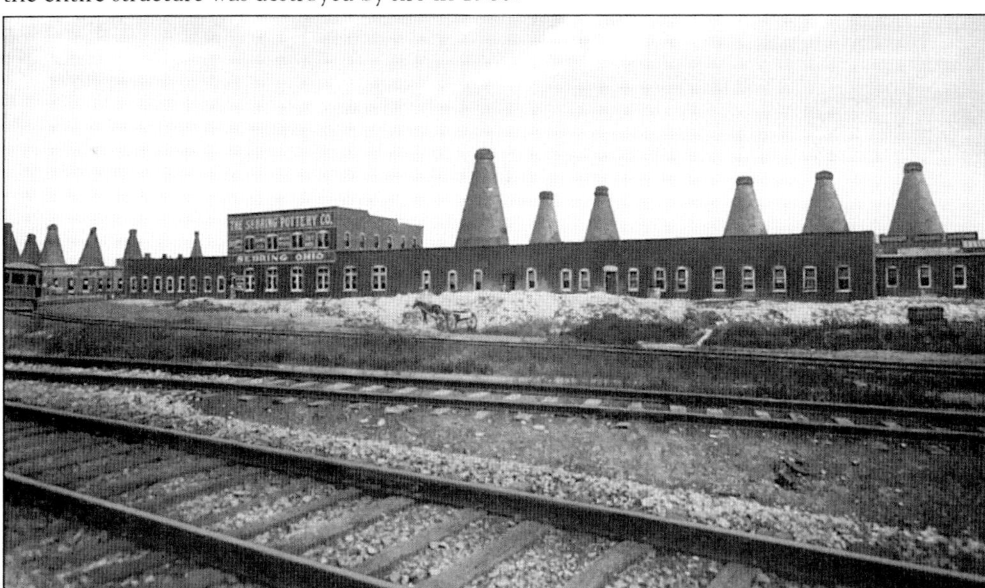

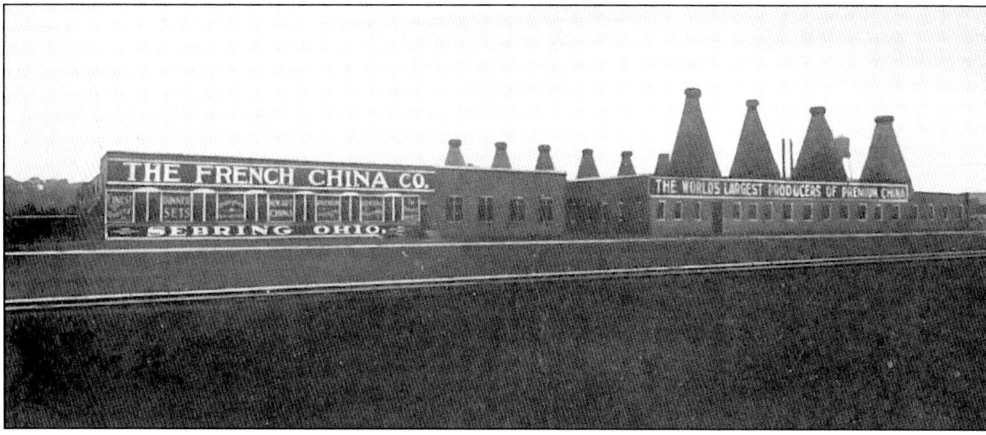

The French China Company was established in 1898 in East Liverpool, Ohio, and it was moved to Sebring at the turn of the century. As advertised on the building, they were the "World's Largest Producers of Premium China." O.H. Sebring took control of this plant in 1916 and formed a holding company called The Sebring Manufacturing Corporation. A bond issue was put into place, and a merchandising plan was set into motion that offered their wares to merchants in the competitive retail field. In 1927, through the urging of a very successful sales distributor named Louis Porter, Mr. Sebring was convinced the newly formed corporation would have a smooth ride to Wall Street. The Crash of 1929 brought this dream to an abrupt end. Through the efforts of the American Chinaware Corporation, a holding company, bonds were secured by several Chicago and Cleveland banks to pay off the mortgage bonds. However, by 1933, the Sebring Manufacturing Corporation went into receivership with the stockholders, losing their entire investments, while the bondholders and creditors recouped about 3 percent of their funds.

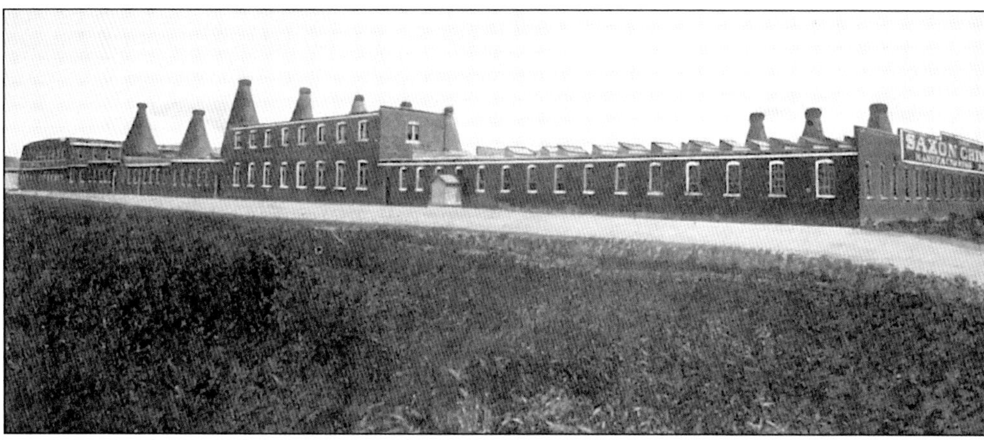

In 1911, the Saxon China Company began operation under the leadership of Fred Sebring, with some assistance from his brother Ellsworth. The plant was sold to Oliver H. Sebring in 1916, giving his son-in-law, Ray Cliff, the opportunity to manage his own business. The plant continued operating until 1932. On April 4, 1934, W.V. Oliver purchased the Saxon plant from the bondholders and, betting on the good name of the old French China Company, organized the French-Saxon China Company. After remodeling, the plant started operations in November 1934 on a very small scale. With the installation of four Allied circular kilns and an eight-line automatic jigger machine in the 1940s, the plant produced nearly 600 dozen pieces of ware per hour. After Mr. Oliver's death, Royal China bought the capital stock in 1964, and operated it as a separate entity for several years.

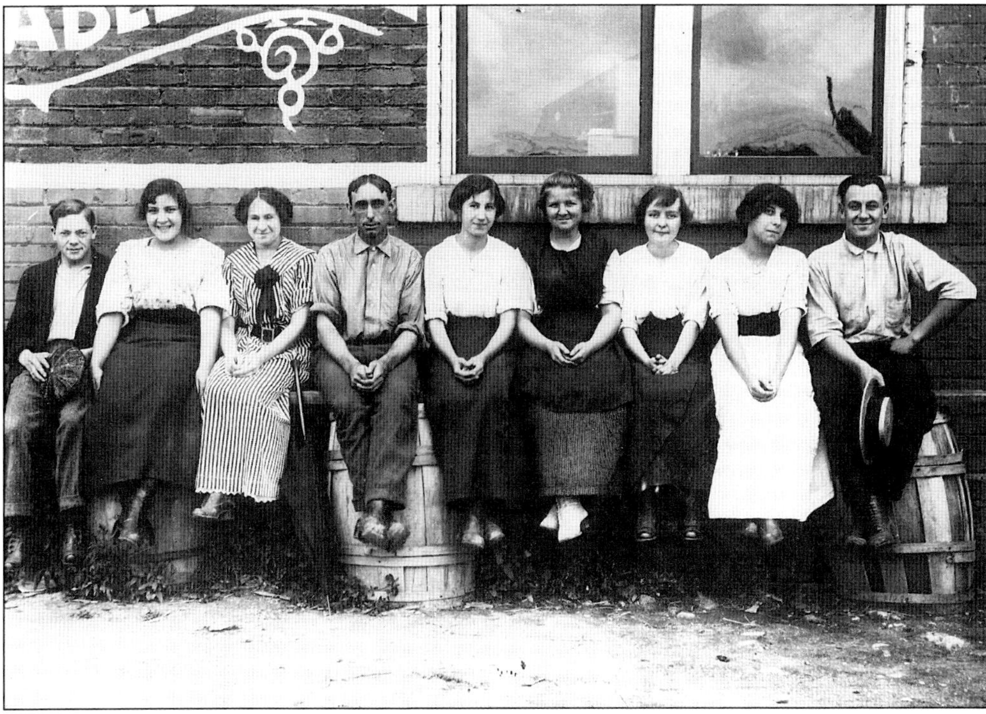

The liners and stampers of the French China Company pose in front of the plant around 1910. The names of the individuals are marked on the back. Time, however, has made some of the names almost illegible. Shown here, from left to right, are as follows: Charles Sherrow, Bertha Karlen Toban, Kathryn Shivley Carner, Homer Rhuderbaugh ?, Gladys Wright Wymer, Flora Buehler Cochran, Alice Twimer Schook, Bessie Cordingly Lower, and Frank Cartwright.

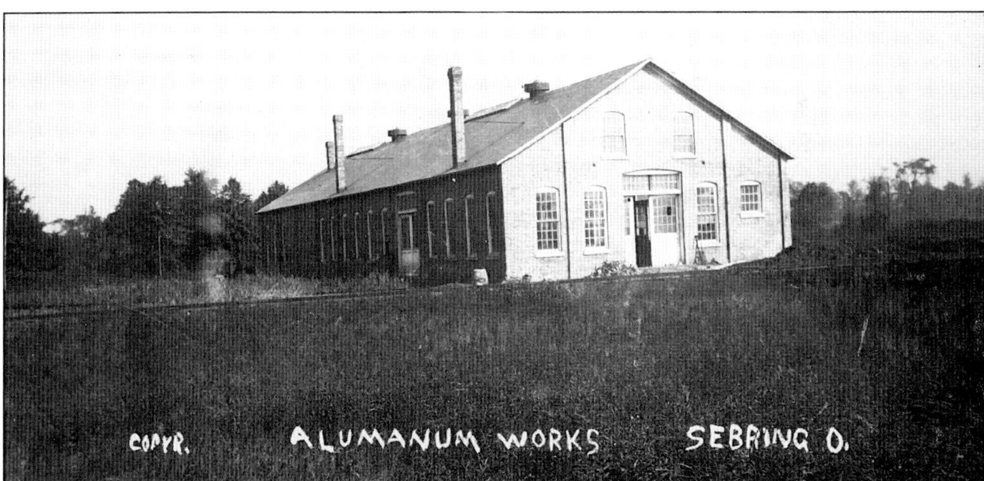

The Aluminum Works (note the spelling error) of Sebring was located on California Avenue and Seventeenth Street, just east of the French Pottery. Little is known of the company. The more famous Strong Manufacturing Company, which is detailed in this chapter, is the only aluminum company mentioned in the various papers and publications on Sebring's history.

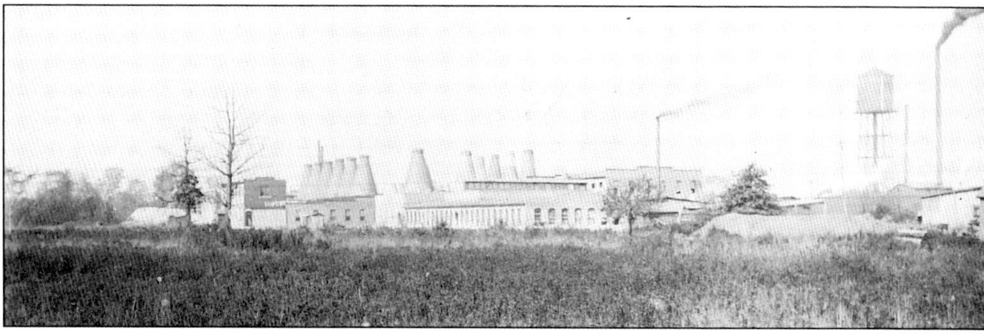

Formed by Frank A. Sebring, The Limoges China Company was established to recreate the fine porcelain china, which had been established in Limoges, France. Originally called The Sterling China Company and later the Sebring China Company, the pottery struggled due to the lack of sales. After a devastating fire in its third year of operation, the company regrouped under the leadership of Frank's brother Fred, and production of earthenware and semi-porcelain began. The first tunnel kilns, which replaced the beehive kilns, were used in this plant. Decal transfers, which are commonplace in the pottery industry today, replaced hand-painted methods of decorating and made their debut in America at this plant. According to excerpts from an article in *Engineering Experiment Station News* published by Ohio State University, "The American pottery industry originally followed, very closely, English methods of manufacture. English raw materials were used almost entirely in the original American potteries. The infant Limoges China Company demonstrated that American manufacturing methods, combined with American raw materials, could produce the equal, if not the superior of any earthware products manufactured elsewhere in the world." Sebring, Ohio, had established itself as the leader in the pottery industry.

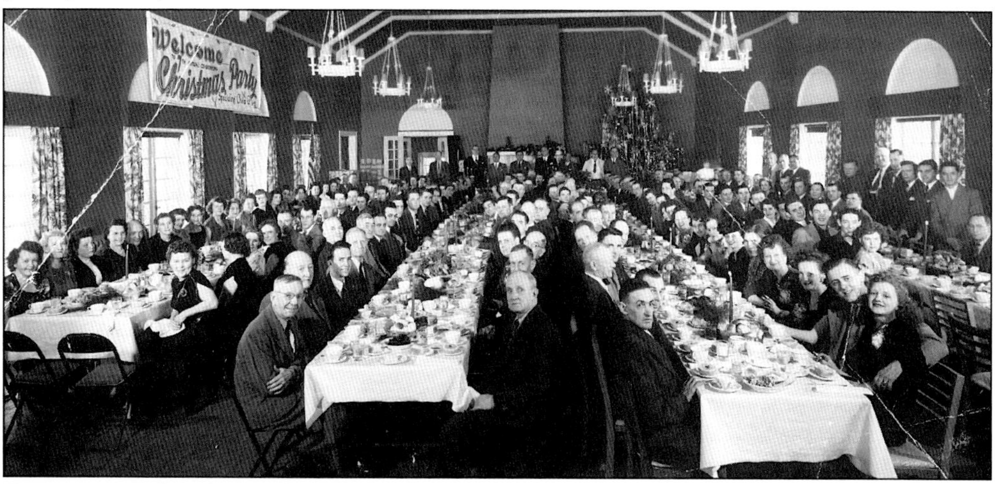

To many outside Sebring, the Spaulding China Company is not recognized by its incorporated name. It is comprised of the trademark names, Royal Copley and Royal Windsor, which overshadow its existence. Beginning in a garage on East Ohio Avenue in 1939, the company eventually employed over 200, and distribution of its ceramic artware encompassed the United States, Europe, and Canada. In today's collector's market, Royal Copley is considered by many to be the most recognized product ever created in Sebring. The airbrush style and brilliant colors created by Spaulding's art director, Miss Margaret Kadisch, are the reasons a flowerpot or coin bank that sold at Woolworth's 5 & 10 command a high price at antique shows and auctions . This photograph of the Seventh Annual Christmas Party was taken on December 10, 1948, at the Alliance Country Club.

Sebring citizens are shown here celebrating the victory in Europe and Japan. Like many communities, Sebring held a parade after V.E. Day and V.J. Day in 1945. This picture shows Buddy Grindley, Art Grindley, Al Flickinger, Freeda Snyder, and other employees of the Grindley Artware Manufacturing Company carrying the United States flag down West Ohio Avenue.

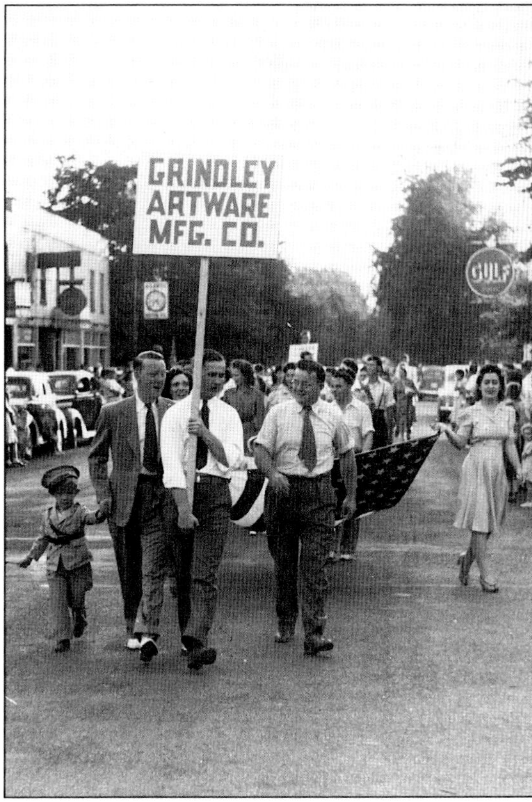

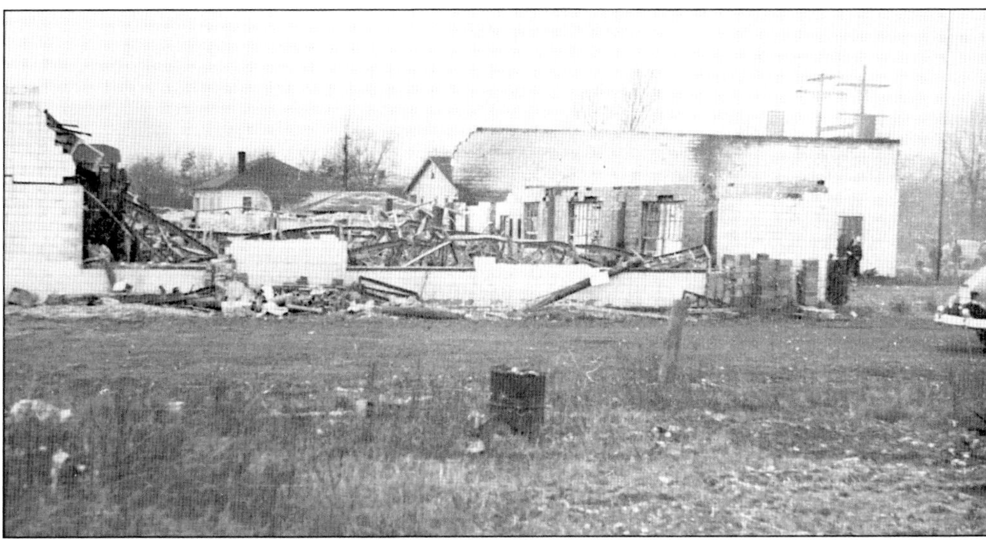

The manufacture of figurines and small art novelties by the Grindley Artware Manufacturing Company was their drawing card of success in the pottery business. With the onset of the Second World War, Japanese and European artware ceased from entering the United States. The Grindley Artware Manufacturing Company business grew by leaps and bounds. Soon a plant was built to meet the demands of the market. In February 1947, a fire broke out, destroying the entire plant within hours. In time, the plant rebuilt and regained much of the stature it had experienced in the past.

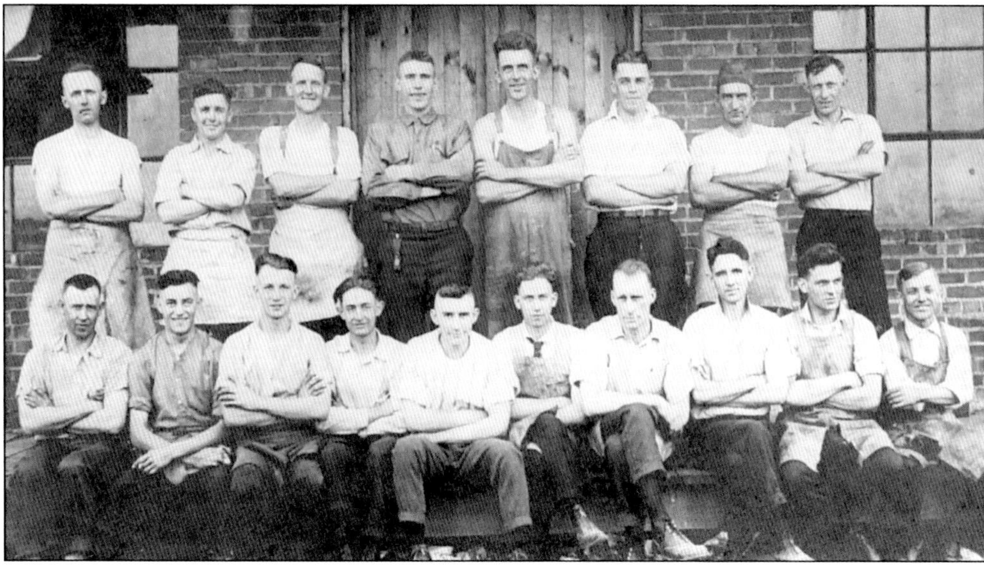

In 1915, some of the employees of the Strong Manufacturing Company pose outside the plant. Founded by Thomas L. Strong in 1903, in Bellaire, Ohio, the company manufactured enameled cooking utensils. Oliver and Orville Sebring heard that Mr. Strong was in search of a new location for his plant. It was a known fact that Mr. Strong had a great disdain for liquor, and in those days Bellaire had many saloons. The deeds in Sebring specified no liquor, and along with the Sebrings' marketing abilities, they convinced Mr. Strong to move his plant to Sebring. It was agreed that the sale of chinaware and cooking utensils would be a great combination.

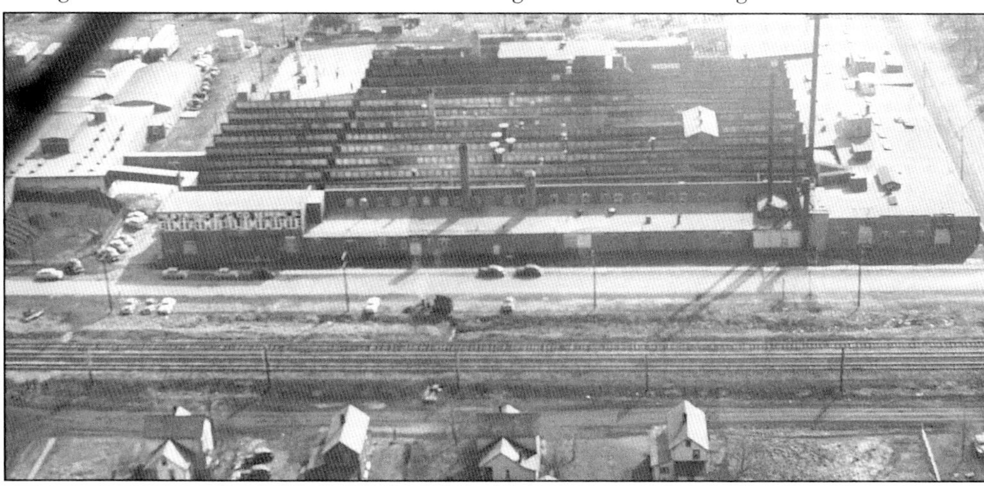

This is a late 1940s aerial view of the Strong Manufacturing Company. By the 1920s, Oliver H. Sebring had purchased Thomas L. Strong's stock and relinquished his control of the company. At that time, the Strong Manufacturing Company was the sole manufacturer of industrial reflectors and fixtures for the General Electric Company and Westinghouse. Mr. Sebring's creation of the Sebring Manufacturing Company, which included the merger of the French and Saxon China Companies with Strong Manufacturing, would be a fatal mistake. With the economic collapse in the late 1920s, the still viable enamel company fell victim to the failure of the pottery businesses and the local bank. In 1932, a group of men from Sebring and Beloit sold 1,000 shares of stock at $50 each, and the plant was purchased from the Central National Bank of Cleveland. Thus the rebirth of Strong Manufacturing was underway.

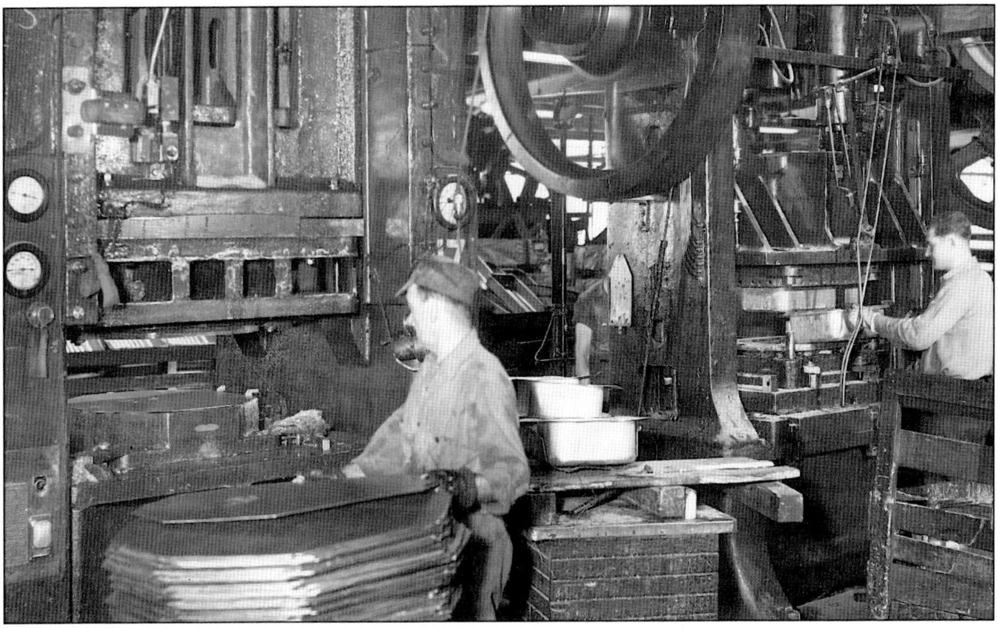

The first two years, 1933 and 1934, were rough for the newly reorganized company. The reflector and fixtures businesses were given to other companies, and the need for utensils was at a bare minimum. However, the year 1935 gave Strong Manufacturing the break it needed. Westinghouse Electric of Mansfield, Ohio, placed a significant order for vegetable pans. The fast turnaround in manufacturing secured contracts from Frigidaire (who developed the hydrator pan to keep vegetables crisp in their new electric refrigerators), General Electric, Philco, Kelvinator, and many more. The top photograph shows men inserting the metal into the stamping machines to mold the pan. The bottom photograph shows the women cutting and rounding the edges of those pans. Strong was also known for the manufacture of mess kits and canteens during WW II. At top production, 10,000 cups and canteens could be produced in 24 hours. In August 1944, Strong Manufacturing received the prestigious Army E Award for its participation in the war effort.

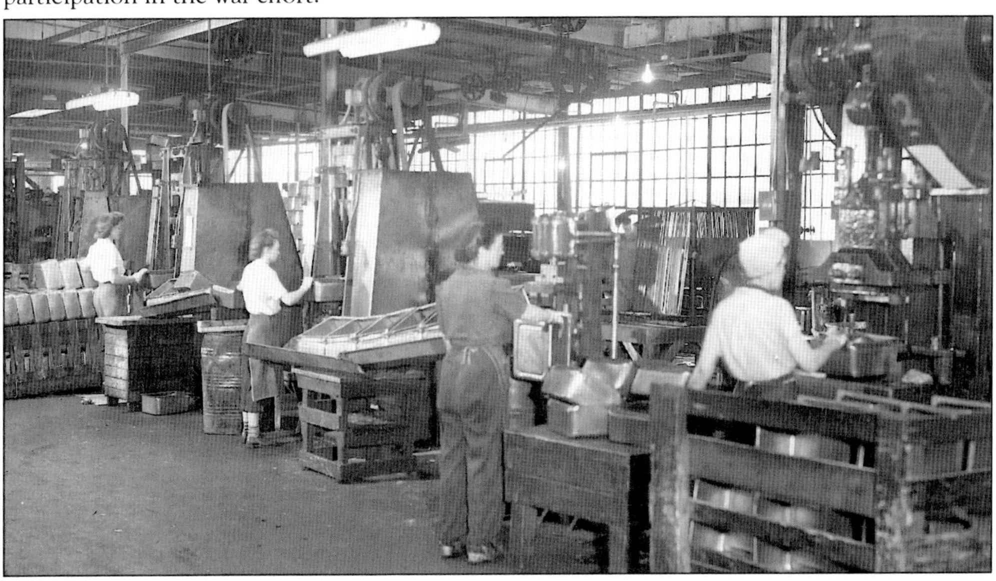

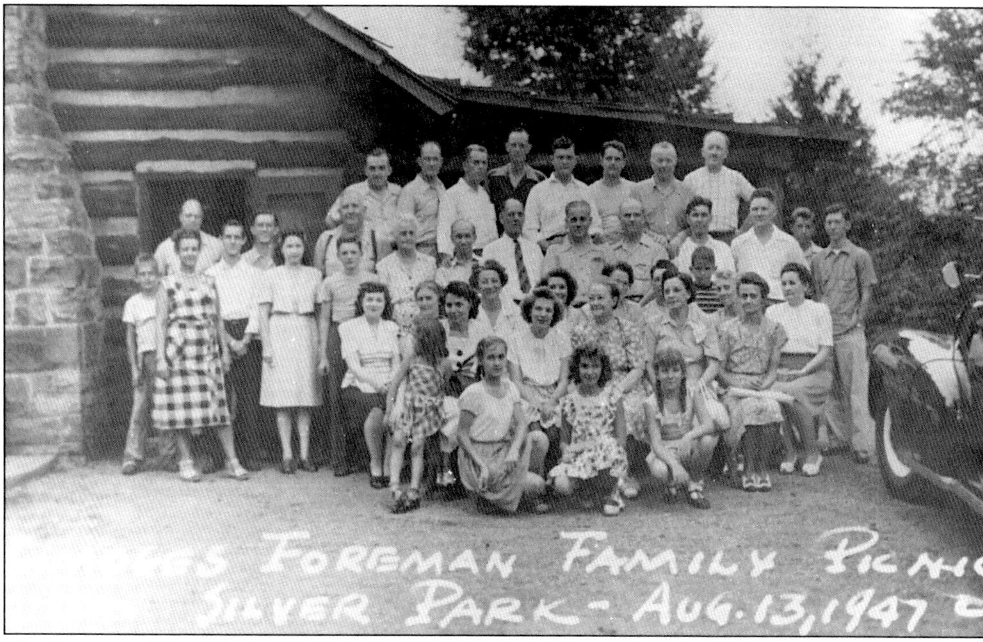

The Limoges China Company Foreman Family Picnic is shown here at Silver Park in Alliance, Ohio, on August 13, 1947.

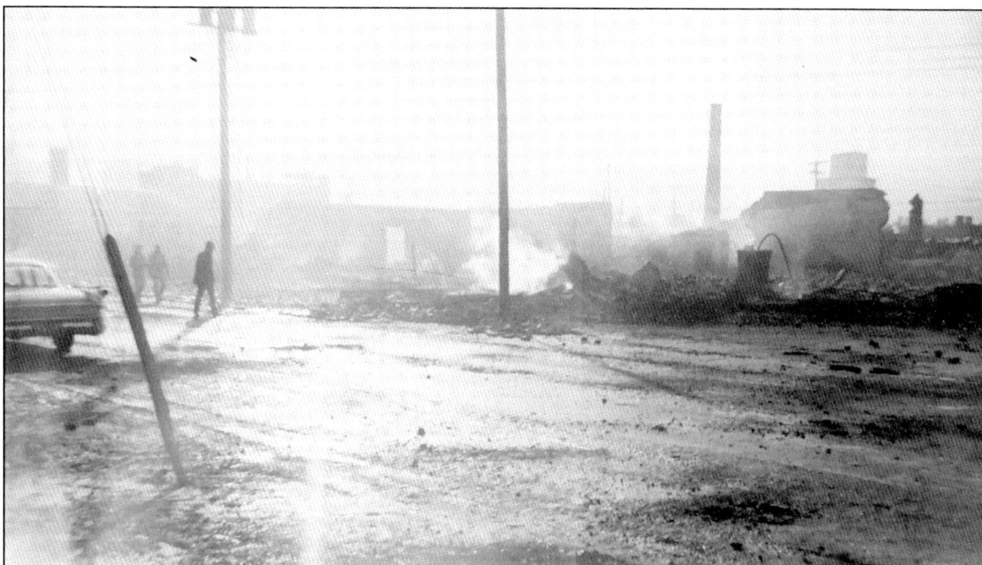

This photograph depicts the remains of the Stanford Art Pottery Incorporated after a devastating fire in late 1960. The blaze also destroyed East Ohio Machinery, a sales engineering firm, and Sebring Container Company, manufacturer of corrugated boxes and packaging. All these businesses occupied the old Sebring Pottery Company building at South Fifteenth Street and West California Avenue. The estimated loss was $765,000. Stanford was noted for the manufacture of planters, lamp bases, clock cases, and figurines. After their Stanford's products were produced, they were shipped to manufacturers for completion. Many of these items were sold in department stores and to discount retailers such as McCrory's, Woolworth, and Kresge's.

The R.M. Strain General Contracting Company was founded in 1935 by Ruskin McCausland Strain. His sons Charles and John ("Jack") worked in partnership for many years. Originally located in town, Strain built a home and office on the Alliance-Sebring Road in 1941. A tin shop and garages were also located on the property. The company did repair work on many of the pottery buildings and Sebring family residences during the 1930s. They were contracted through several Youngstown Banks, which held the mortgage on the potteries during the Depression. The name changed in the late 1940s to The R.M. Strain and Sons General Contractors. In the years that followed, Jack went on to other business ventures, and Mr. Strain and Charles focused on plumbing and heating. Thus the name was changed again to R.M. Strain and Son Plumbing and Heating. After Ruskin's death in 1981, Charles remained in business for several years. After he retired, the family sold the business to Dale Mohr. After his death, the business was sold to Jack's son, Bruce Strain, and it is still in operation today.

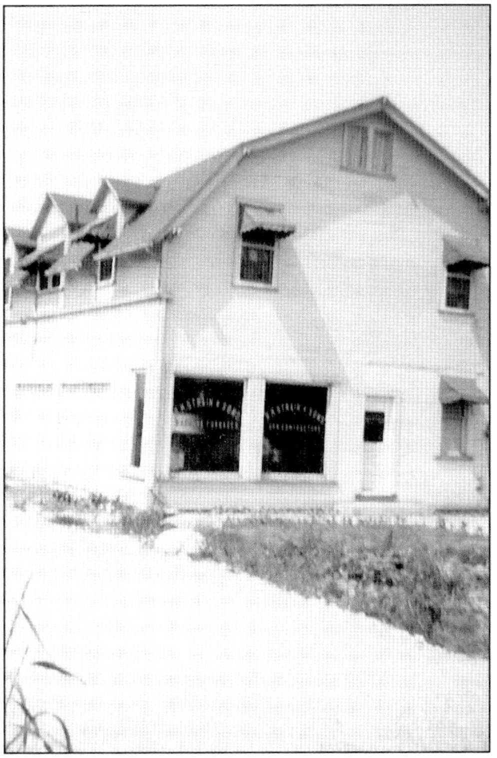

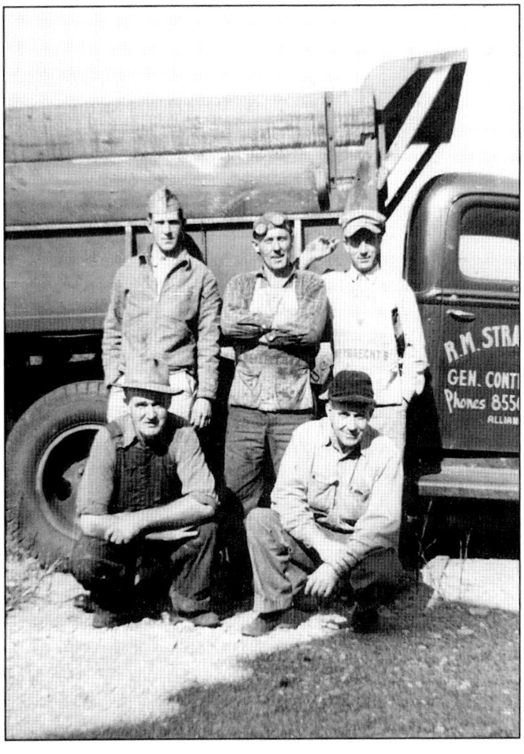

The crew of R.M. Strain General Contractors poses in front of one of the company trucks in 1943. Shown in this photograph are, (kneeling) W. Floyd Strain and Ruskin M. Strain; (standing) Charles K. Strain (home on furlough), Cy Heslep, and John F. Strain.

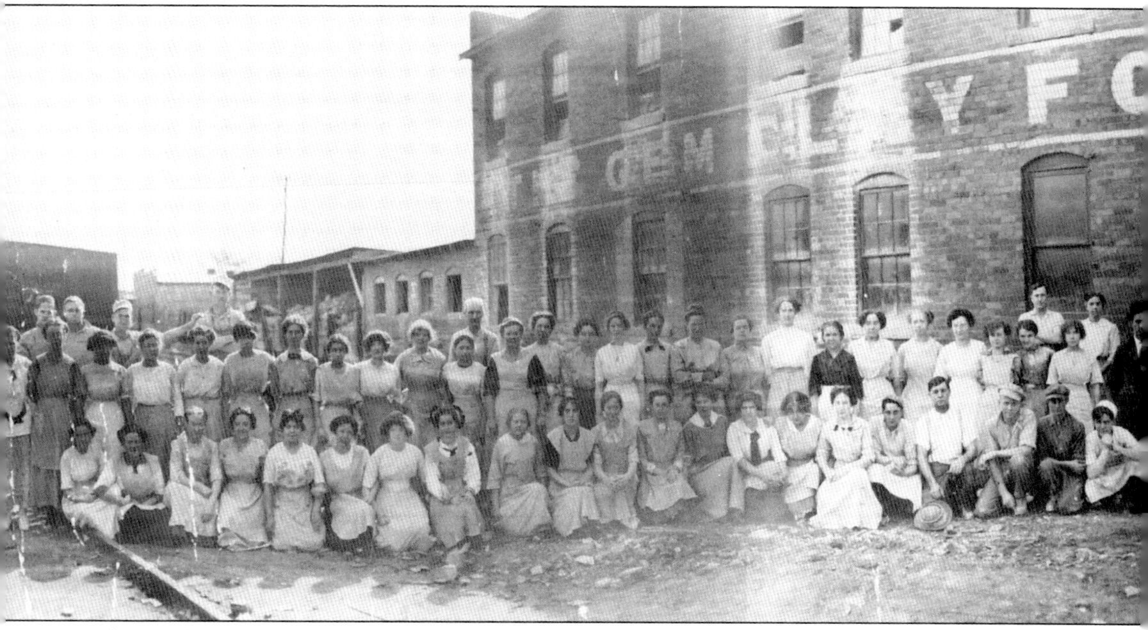

The employees and management of the Gem Clay Forming Company piled outside the plant for this picture in 1910. The company came to Sebring in 1907 and built a plant where the Strong Manufacturing building is today. The building was destroyed by fire in 1908. A new location was

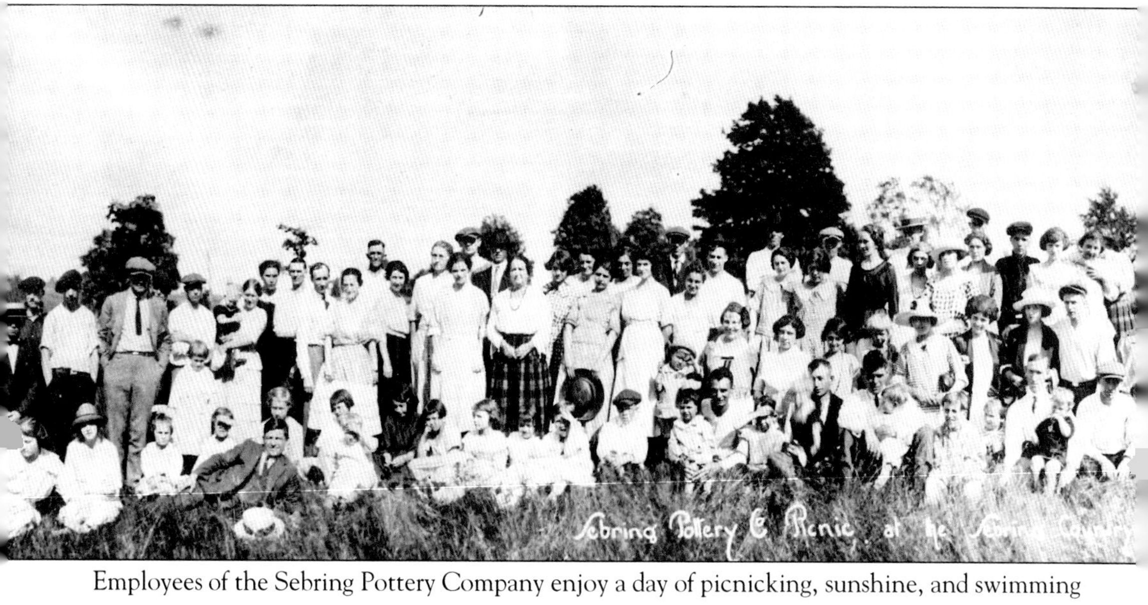

Employees of the Sebring Pottery Company enjoy a day of picnicking, sunshine, and swimming

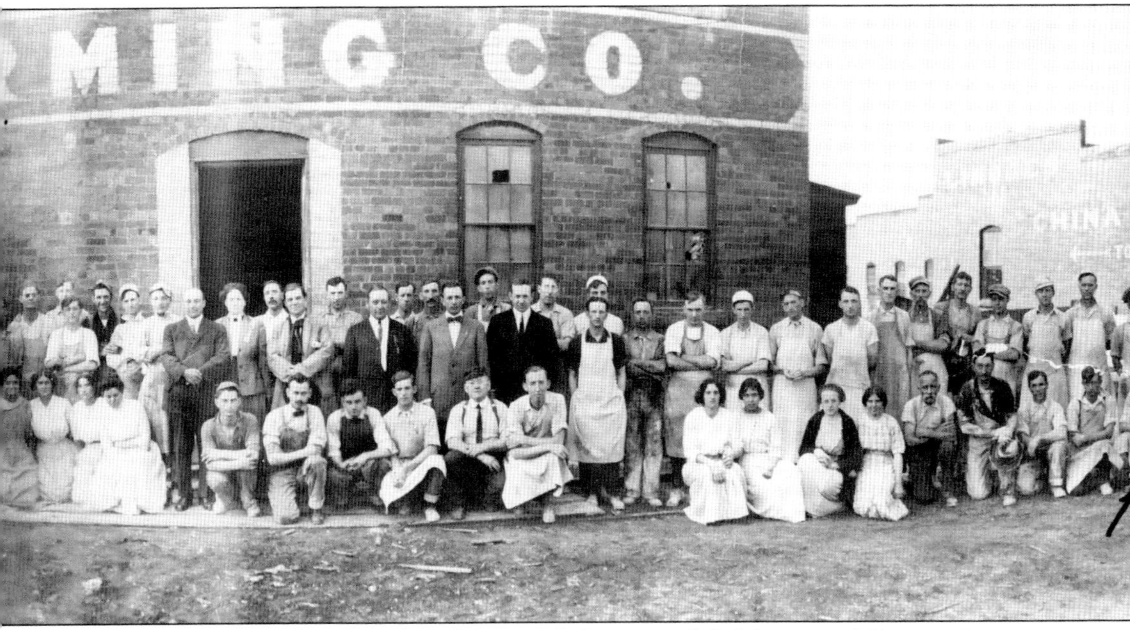

selected between South Fifteenth and Sixteenth Streets and California and Georgia Avenues. They manufactured gas mantle rings, electrical porcelains for the electrical trade, timer cases, and light housings for the cooking range trade.

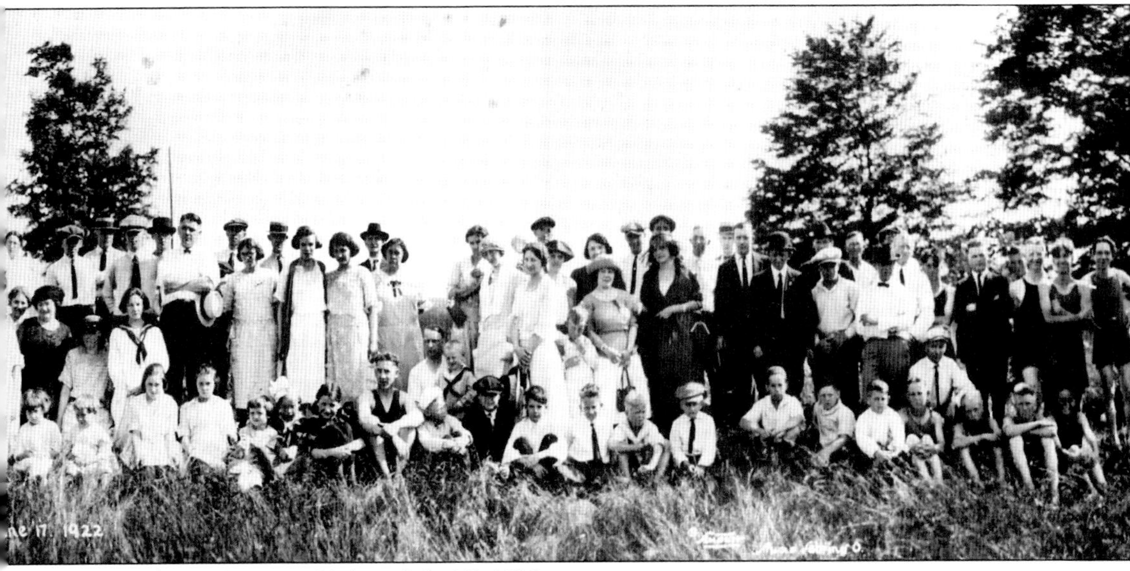

at the Sebring Country Club on July 17, 1922.

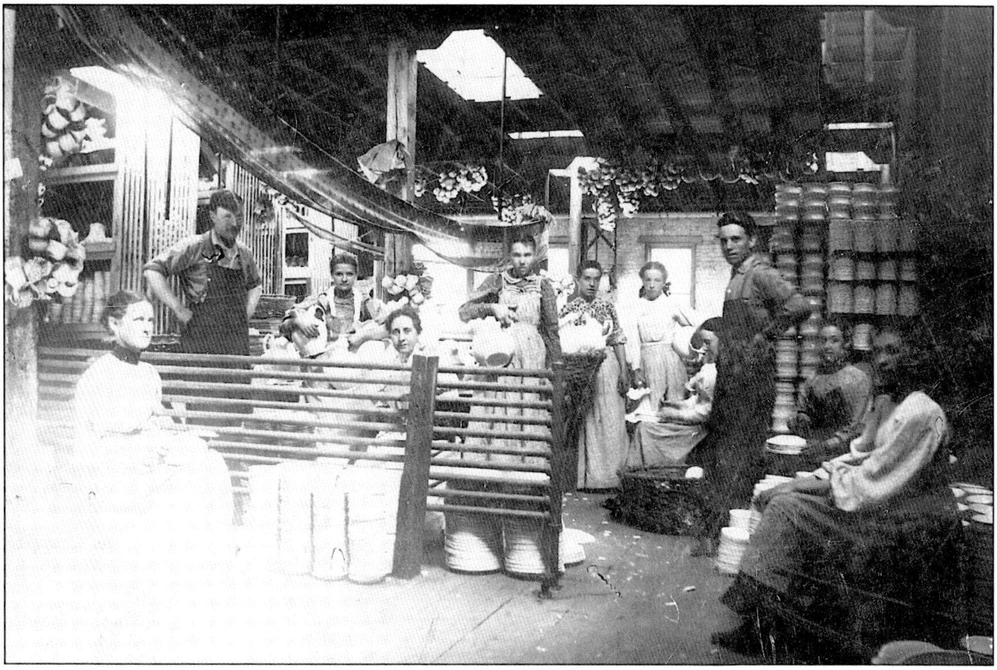

This is an early photograph of an unidentified pottery in Sebring. Taken around 1901, it is one of the earliest known photographs in the Sebring Historical Society's collection and shows the interior of the factory with its workers.

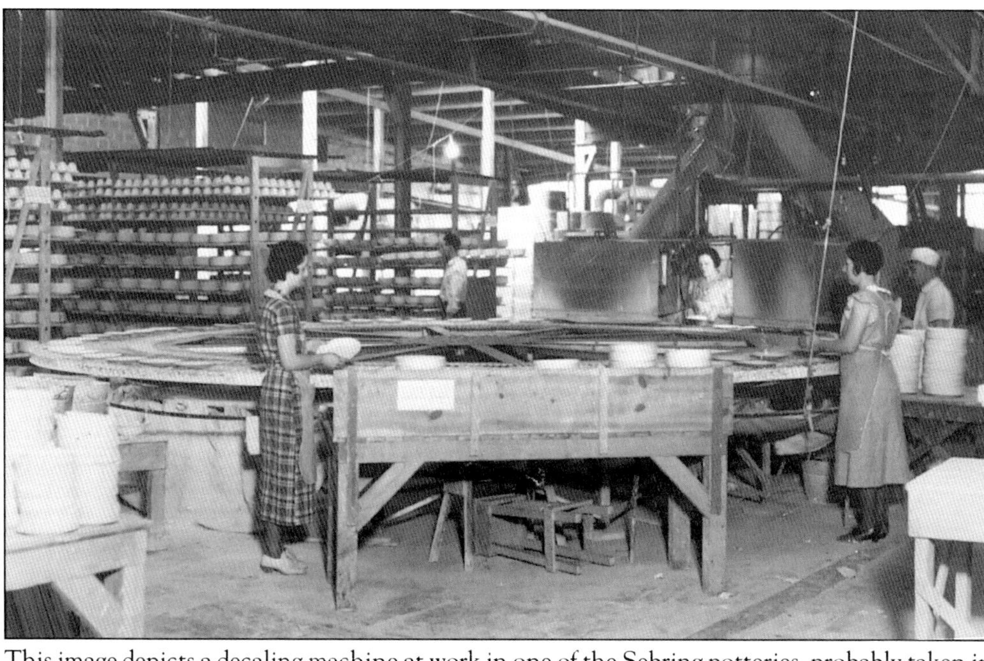

This image depicts a decaling machine at work in one of the Sebring potteries, probably taken in the late 1930s or early 1940s. Decaling became an inexpensive way of producing tableware, and the Sebrings were pioneers in this process. Handpainting was the custom in the manufacture of dishes.

Three

DEVELOPMENTS:
MIND, BODY, AND THEOLOGY

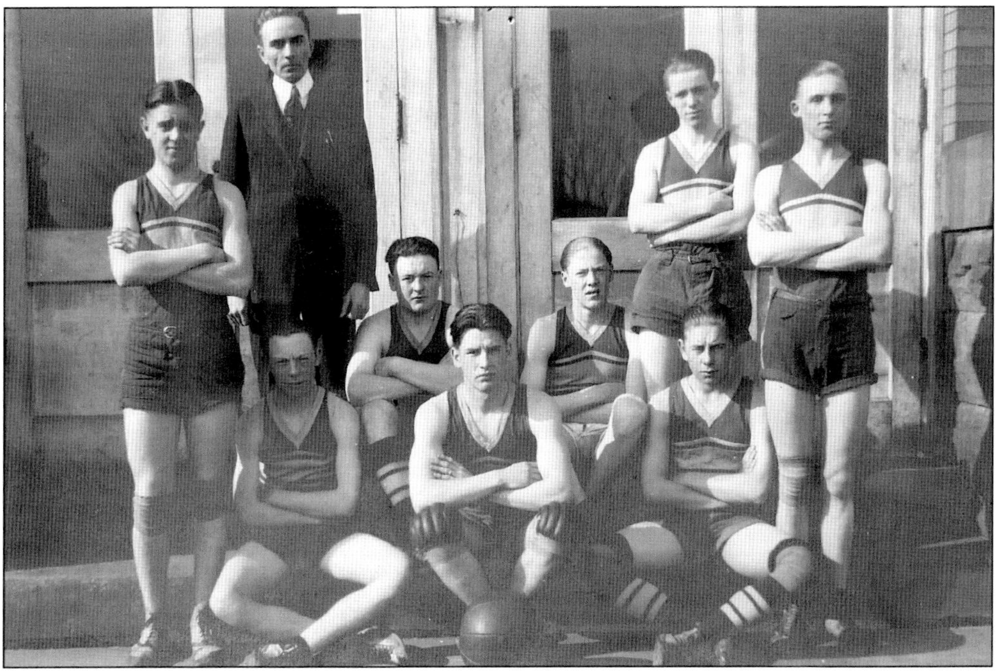

The first indoor basketball game played in Sebring was in a roller skating rink operated by Louis Kuntzman. The rink was located on the corner of Indiana Avenue and Fourteenth Street. This photograph shows the 1921-22 team who won 11 games in a row. They beat all the county teams and lost only to Columbiana, in the Northeastern Ohio tournament, and Berlin Center, in the county tournament. Pictured here are Kenneth Mills, "Red" Nigel, Dick Alvis, Lorenzo Brimlow, Bus Forbes, Bud Blumenstiel, and ? Trimmer.

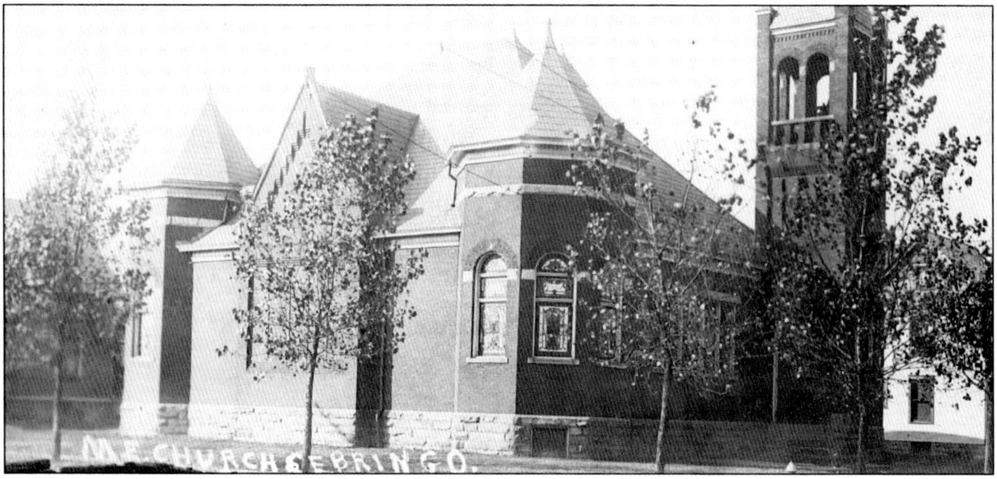

The Methodist Episcopal Church was the first religious organization established in Sebring. The first meeting was held in September 1899, in the barn of the old Gray property. The Sebring family realized that the success and development of their community not only depended on the pottery business but also on the Christian faith of the residents. Nearly 200 people attended the services each week. In 1900, $20,000 was raised for the construction of a church building. This building was dedicated February 27, 1901, just in time for the marriage of Mr. and Mrs. Oliver H. Sebring's daughter Pearl to Homer Taylor.

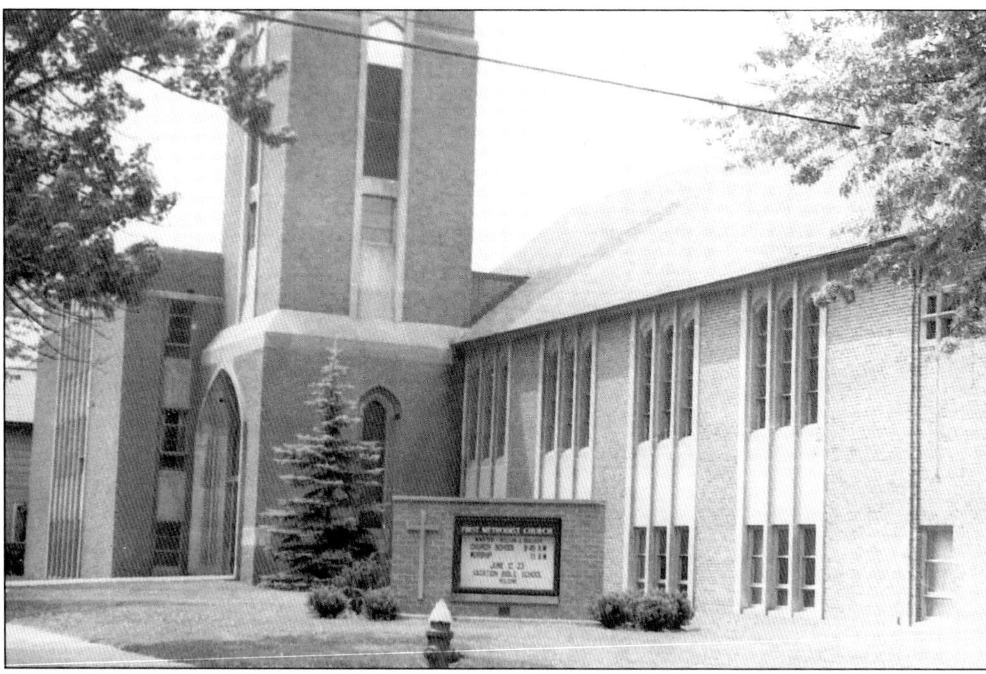

The First United Methodist Church of Sebring, located on the corner of Fifteenth Street and Indiana Avenue was built in the 1950s, replacing the original structure, which was destroyed by fire in 1955.

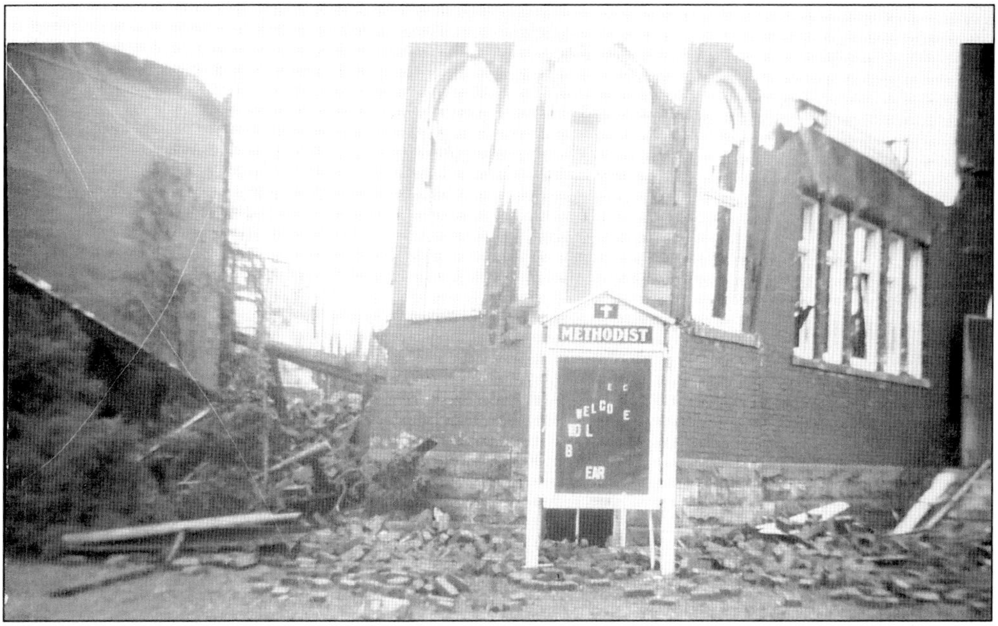

These snapshots show the aftermath of the devastating fire that destroyed the historic Methodist Church in March 1955. The fire was so intense that many observers remembered the bell tower, on the northeast side, looked like an enormous candle. The bell was removed and now sits in front of the fire station.

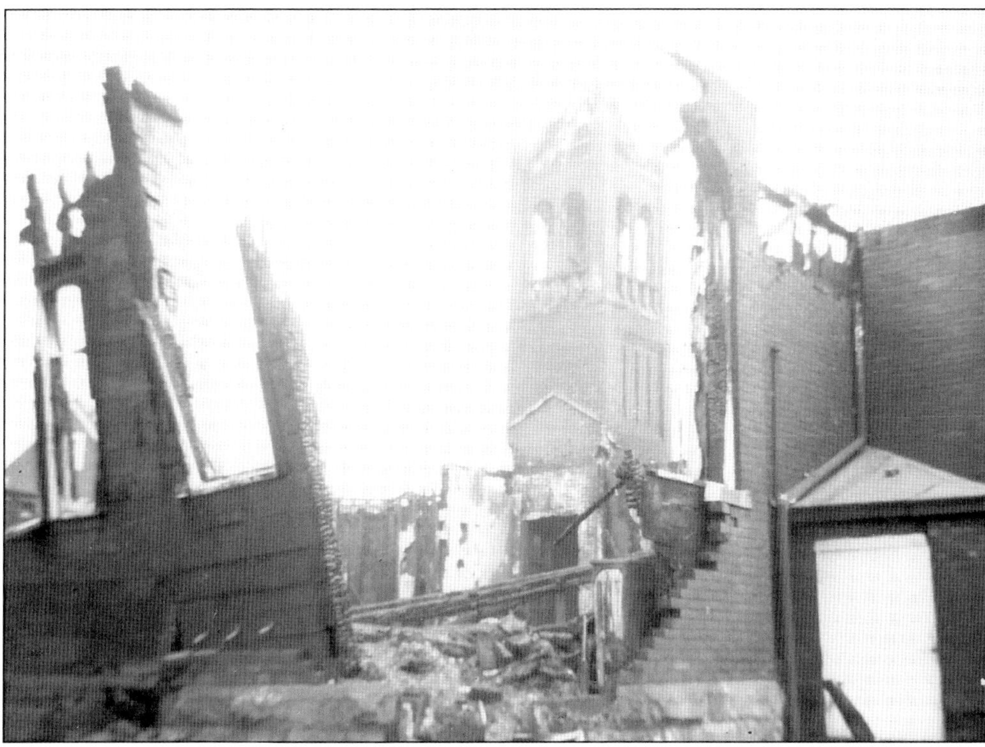

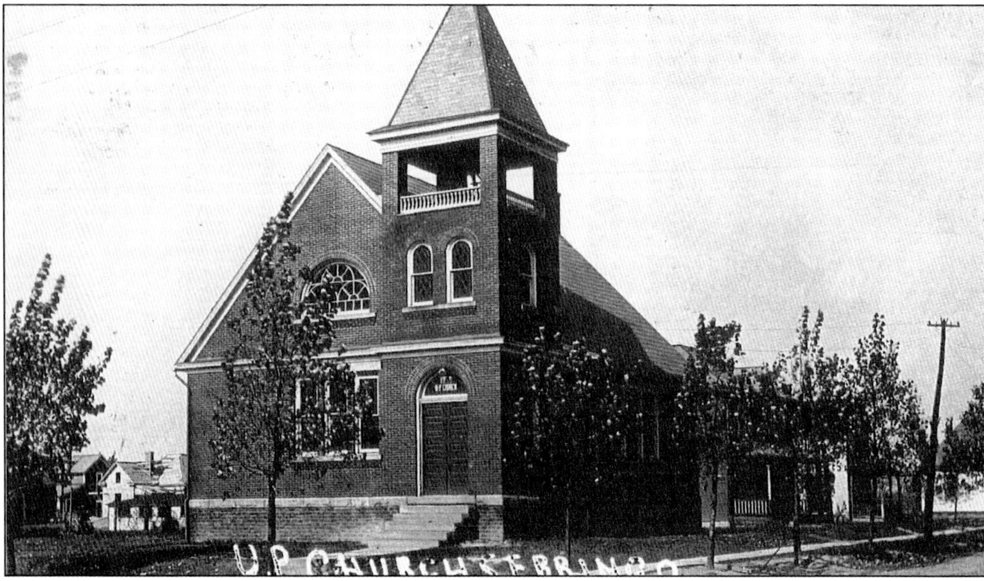

Organized in 1901, The First United Presbyterian Church (renamed The Faith United Presbyterian Church) held their first service in a sheep barn at the corner of Fifteenth Street and Oregon Avenue. Soon after, services were held in the rooms over a barbershop. Worship was conducted by The Reverend E.E. Douglass and the Session of the East Palestine United Presbyterian congregation. In 1902, the south and main portion of the church building, as viewed in the top photograph, were constructed at a cost of $4,500 on the northwest corner of Sixteenth Street and Maryland Avenue. In a few years, with the help of E.H. Sebring and Fred Sebring, the land north of the edifice was donated, and the building was enlarged to include the east entrance. In the photograph below, those additions and the parsonage, which was built in 1915 to the west of the church, can be seen. In 1948, an extensive interior remodeling program took place, and the installation of chimes in the belfry was made possible by the generosity of Mr. and Mrs. Carl Hamilton and their son-in-law and daughter Bill and Belva Mercer. In 1973, the Faith United Presbyterian Church merged with the First Presbyterian Church. The building remained empty for a period of time, and over the years it has been occupied by various denominations.

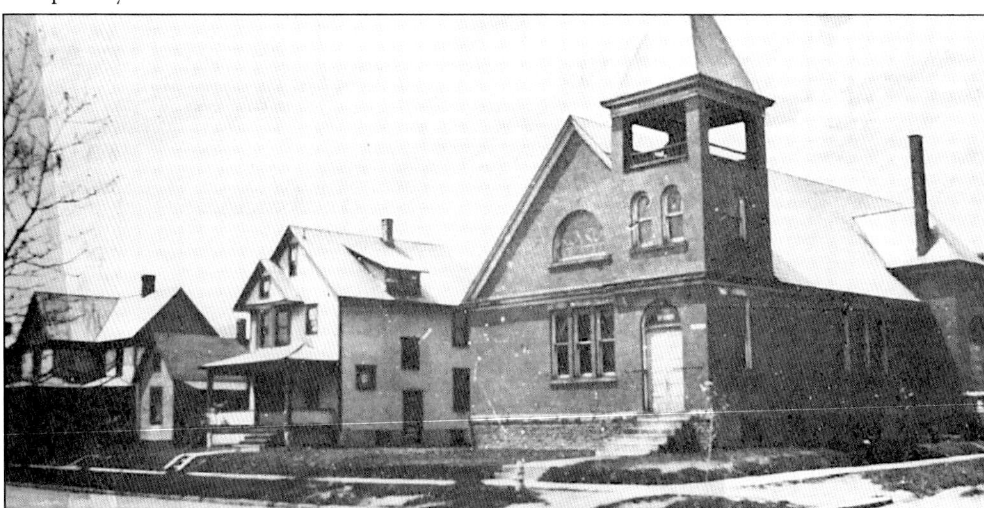

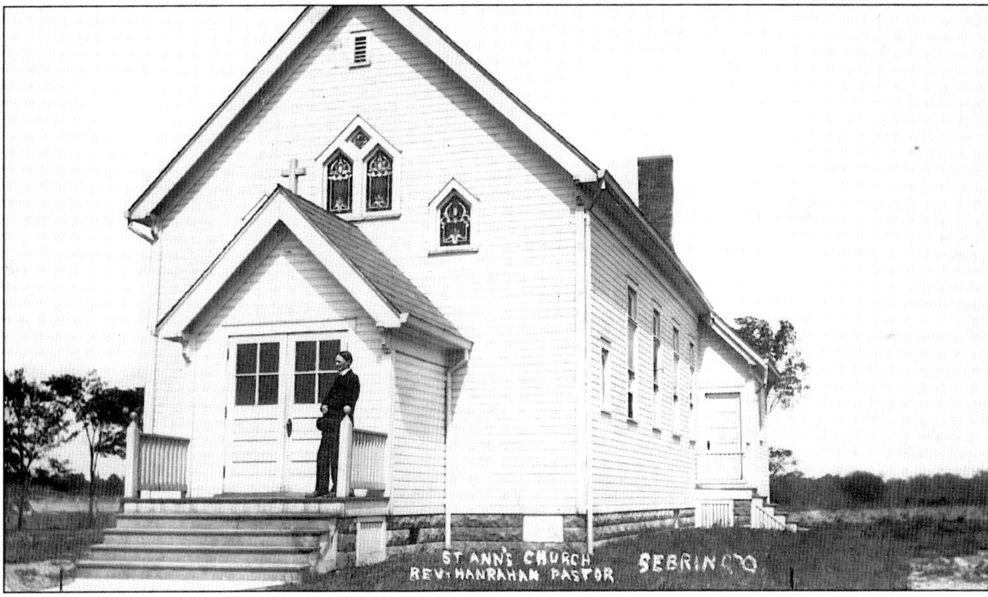

The first spark of Catholicism in Sebring emerged in 1908 when approximately 75 individuals assembled in the city hall to hear Father Francis Hopp. In that same year, a building was rented on Seventeenth Street between Pennsylvania and Oregon Avenues. The diocese appointed Father George C. Schoenemann as pastor and named the church in honor of St. Anne. The cornerstone of this edifice was laid on July 31, 1910. In the early 1930s, a tower was added to the northwest corner through the efforts of Father Studer. According to the church history, Studer begged for a bell from the Holy Name Parish in Cleveland and was successful in obtaining it.

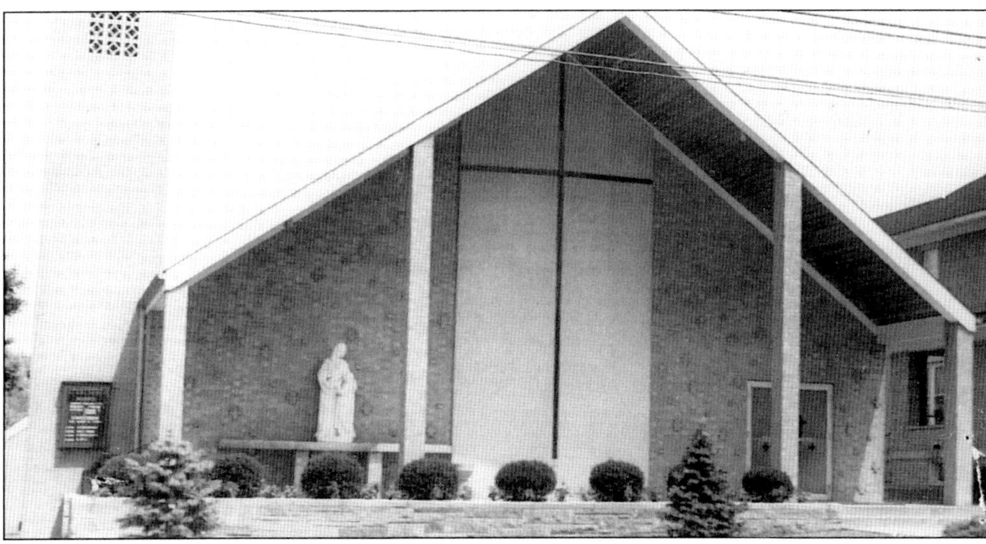

In April 1960, the old frame edifice was moved to a back lot to make room for a new church building for St. Anne's. Designed by Leonard S. Friedman, it was constructed by Paul A. Kintz Construction Company of Alliance, Ohio. It was the dream of Fr. Ferris Petros that the new church become a reality. On the day of Petros's death (September 8, 1960), the bell that Father Studer received for the church in 1930 was installed in the tower of the new church and was tolled to announce his death.

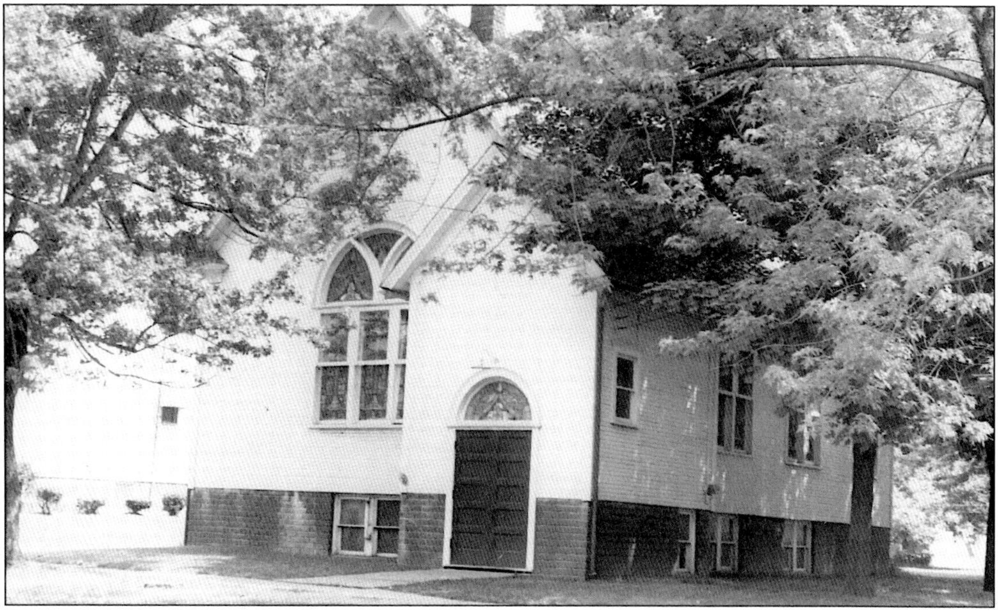

In February 1913, the Trinity Lutheran Church was organized in Sebring through the efforts of Rev. W.W. Kennerly of St. Paul's Lutheran Church in Alliance, Ohio. In the beginning, the services were held in various locations including city hall. In May 1915, the frame structure (shown above) was dedicated. In December 1915, the Sebring congregation united with New Baltimore and North Georgetown as services were held in Sebring. After several years, the New Baltimore agreement was terminated, and North Georgetown formed a parish with New Franklin. In 1935, North Georgetown again united with Sebring. The congregation outgrew the small church, which was located on East Indiana Avenue and Eighteenth Street, and was closed in the 1970s. In the 1990s, the building was sold at auction. Today, it is privately owned.

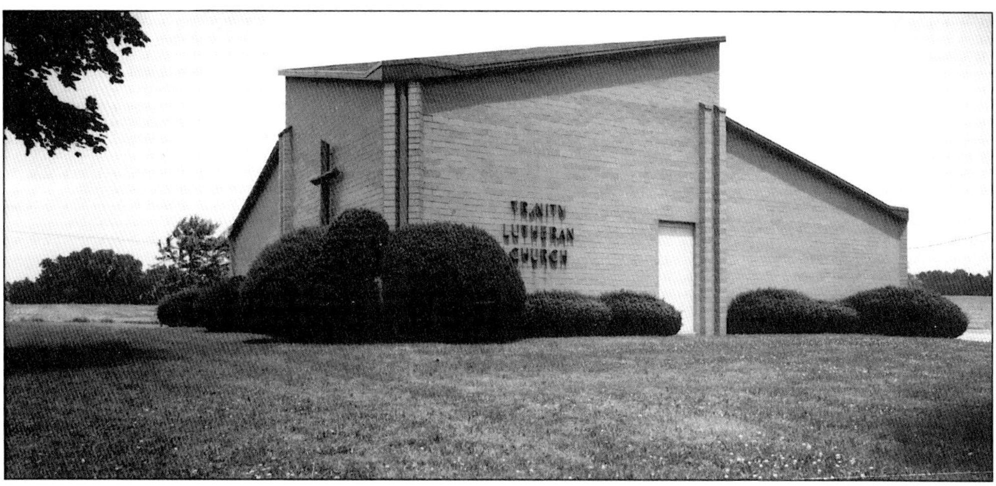

With the growth of the congregation, the Trinity Lutheran Church built a new edifice on the corner of Twelfth Street and Pine Lake Road in the 1970s. Constructed by Cartwright Construction Company, it is a typical example of the modernized style of architecture that many church congregations used in the 1960s and 1970s.

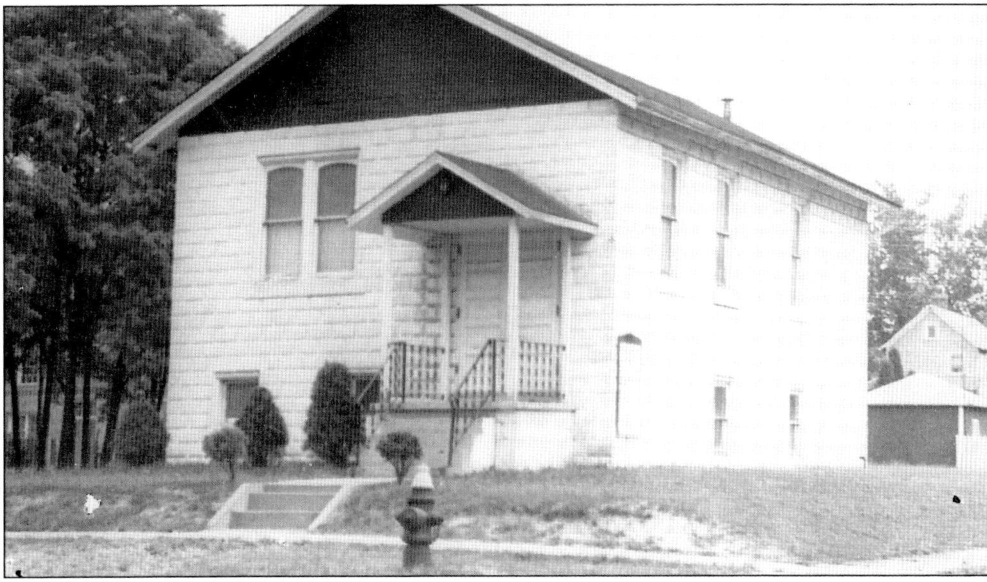

The Virginia Avenue Church of Christ is located on the corner of East Virginia Avenue and Fourteenth Street. They established their congregation in the 1940s.

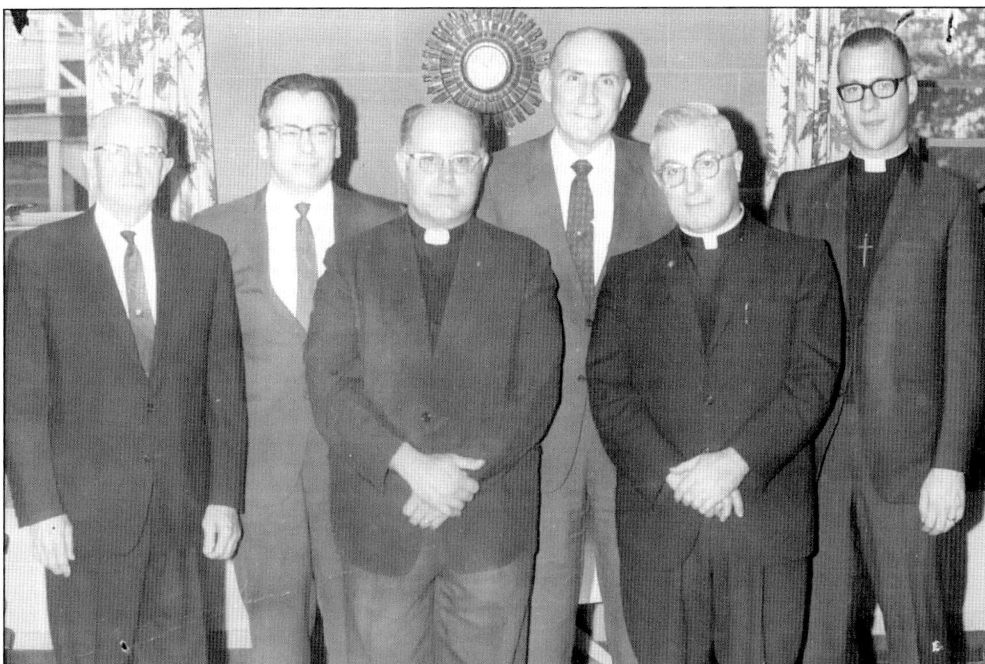

The members of the Sebring Ministerial Association gathered for this picture in the 1960s. Pictured here, from left to right, are as follows: (front row) Rev. Chester Stanley (Faith United Presbyterian Church), Rev C.O. Armstrong (First Presbyterian Church), and Rev. Frederick Anzivino (St. Ann's Catholic Church); (back row) Rev. William Waltz (Quaker Hill Friends Church), Rev. Edwin Eshelman (First United Methodist Church), and Rev. Paul Swartz (Trinity Lutheran Church). Not present for the picture was Rev. Bernard Younce (Nazarene Church).

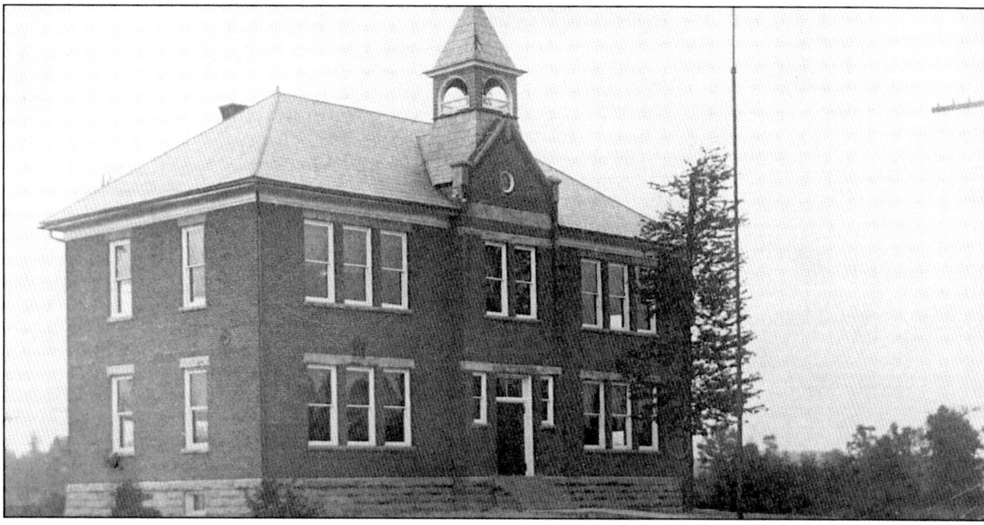

The Ohio Avenue School building was constructed in 1901 at a cost of $6,000. Prior to the construction of this building, the first public school room opened in 1900 in the old barn on the Gray farm. It was a one-room structure located on the southwest corner of Oregon Avenue and Fifteenth Street. The Ohio Avenue building, which was a three-year high school, enrolled ten students the first year. The first graduating class in 1904 included four students. This building was torn down in the late 1930s.

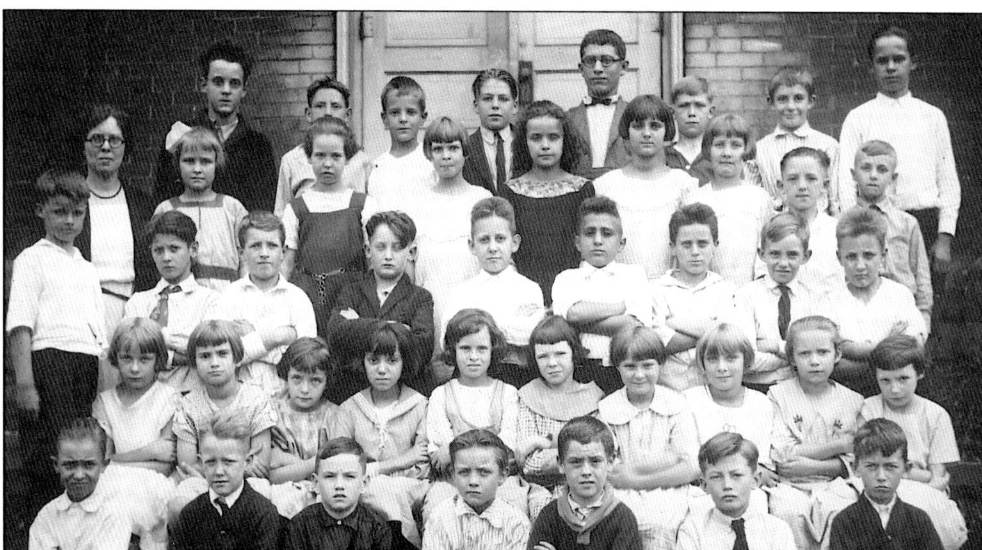

The fourth grade class poses in front of the Ohio Avenue School in 1923. They are shown here, from left to right, as follows: (first row) J. Mitcheltree, H. Pennick, E. Evans, H. Sanford, Dick Eans, George Grindley, and C. Barnhart; (second row) S. Brown, B. Edie, M. Sullivan, M. Calderone, N. Williams, ?, D. Yeagley, V. Pinkerton, P. Slagle, and M. Perkins; (third row) G. Shaffer, Don Hall, C. Hinemann, J. Hall, G. Halverstadt, J. Lee, Al Brindlinger, ?, and Glenn Halverstadt; (fourth row) Mrs. Shaffer, F. Wheeler, M. Keener, E. Dawson, Sanford, M. Fryfogle, R. Cummings, L. Schindler, and unidentified; (fifth row) three unidentified students, Shuster, T. Attamis, R. Pinkerton, Jack Marshall, and Edward Baker.

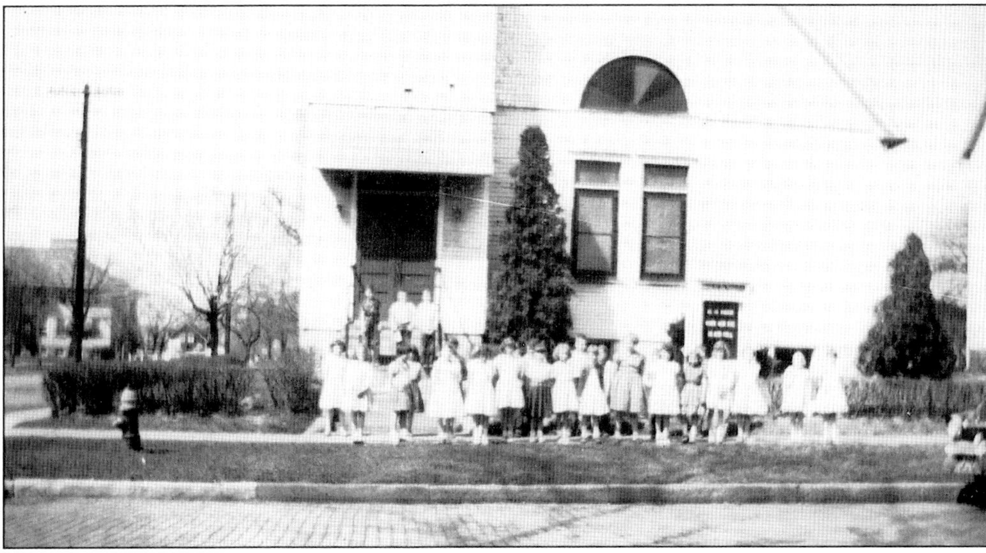

Members of the Nazarene Church Sunday School pose in front of their church in the 1940s. The church was organized in 1928 after a revival campaign. For a number of years worship services were held in the old Church of Christ building on the corner of Maryland Avenue and Seventeenth Street.

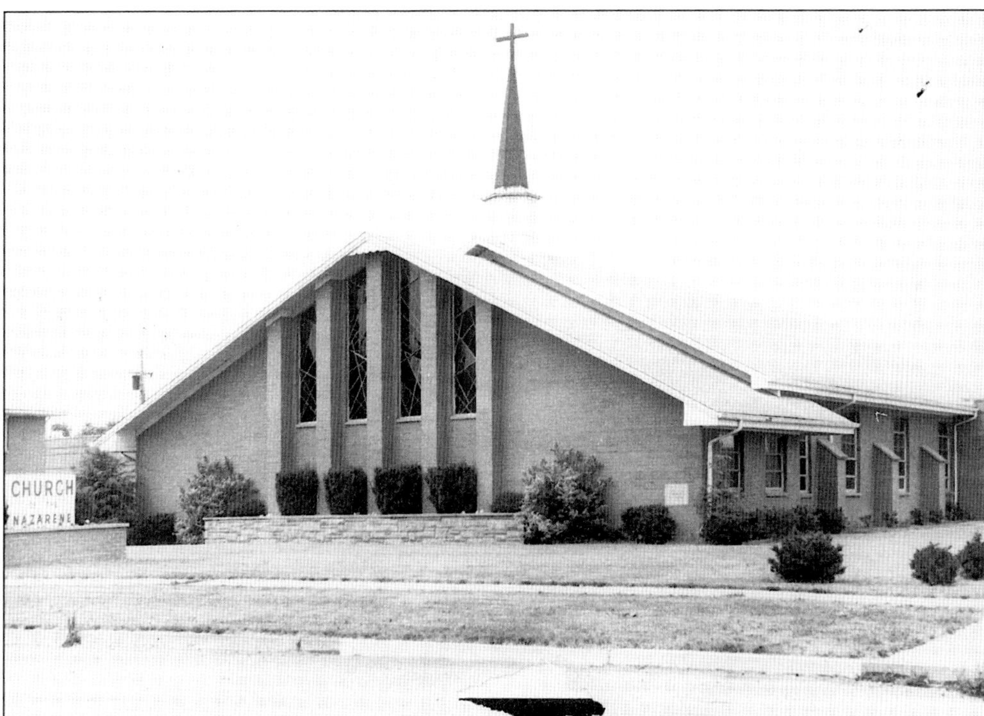

The Nazarene congregation grew considerably during the 1950s. In 1960, this edifice was built at 626 East Maryland Avenue.

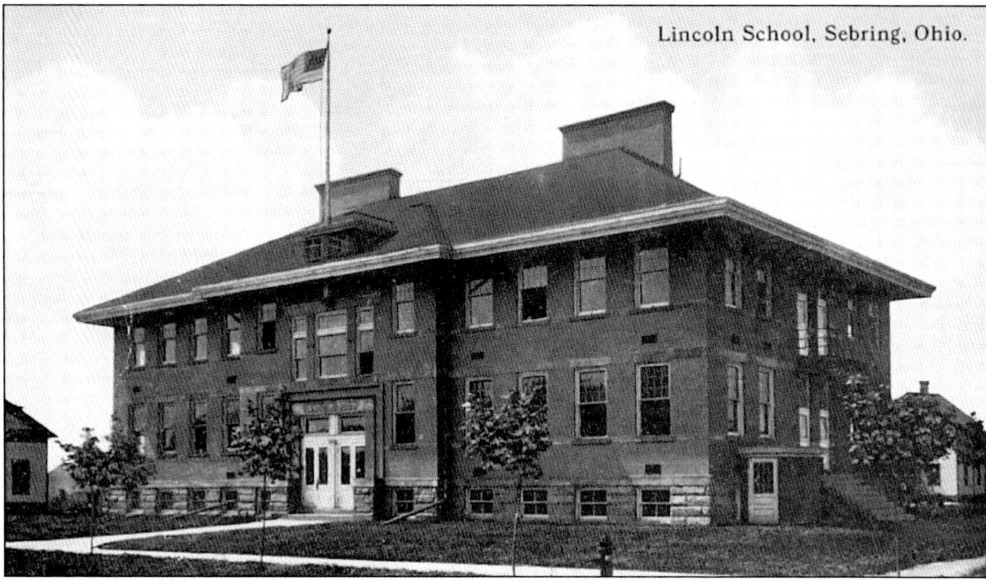

The Lincoln School building was located on the northwest corner of Indiana Avenue and Seventeenth Street. Built in 1909 at a cost of $20,000, the brick structure originally served as the high school until the McKinley School was built in 1914. The building is still in use today as an apartment complex.

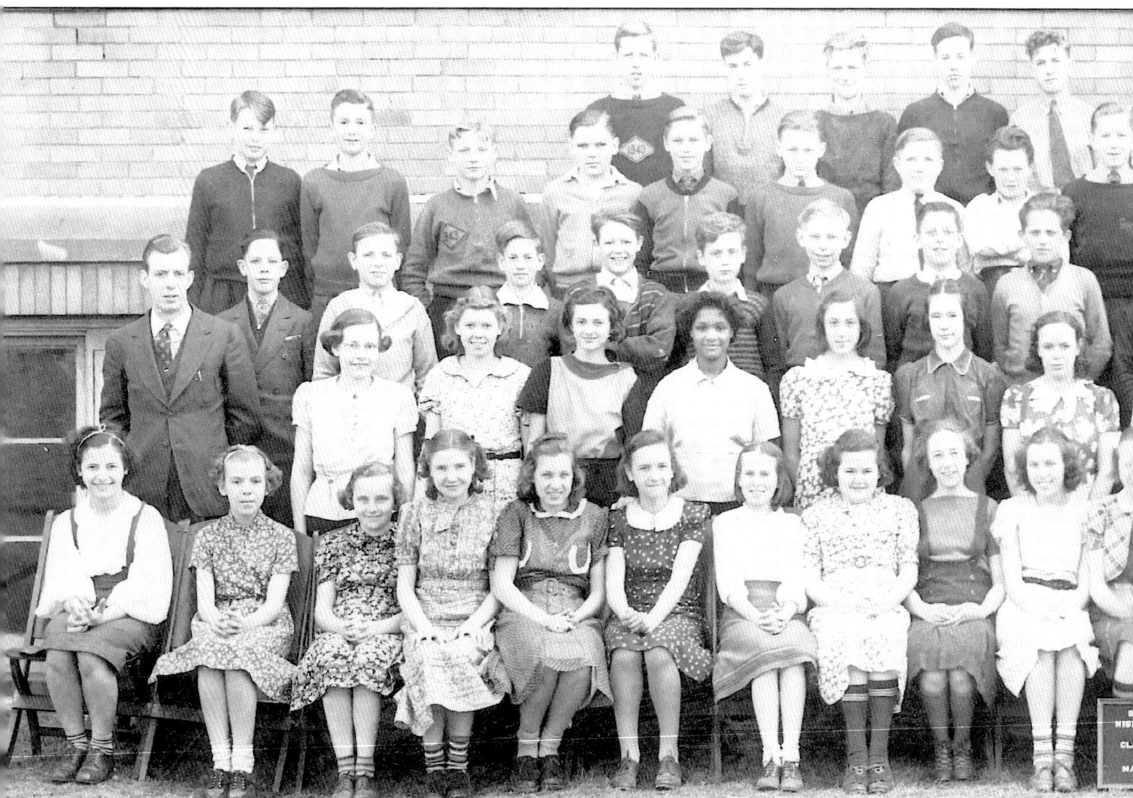

The future class of 1943 pose, during the seventh grade, outside the McKinley High School

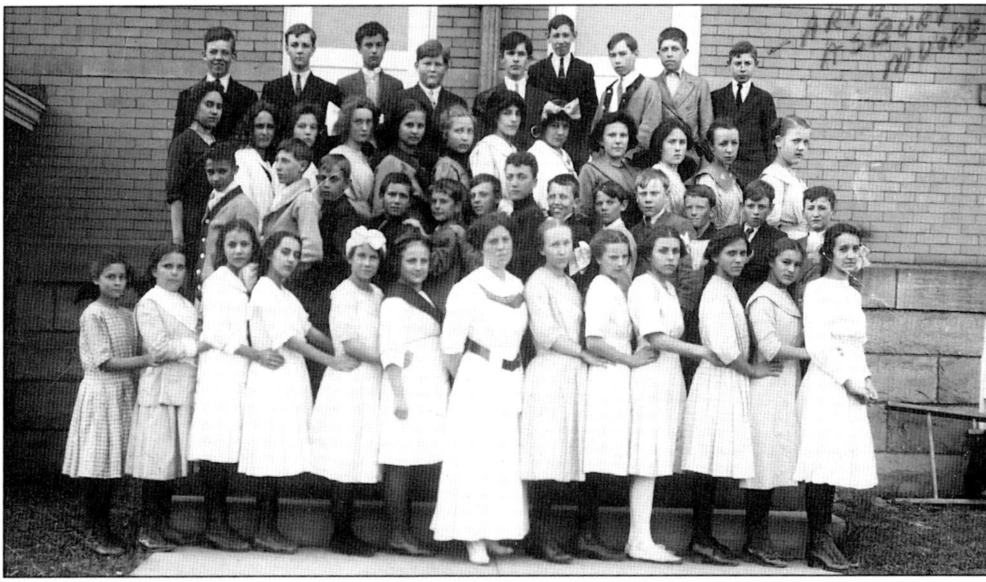

The seventh and eighth grades at Lincoln School lined up for this picture in the early teens. The only identification on the picture is Arthur Asbury Moore, first on the right, top row.

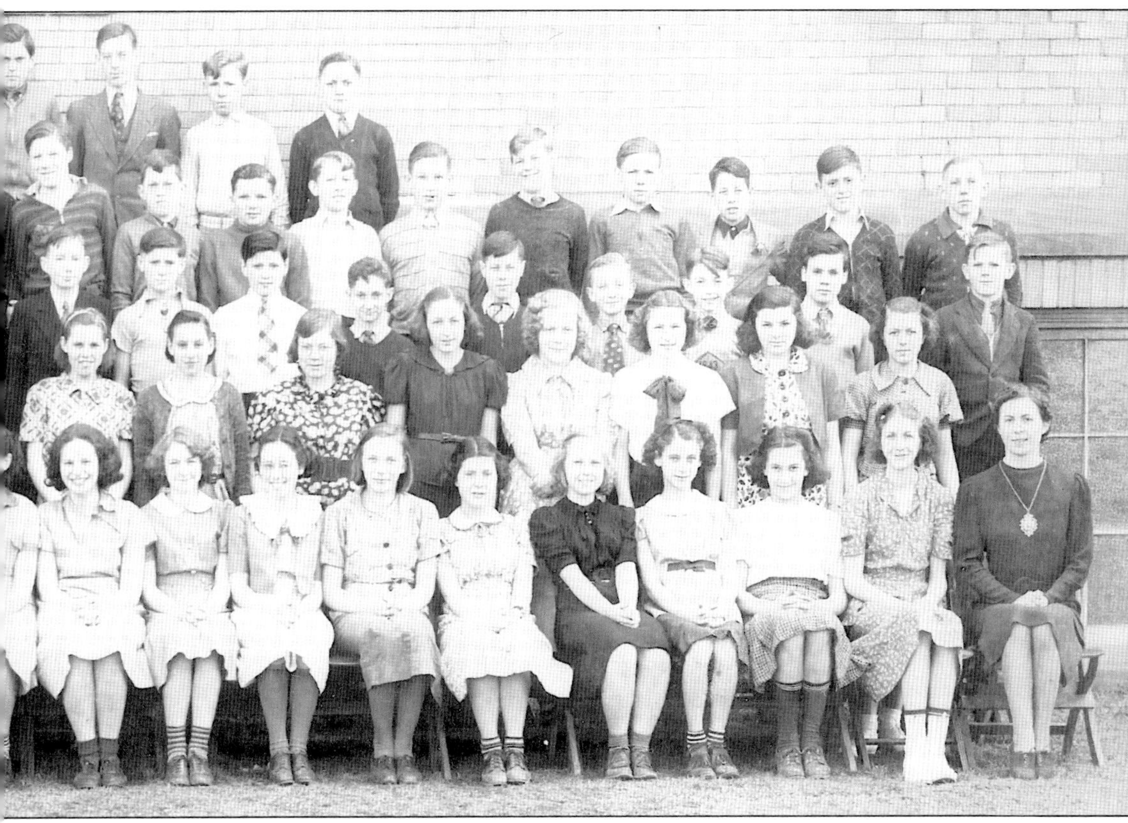

building on March 25, 1938. The teacher, seated on the far right, is Esther Smith Ray.

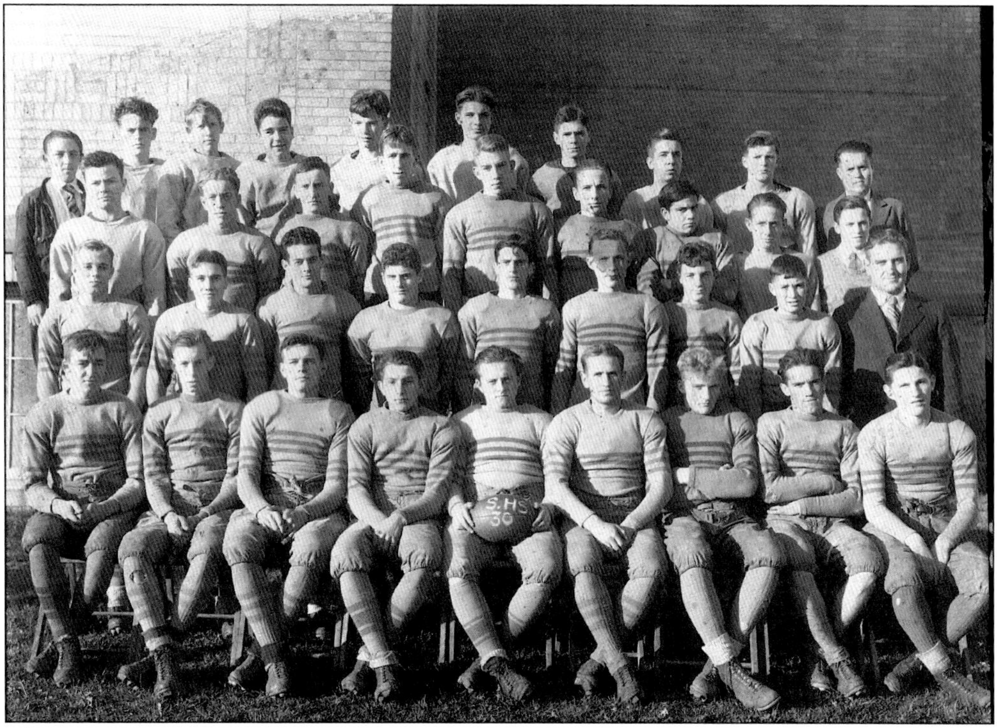

The 1930 Sebring High School football team is shown here, from left to right, as follows: (first row) Bob Warth, Harry Crewson, Kenneth Elliott, Willard Close, Oliver Edwards, Victor Burgess, Jack Henry, John Eells, and George Brimlow; (second row) Art Cannell, Ed Oliver, Jack Beech, Dick Ward, Al Brendlinger, Bob McClure, Leonard Bye, Robert Akenhead, and Arnold Karsen (coach); (third row) Melvin Ritter, Delbert Leasure, Roy Reedy, Jack "Popeye" Erb, Red Yothers, Don Burgess, Alton Bandy, George Goodballet, and Dean Iddings (manager); (fourth row) Sam Schindler, Ed Evans, Jules Gossiaux, Bob Stanford, Joe Woods, ? Fryfogle, Charles Bumgartner, Gale Myers, George Clark, and Mr. Rupert (principal).

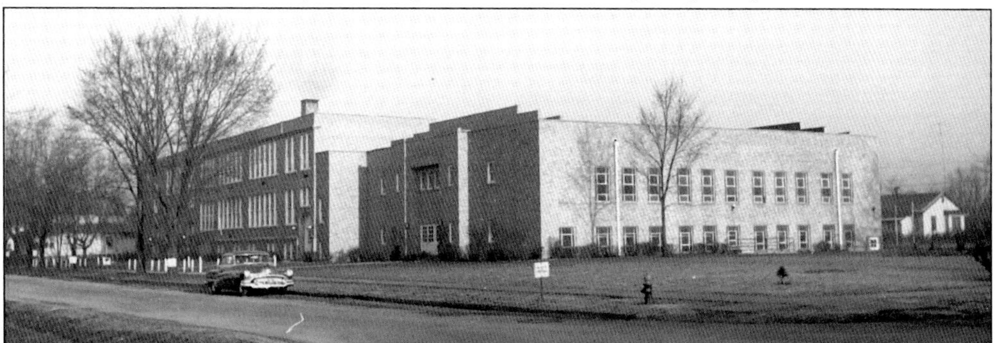

The McKinley High School developed in various stages. Originally built as an elementary school in 1914, it became the high school in 1924. Numerous additions have been made over the years including the auditorium and classrooms in 1924, and gymnasium, classrooms, and offices in 1937. The additions cost approximately $205,000. The W.P.A. and P.W.A., both Roosevelt Administration agencies established during the Depression, subsidized the cost of an athletic field in 1937. In 1998, a bond issue was passed to make way for a new structure, and with the exception of the 1955 addition, the building will be demolished.

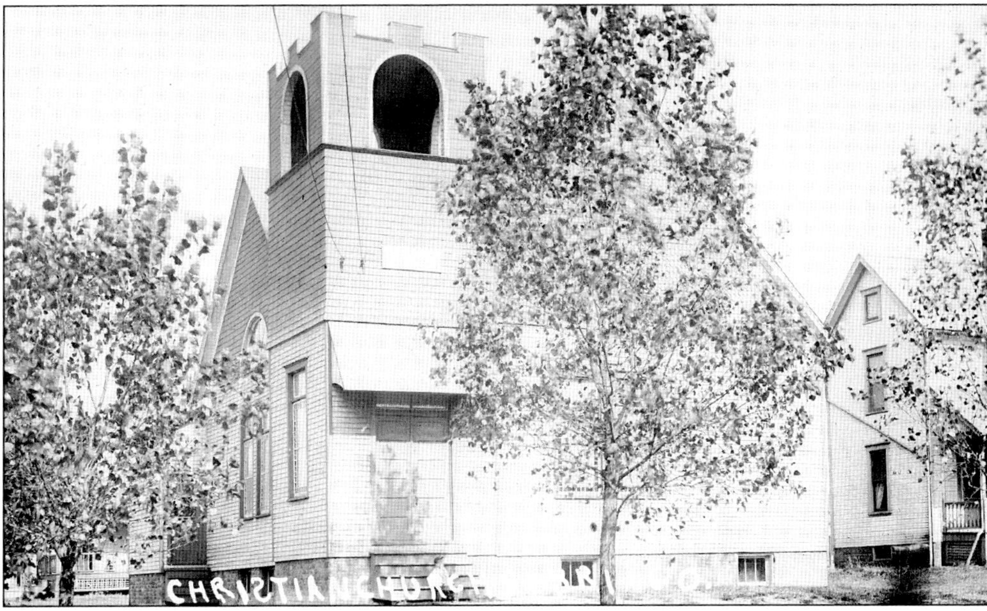

After several prayer meetings and revivals, the Church of Christ was organized on January 29, 1902. The congregation met in the Pythian Temple on Fifteenth Street until the construction of their church was completed. Built on the corner of Seventeenth Street and Maryland Avenue, on land donated by the Sebring Land Company, the Church of Christ building was dedicated on September 18, 1904. The congregation's expansion in membership through tent meetings and the "Saving of Souls" posed a problem in the early 1920s. The small frame structure could no longer meet their needs.

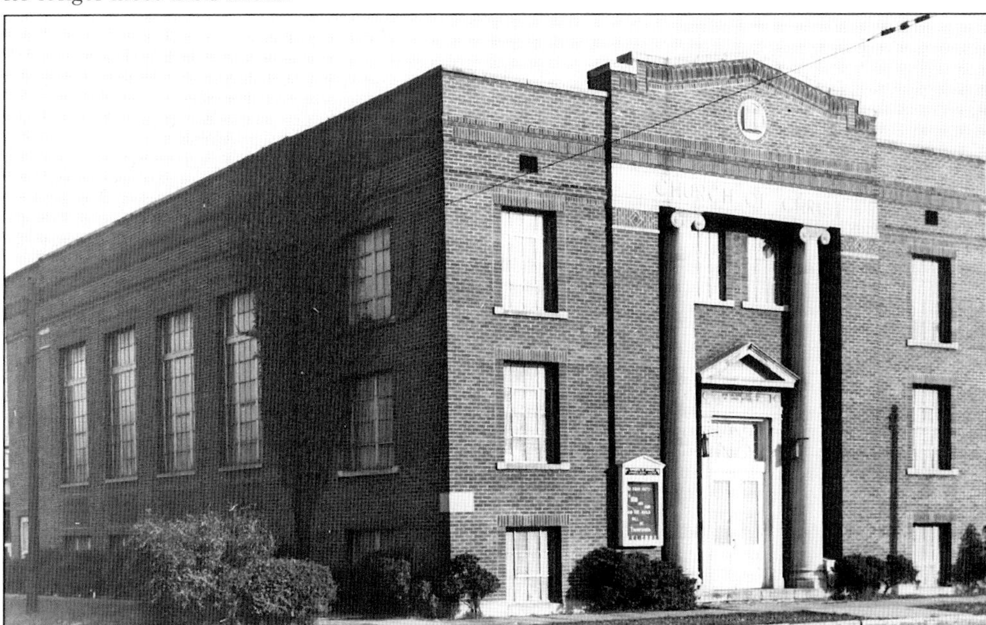

In 1924, the ladies of the Home Circle purchased two lots on Fifteenth Street and Maryland Avenue, and the cornerstone was laid on June 13, 1926. The new church was dedicated on May 22, 1927.

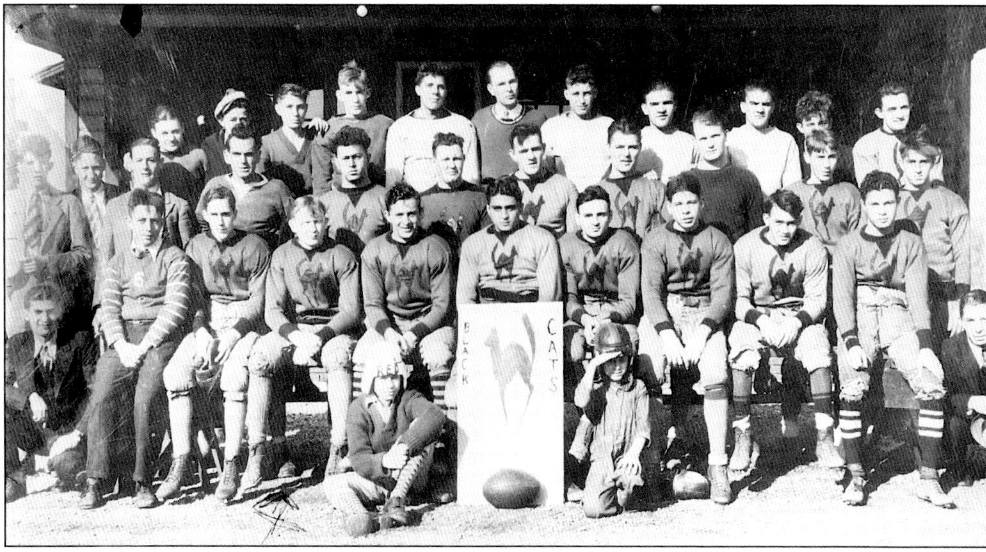

The Black Cats were a semi-pro team in Sebring during the 1930s, and they competed against teams in Canton, Ohio; Massillon, Ohio; and Alquippa, Pennsylvania. Although home field was located at the Sebring Race Track, they also played at a field located south of the Mile Branch Grange where the Clinton Heacock home stands today. The players shown here, from left to right, are as follows: (first row) ?, Mike Conny, ?, Red Beaton, ?, Jim Lee, Sailor Lee, ?, Melvin Welch, and Paul Demark; (second row) four unidentified players, John Palermo, Lloyd Cobbs, ?, and Hershal Harris; (the two players on the right) Ron Wayt and Richard Wayt.

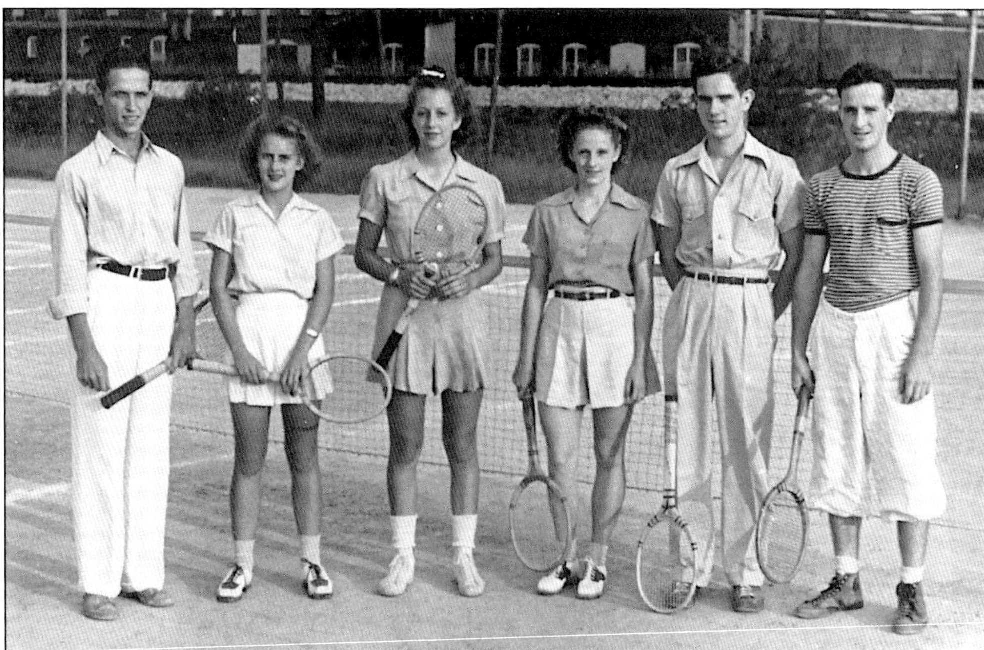

Players shown here enjoying a game of tennis, from left to right, are Joe Rittenhouse, Betty Stanley, Jean Applegate, Enid Miller, Bill Miller, and Charles Hawkins.

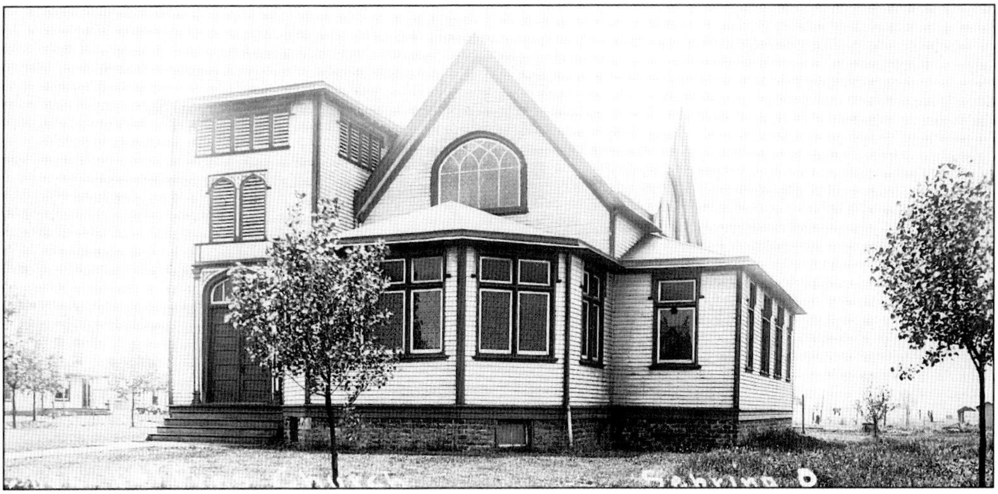

The organization of the First Presbyterian Church began in the latter part of 1900. Through the assistance of the Presbytery, a petition was given on February 5, 1901, to establish the church. The Sebring Land Company donated land on the northwest corner of Sixteenth Street and Indiana Avenue to be used specifically for a church building. With the help of a $1,000 grant from the Board of Church Erection, F.D. Sewell was contracted to build a suitable house of worship to seat 350, heated by a warm-air furnace, carpeted, and lighted by electricity. The cornerstone was laid on July 5, 1902, and the church building was dedicated on November 23, 1902.

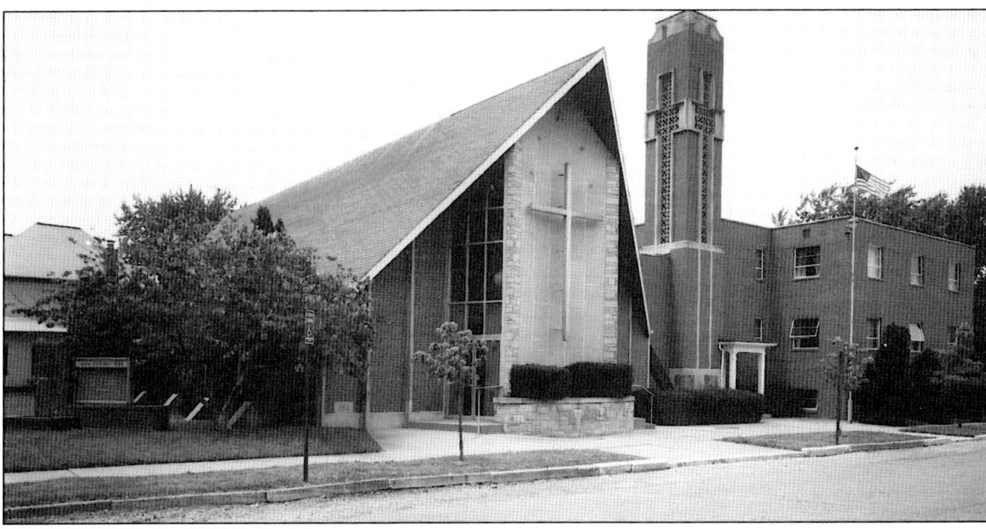

Throughout the years, the growth of the First Presbyterian Church made it necessary to expand the building. A basement was placed under the frame structure in 1914. In 1946, the sanctuary was remodeled with new pews and carpet, and new chancel furnishings were added. The Emmett Albright family presented a memorial organ and chimes. In 1952, the congregation named two study committees for the erection of an educational building, and on March 29, 1953, the Building Fund campaign was completed with $50,000 pledged. Construction began on September 13, 1954, with the laying of the cornerstone on October 17, 1954, and dedication on October 16, 1955. In the early 1960s, plans for a new sanctuary were drawn up by prominent Alliance architect Richard Zuber. Construction began in 1964 by Charles Cartwright Construction Company, and the dedication services were held on March 28, 1965.

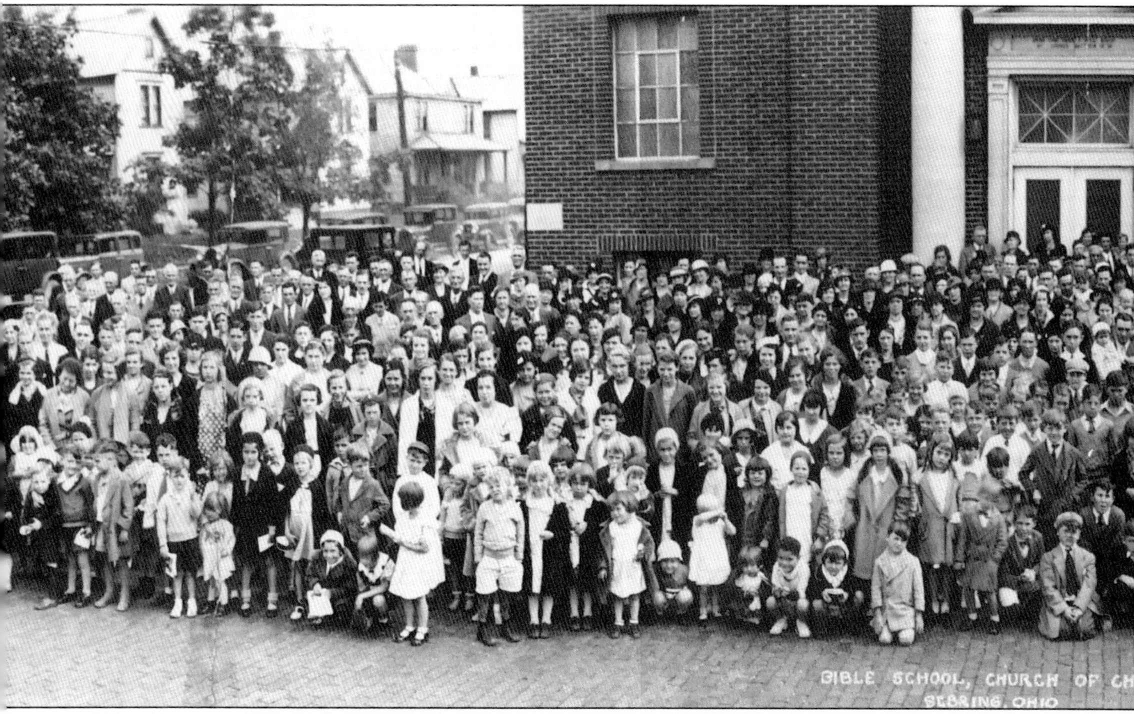

The Church of Christ has always had the largest Bible school class throughout Sebring's history, as the classes were open to everyone in the community. The success of the class is depicted in

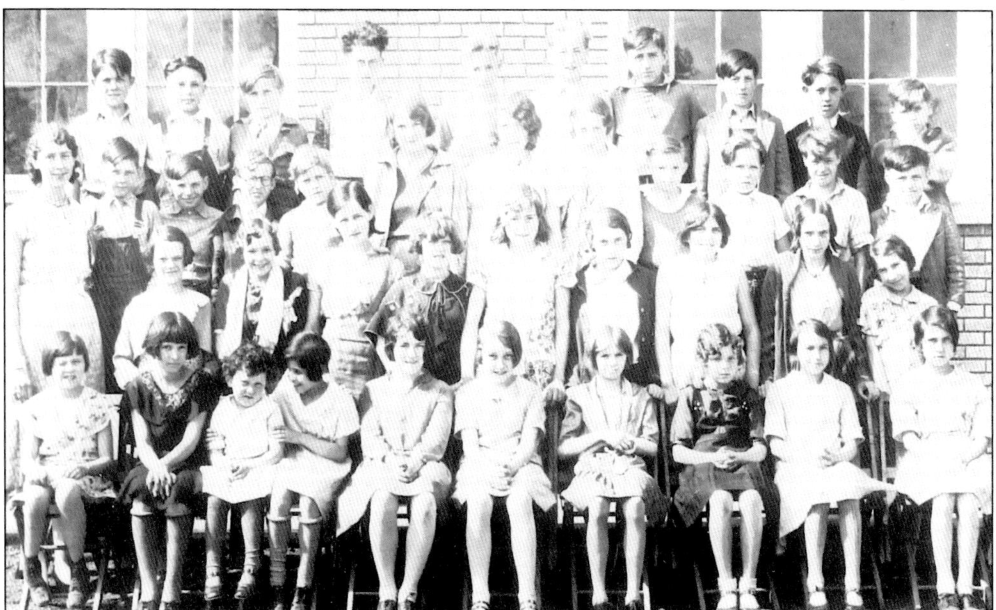

Maple Ridge School, which opened in the fall of 1925, was established through the consolidation of the surrounding one-room schoolhouses. Fish Creek, Bandy, and Quaker Hill eventually closed in the 1920s and 1930s. Hazel Phillips's students include Mrs. Charles (Hazel Brunie) Strain, second from the left in the second row, and Mrs. Eddie (Evaline Brunie) Oliver, seated in the first row third from the right.

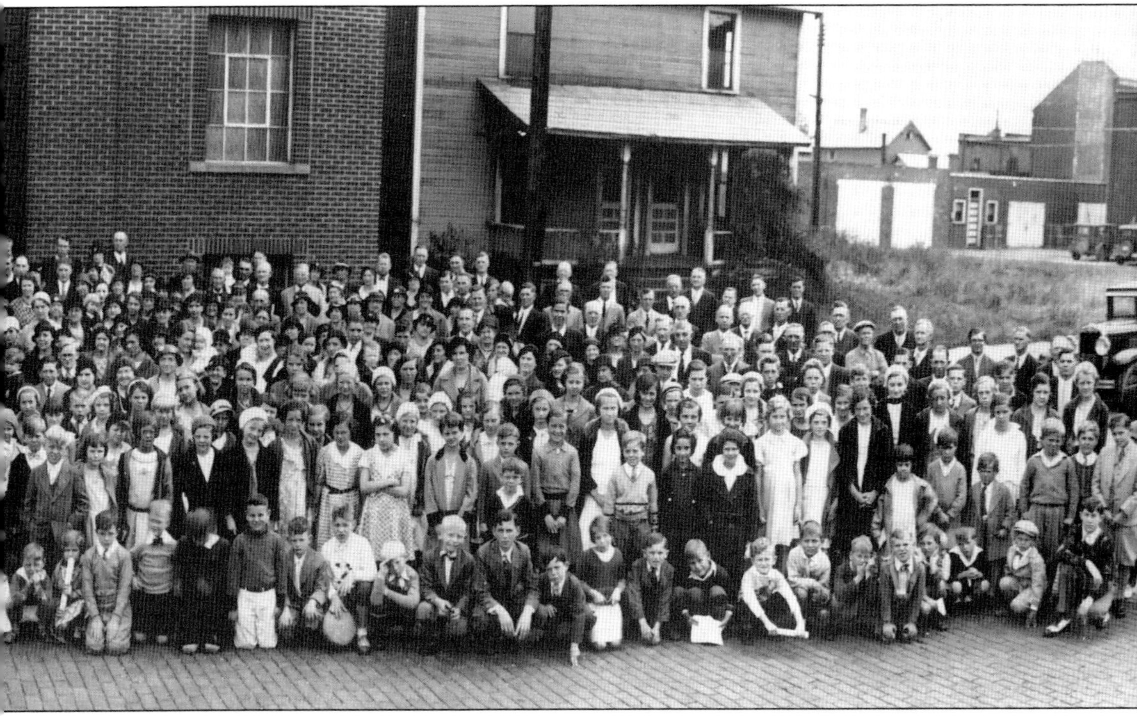

this early 1930s panoramic photograph.

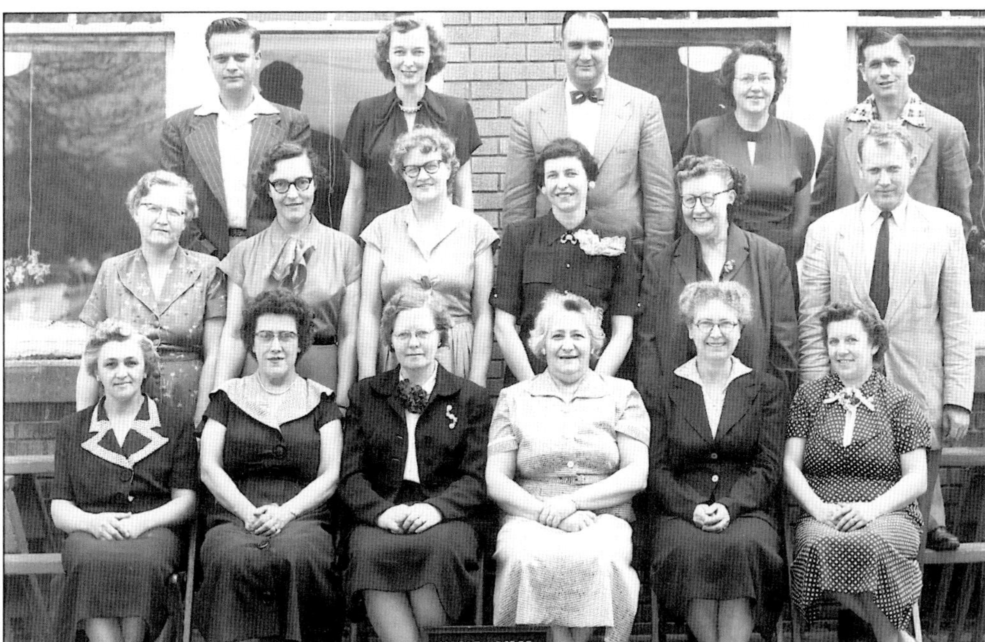

Maple Ridge Staff, who posed for Wilbur Dimit on April 30, 1954, from left to right, are as follows: (seated) Virginia Rill, Phoebe Fasnaught, Jesse Brunie, two unidentified, and Gladys Byham; (center row) three unidentified, Elizabeth Boehm, Dorothy Jolley, and unidentified; (back row) ?, Helen Hodge, Robert Ackenhead, and two unidentified.

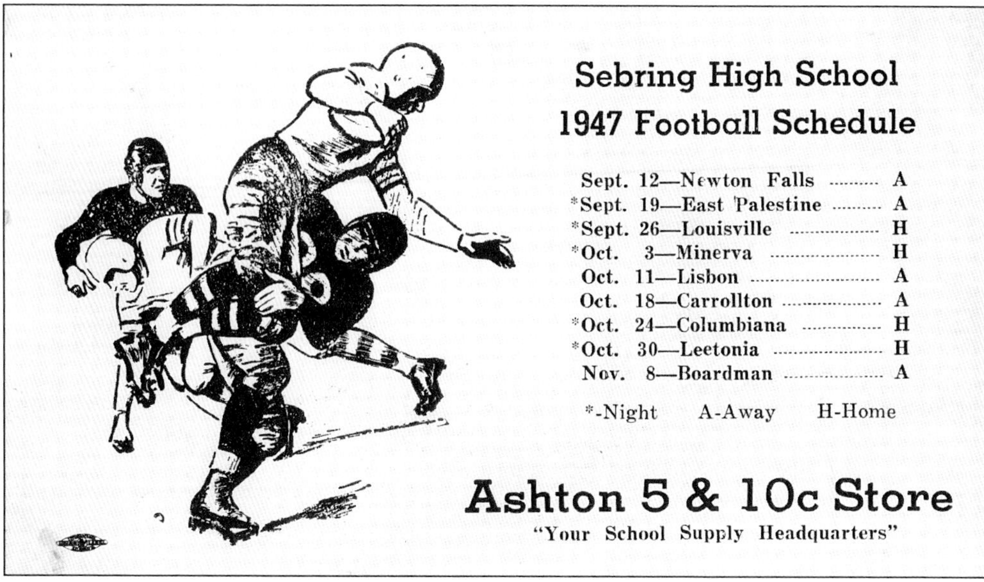

Shown here is the game schedule for the Sebring High School 1947 football team, which was given out by Ashton's 5 & 10 cent Store.

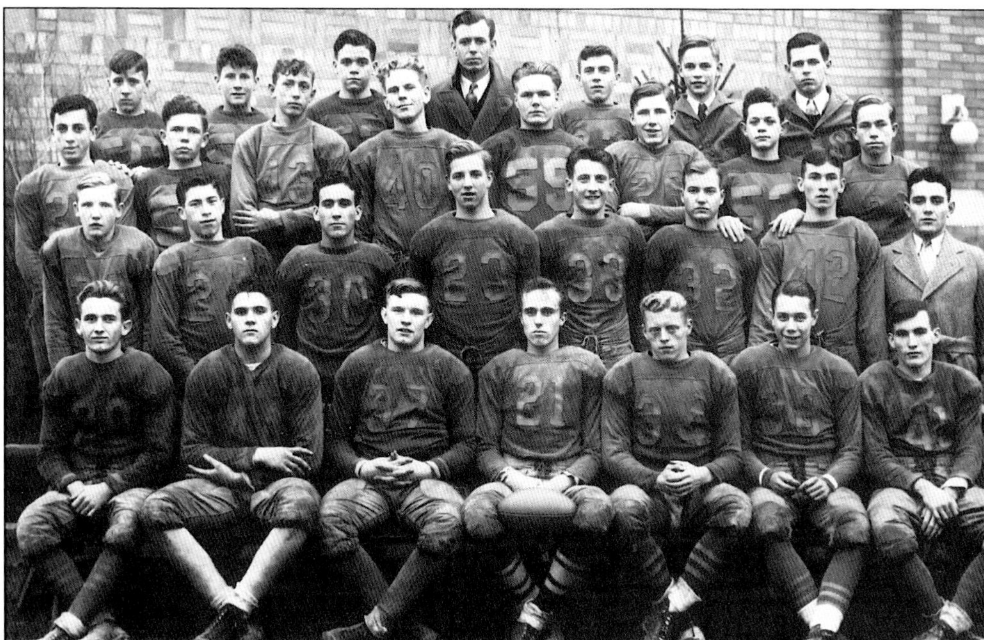

The Sebring High School Tri-County Champs of 1935 are, from left to right, as follows: (first row) Earl Ells, Ken Armitage, George Freetage, Scotty Burns, Bob Iddings, Sonny Campbell, and Art Fullerton; (second row) Bob Falkner, Jim Campbell, Bob Howell, Church Mercer, Gene Rogers, Carlos Craven, Jack Cardinal, and James Hostetler (coach); (third row) Frank Conny, Wayne Hoptel, David Messinger, Steve Tucker, Schlenbargarl, Bill Workman, Lower, and Dale Becker; (fourth row) Bob Cardinal, Denny Steed, Wade Rittenhouse, Huck Crewson (assistant coach), William Smith, Colin Anderson (assistant manager), and Robert Lower (manager).

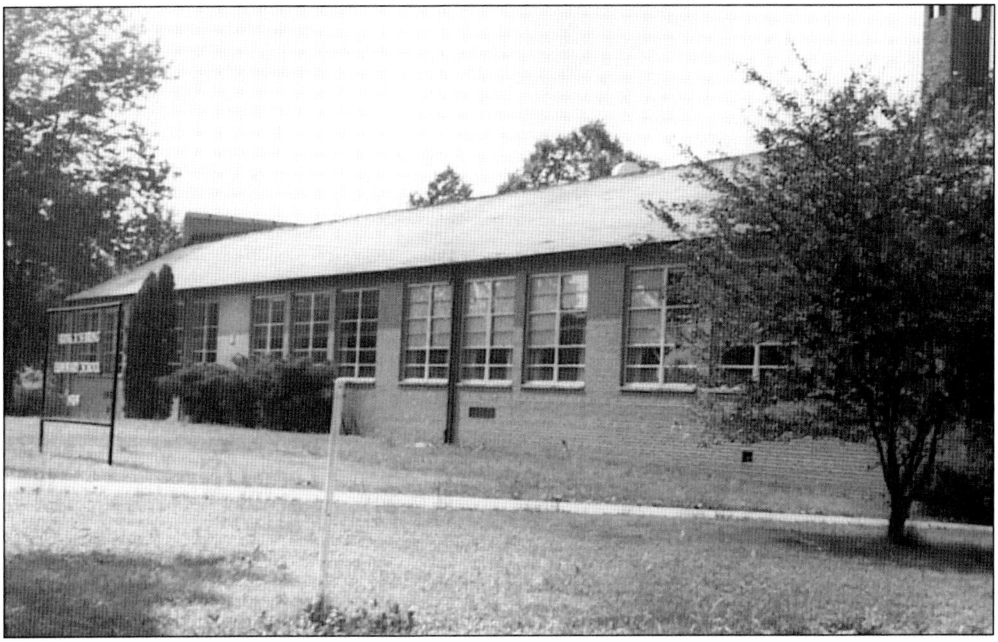

The Frank A. Sebring School was built in 1949, replacing the old South Side School. Located on West Texas Avenue, it was constructed at a cost of $150,000.

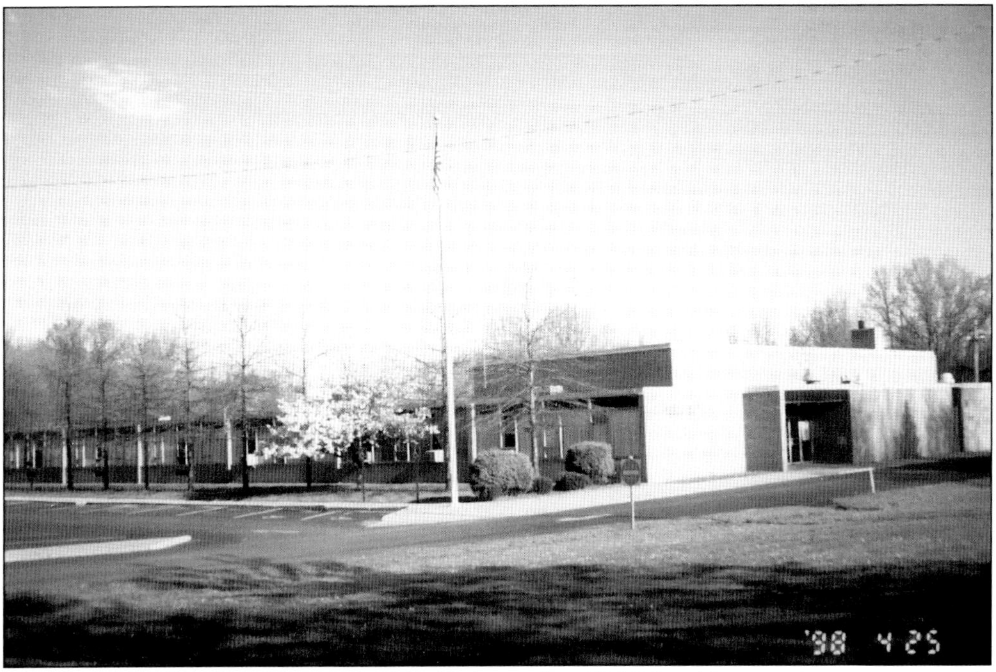

The Beatrice L. Miller Elementary School, located at 506 West Virginia Avenue, was made possible by its namesake, through her generous donation of $20,000 in 1967 and a bond issue that was paid off in 1992. Beatrice L. Miller was a founder and head of the Royal China Company. Miller was very generous to the community and her church. She set up a scholarship fund at the Sebring United Presbyterian Church, which has given many youth the opportunity to attend college.

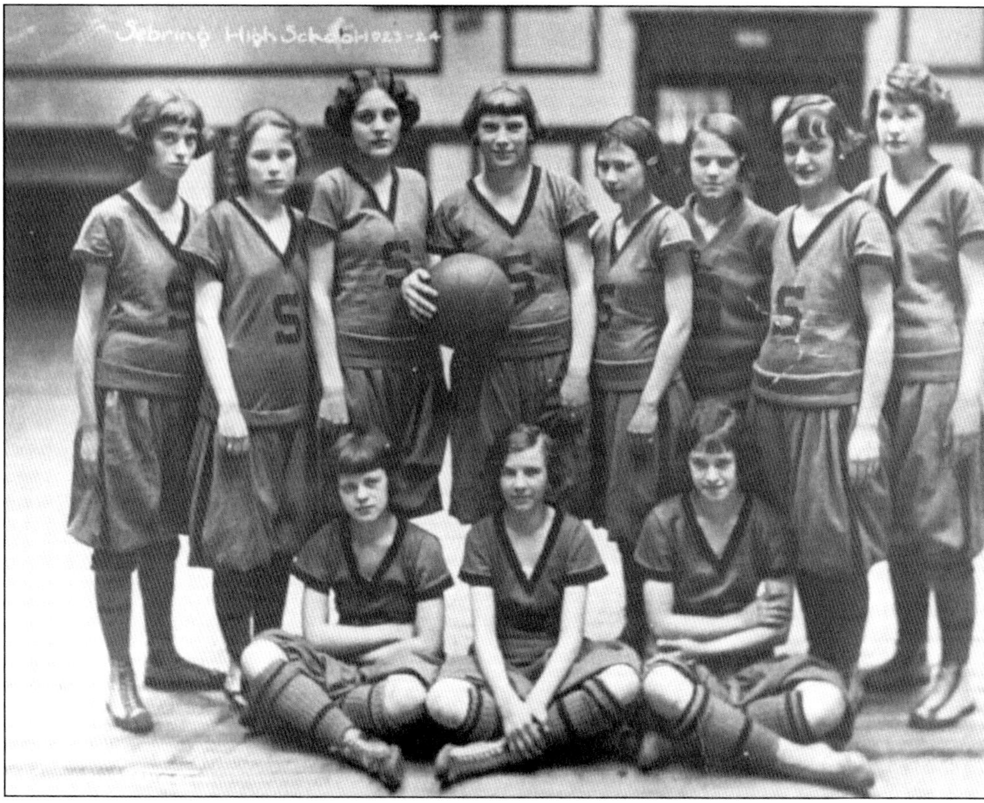

This photograph illustrates the 1923 and 1924 Sebring High School girl's basketball team. Not much has been written about this and other girls' teams in Sebring's history, and only a few names can be identified. Lenora Patton (standing at the far left), Gladys Dairyman, Charlotte (Jones) Daugherty, Alda (Patton) Watson, and Mildred (Welch) Hineman are shown here.

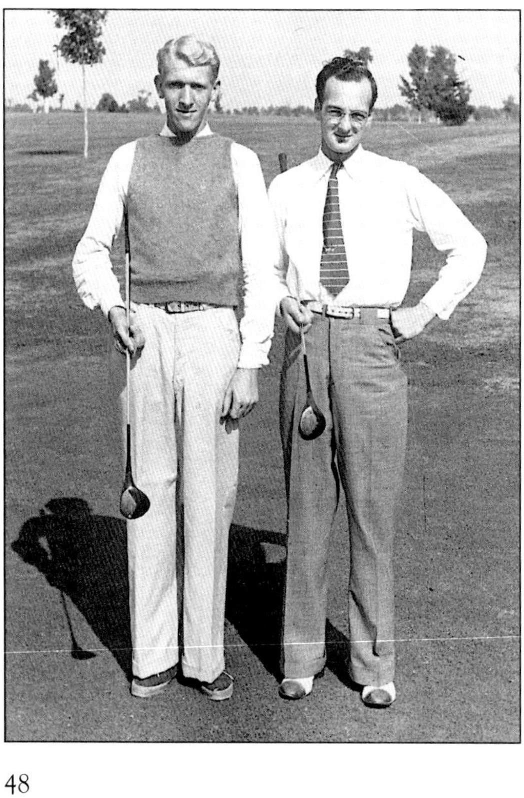

Bob Maus and Ed Eddy take time out during a golf outing to pose for this 1940s snapshot.

THE PURGOLDRA MASQUE

OF

THE SEBRING McKINLEY HIGH SCHOOL

UNDER THE AUSPICES OF THE ROTARY CLUB

Presents

"WE SHOOK THE FAMILY TREE"

McKinley High School Auditorium

WEDNESDAY and THURSDAY, DECEMBER 1 and 2

Estella Crewson, Director

Cast of Characters

Hildegarde, who is tired of being a wallflower .... MARILYN EASTHAM
Mr. Dolson, her father .... BRUCE FINK
Mrs. Dolson, her mother .... SARA JANE CARTWRIGHT
Sally, her younger sister .... JANET PETTIT
Bob. her older brother .... DICK BURSON
Jimmy, the younger brother .... RODGER CARSON
Paige, who likes to play postman .... GRETCHEN ERB
Ellie - May, Bob's heartthrob .... MARCIE BRADLEY
Jill, her friend .... VAUNDA LEE MOORE
Freddie Shermer, who wears knickers .... BOB POLEN
Mr. Shermer, his father .... JIM DANIELS
Mrs. Shermer, his mother .... BARBARA McCUNE

Place: The living-room of the Dolson home.
Time: The present. Spring.

Synopsis

Act One: Afternoon.
Act Two: Saturday afternoon, the day of the Prom.
Act Three: Eight o'clock, the evening of the same day.

Stage Crew

(Different Crew for each performance)

Stage Manager—Rodger Carson; assisted by Don Justison.
In Charge of Dressing Rooms—Marcie Bradley.
Prompters—Willa Mae Andrie, Marilyn Gartrell, Deloris McBride, Joan Folk, Ruth Shively, Elanor Reynolds.

Make-up—Maxine Heverly, Ruth Buehler, Esther Krahling, Florence Ellis, Maxine Theodore, Grace Herron, Mary Jane Jordan, Ruth Ann Kintner, Doris Fobean, Carole Hannen, Barbara Locke, Dorothy Fairbanks, Norma Gorby, Martha Sweeley, Nelda Myers, Thelma Knecht, Rosella Martin, Norma Dorsey, Donna Herren, Frances Welsh.

Music furnished by McKinley High School Orchestra, Under the direction of F. J. Conway.

Produced by special arrangement with The Dramatic Publishing Company, Chicago, Illinois.

This high school is a member of the National Thespian Honor Dramatic Society for High Schools—Troupe No. 666

Shown here is the playbill from a Sebring McKinley High School play.

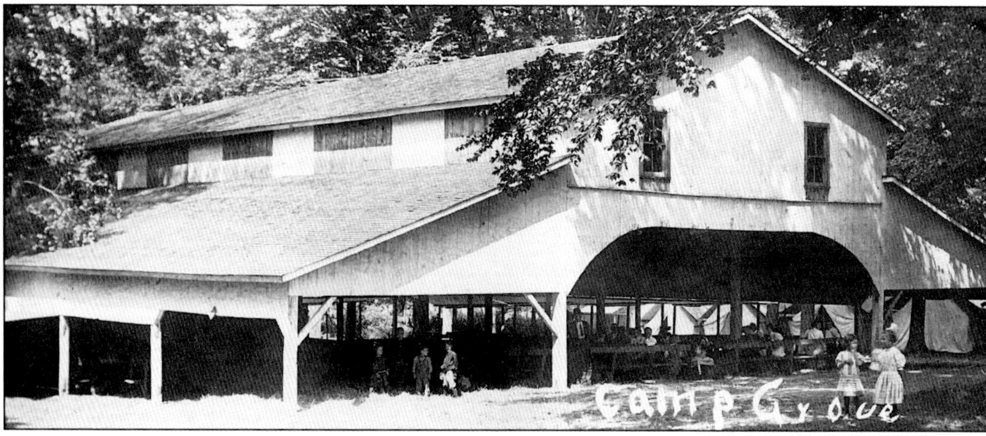

In 1904, George Sebring and Sebring's first mayor, Richard Albright, took a walk in a grove near Quaker Hill. As the two friends discussed their faith in Christ, they came upon a little sugar house in the maple grove. After entering the building the two men kneeled down to pray, and this was the beginning of the Sebring Camp Grounds. Mr. Sebring gave 19 acres of property for the sole purpose of "preaching salvation to a lost world," according to text from the 50th anniversary book. Shortly after that meeting, Anne Murphy, daughter of O.H. Sebring and a niece of George Sebring, invited Dr. George F. Oliver, a Methodist minister, to preach at the first meeting. One large tent served as the auditorium and several small tents were placed in the grove for campers. In July 1905, approximately 85 people attended the first meeting. The second meeting attracted over 250 individuals seeking salvation, and by the fifth meeting, 2,000 people passed through this once quiet sugar grove. Soon afterward, a building and many cottages were erected to accommodate the crowds.

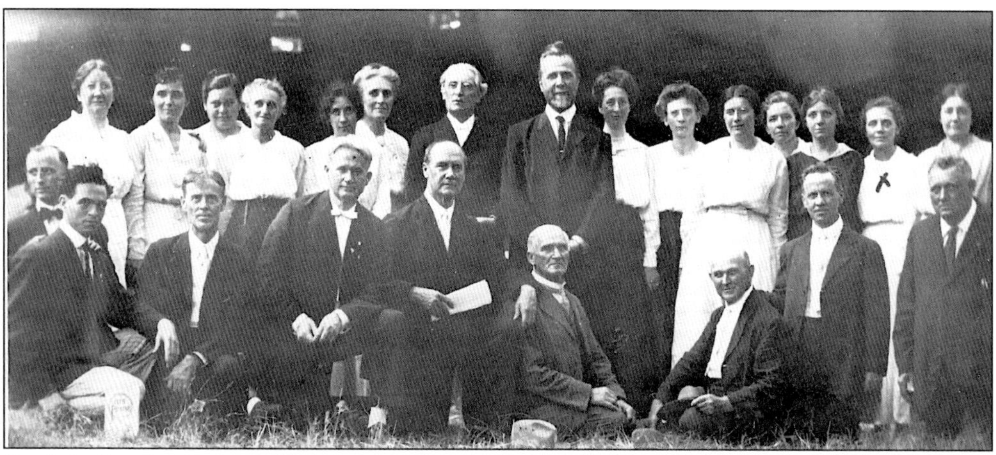

On July 27, 1918, a formal group of men and women took time out to gather together for this photograph at the Sebring Camp Grounds. According to Stella McNutt Purviance's story, in Sebring's 50th anniversary publication, "A great many of the world's best workers have had a part in its [camp meetings] success. God has been pleased to bless and own the efforts put forth for the upbuilding of His Kingdom and His glory. Many have gone out on the King's business to South America, Africa, Japan, India. Hence the fragrance of the prayer which went up to God from the 'sugar house' lingers over many a life, many a home, and many a land. Countless thousands of men and women have attended Sebring Camp, and have now gone to their reward. What will Eternity hold?"

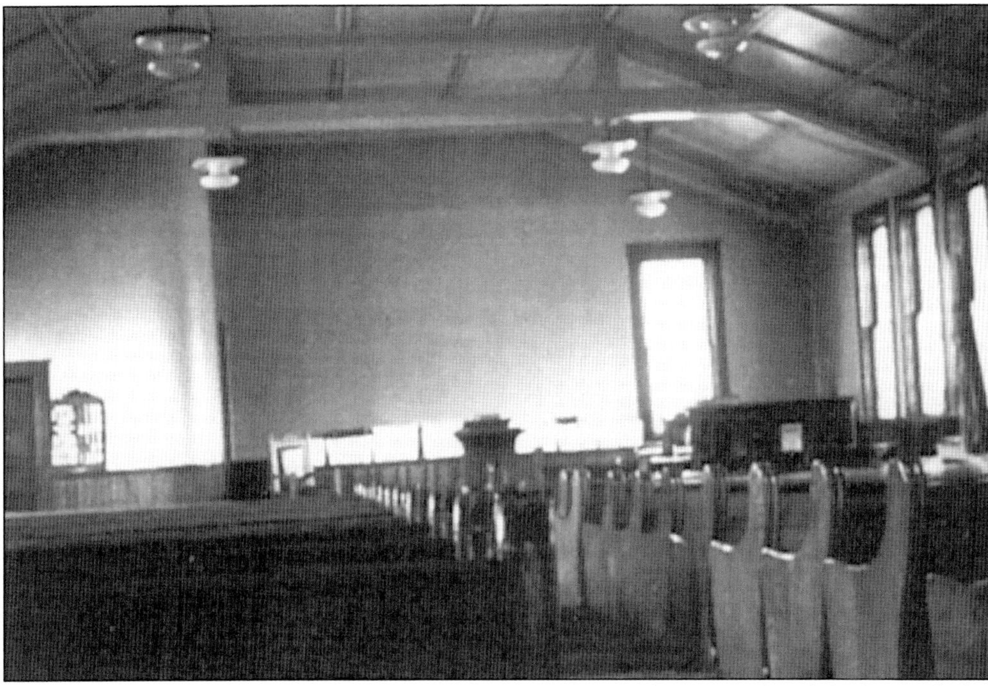

These are interior shots of the First (later Faith) United Presbyterian Church before and after the 1949-50 remodeling. The rooms to the left and right of the pulpit and chancel were used for Sunday school classes and the minister's study.

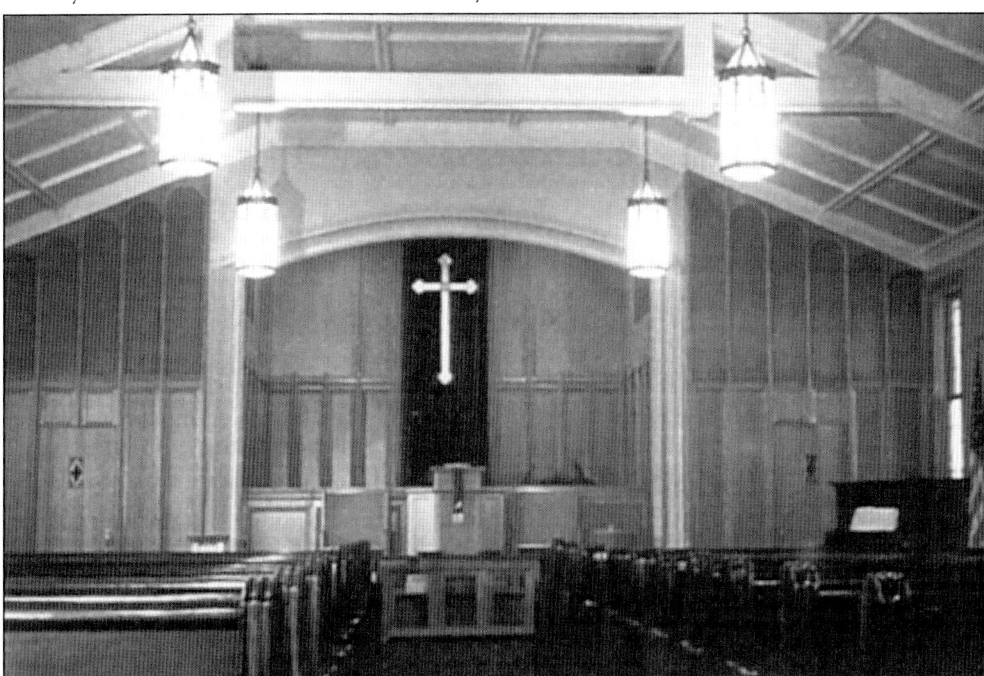

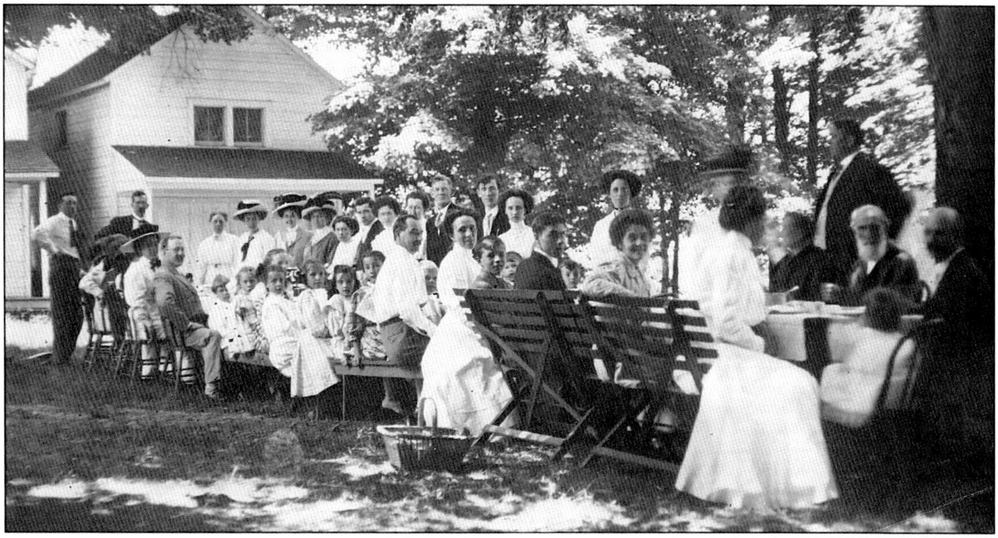

In this early view of the Sebring campground meeting, we see members of the Sebring family and other worshipers taking time out to eat. George E. Sebring Sr. (seated second from right), the thin man with the beard, looks toward the camera, and Fred Sebring is the rotund gentleman standing.

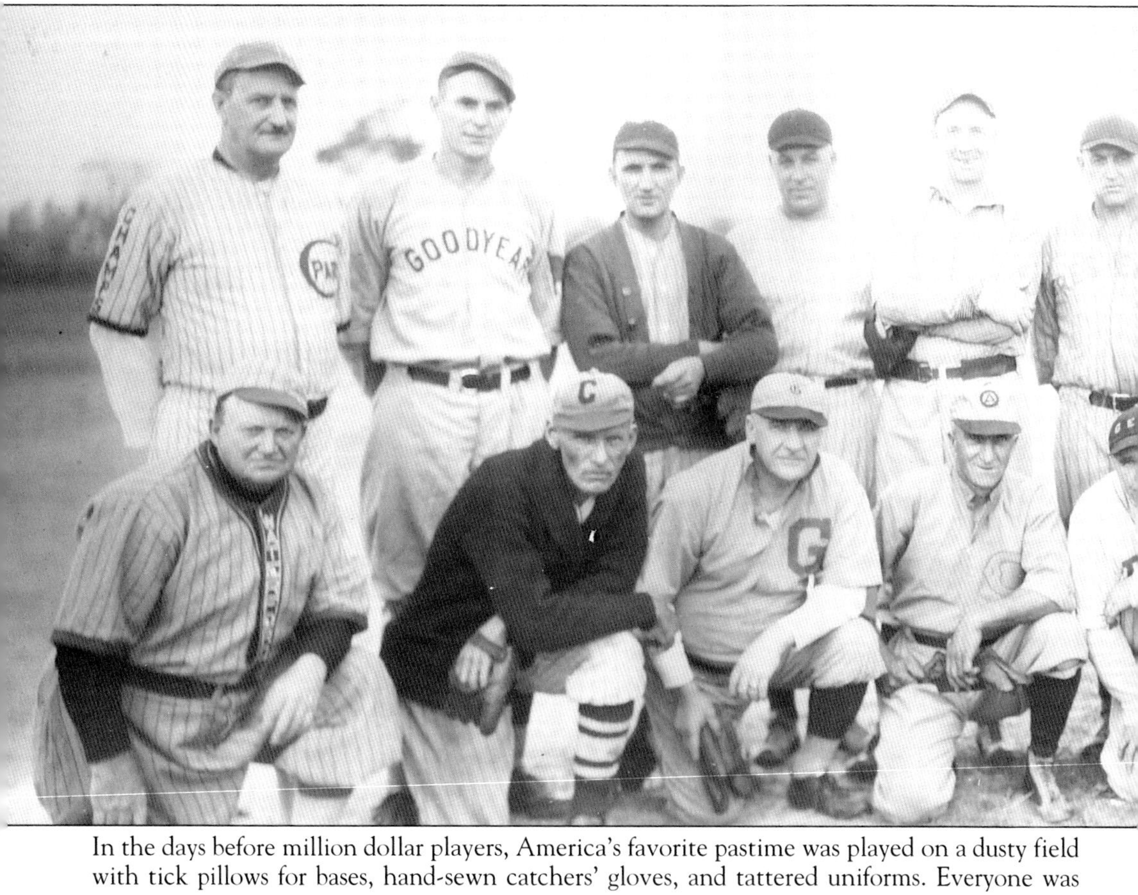

In the days before million dollar players, America's favorite pastime was played on a dusty field with tick pillows for bases, hand-sewn catchers' gloves, and tattered uniforms. Everyone was

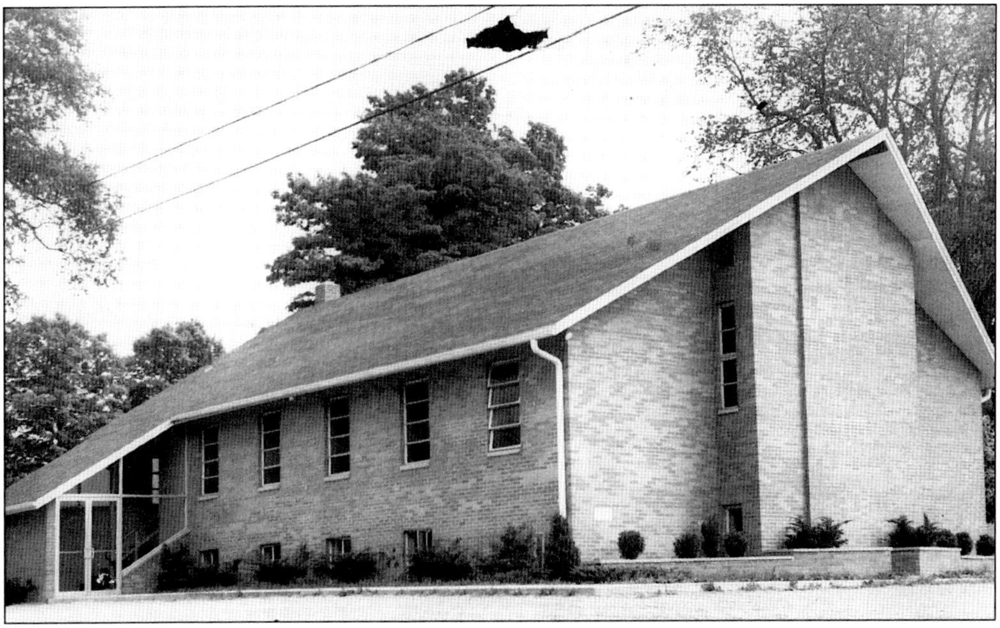

This photograph depicts the Quaker Hill Friends Church in the 1960s.

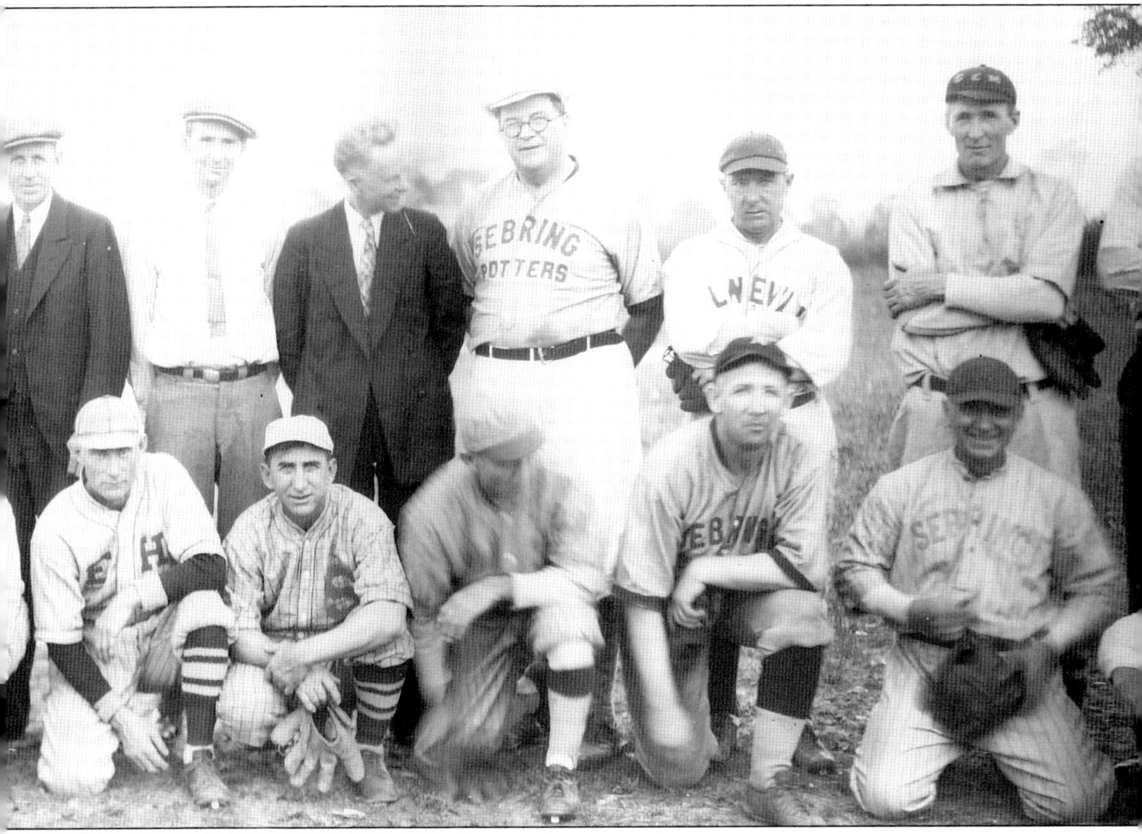

welcome to play, and the spirit of just having fun was goal.

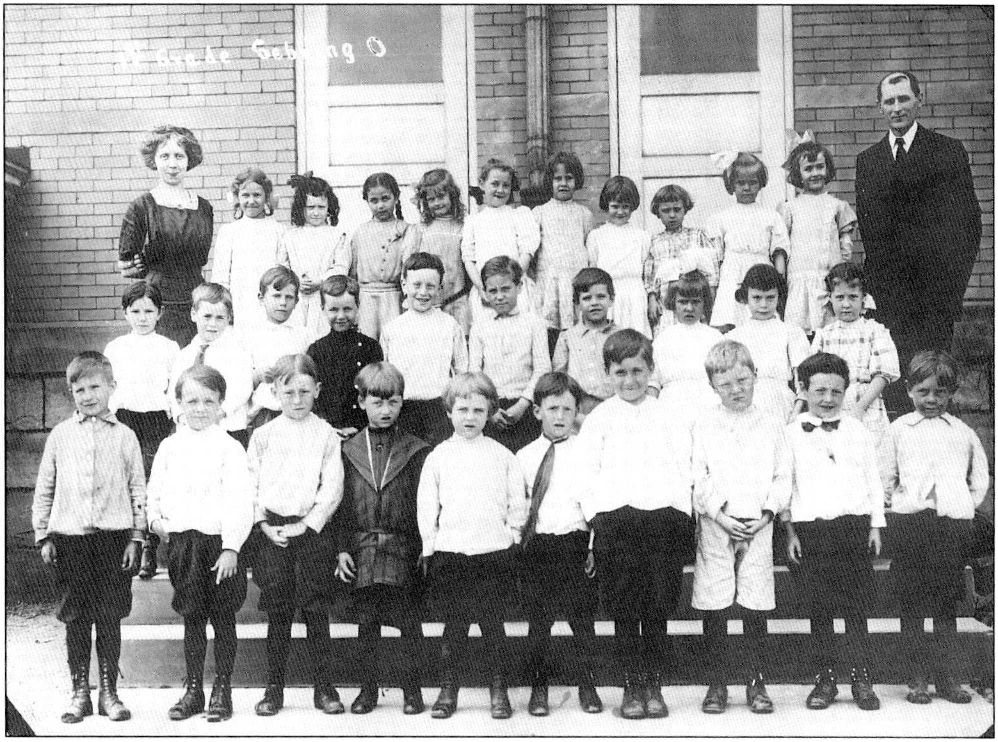

This is an early photograph of the first grade class at the Lincoln School building. One person identified on the back row is Franklin Henry LeFevre (first row, fourth from the left). LeFevre's father, Frank T., entered the insurance business in 1910 and was prominent in the community for many years. F.H. LeFevre continued in the business for many years.

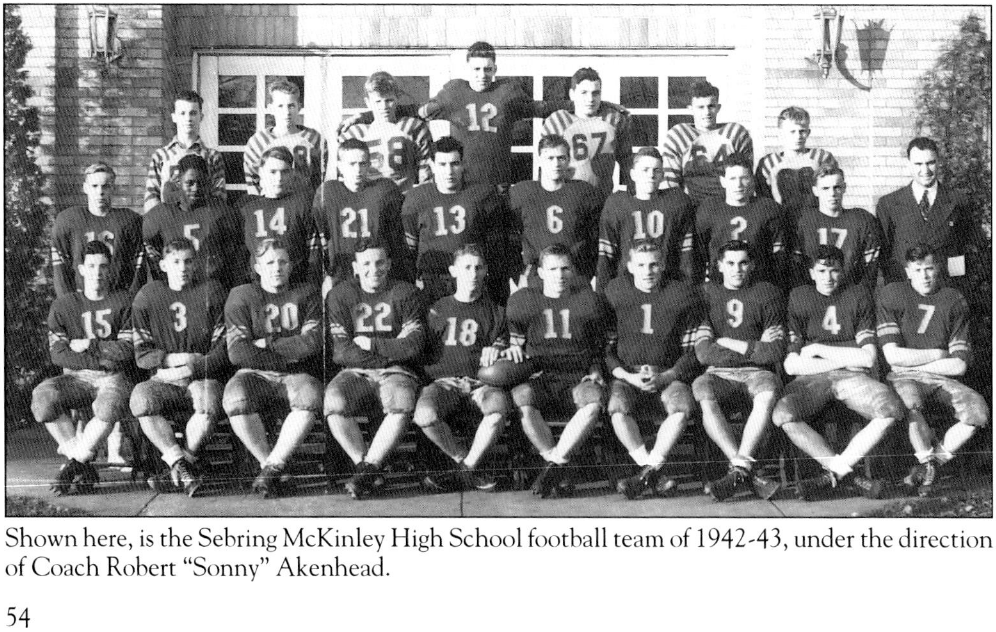

Shown here, is the Sebring McKinley High School football team of 1942-43, under the direction of Coach Robert "Sonny" Akenhead.

Four

MUD, PLANK BOARDS, AND BRICK STREETS

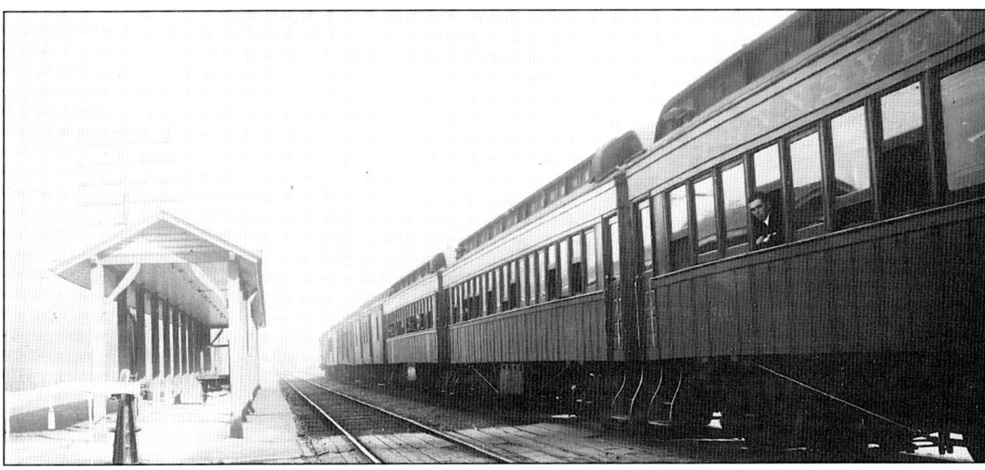

At the time our country was established, and in the decades that followed, men and women from the British Isles and Europe envisioned the chance for a better life in America. First impressions are always an important factor in maintaining hope and opportunity, and the arrival at ports in Philadelphia, Baltimore, and New York left a lasting impression on all. Seeing the stern but determined Statue of Liberty and the quaint Hall of Independence were reassuring signs, however, arrival in Sebring was not so impressive. The men and their families, many of whom were unemployed due to the poor economic conditions in West Virginia, were greeted by the black billowing smoke of the pottery's beehive chimneys, hastily constructed frame structures, and very muddy streets with plank board walks. This left many wondering what their futures would hold. As you will see in this chapter, the Sebring family's aggressive determination to build a better life for all would be realized. The community became an official stop for the railroad in November 1899, and the first station was housed in an old boxcar until the new station was completed in 1900. In this *c.* 1905 postcard, a passenger train has stopped at the Pennsylvania Station. In the distance, another train is arriving.

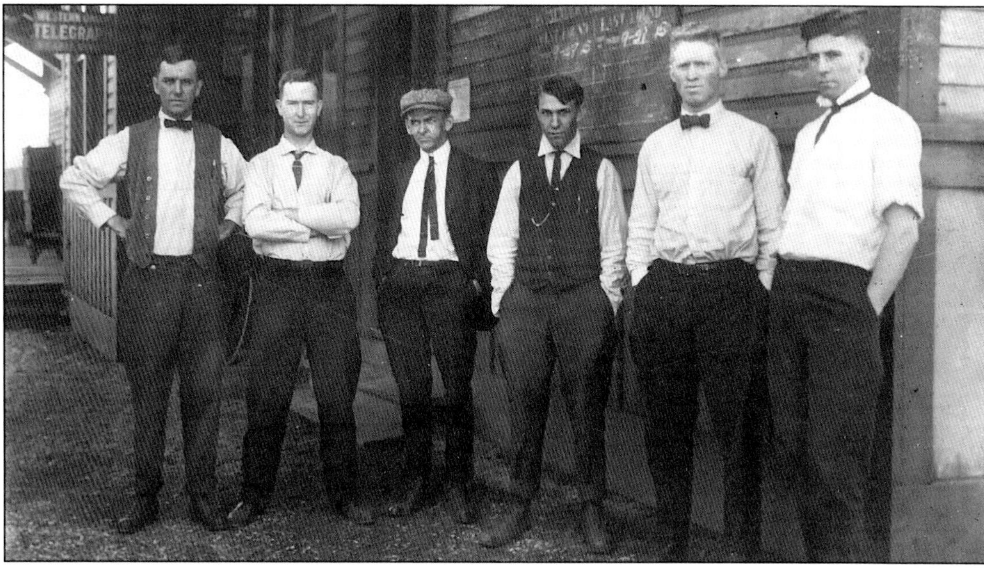

The men who worked in the Pennsylvania Railroad Station shortly after the turn of the century included railroad clerks, operators for Western Union Telegraph Company, and an official for the Railway Express Company. Pictured, from left to right, are Jim Meek, chief clerk; T.D. Keenan; Matthew A. Sutherin, railroad agent; Emerson Heacock; Howard Cook; and E.T. Whiter. The Western Union Telegraph Company was located in the station until it established its own office in 1920. One employee, Lloyd Strain, also served as telegraph operator in the famed "Lost Battalion," during WW I. He was the first enlisted soldier to receive word that the American troops were going home after a year-long occupation in Europe. Strain, who was exposed to the Germans' poisonous gas, never fully recovered, and he took his own life in 1941.

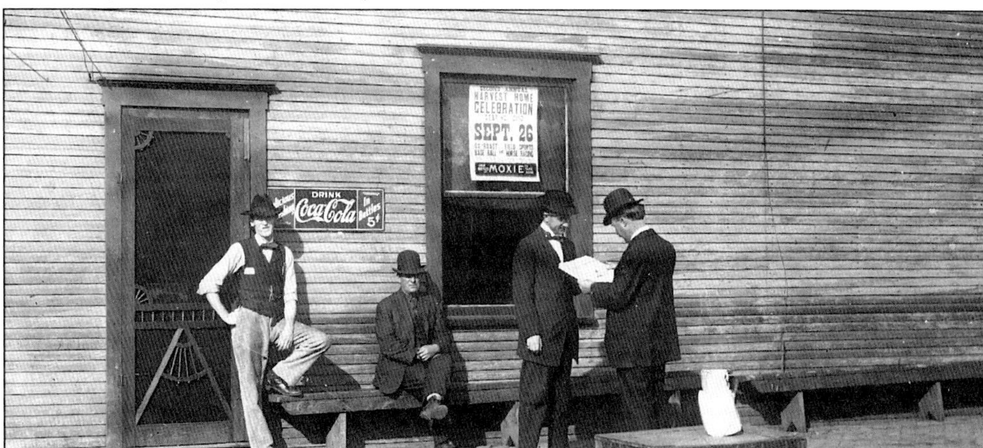

Five-cent bottles of Coca-cola greeted the passengers as they arrived at the railroad station in Sebring. Also posted on the window was an invitation to the Second Annual Harvest Home Celebration on September 26, and at the bottom of the sign, an advertisement read: "Cold bottle of MOXIE to take home." In the 1949 anniversary book, the caption of this picture states: " Sebring Brothers [sic] Take A Trip." They are probably the two men standing with the newspaper; however, the exact identification is uncertain. The back of this card also indicates that Jacob Smith is pictured. The items on top of the trunk appear to be carefully wrapped samples of pottery; perhaps the men were sales representatives for one of the local potteries.

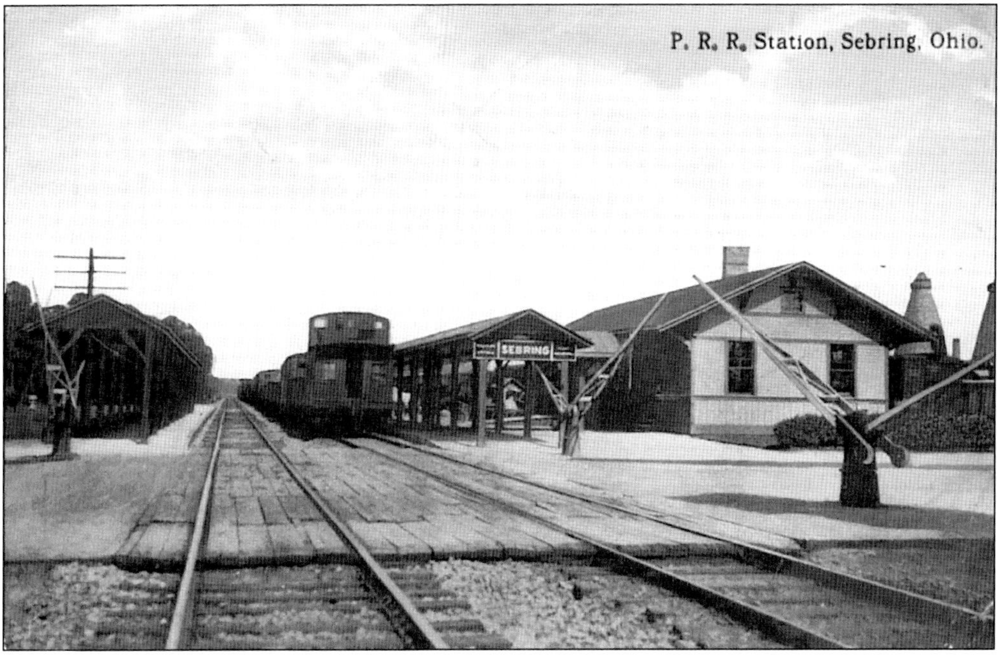

This postcard view, taken between 1910 and 1912, shows the Pennsylvania Station at the Fifteenth Street crossing. The manual crossing gates are visible in this picture, as are some of the beehive stacks of the E.H. Sebring Pottery Company. When the station was in danger of being razed, the Salem Model Railroad Club moved the building to the north side of the railroad tracks (along Pennsylvania Avenue) in the 1970s. This event made quite a spectacle, since all trains were stopped in order to slowly transport the delicate frame structure across the tracks.

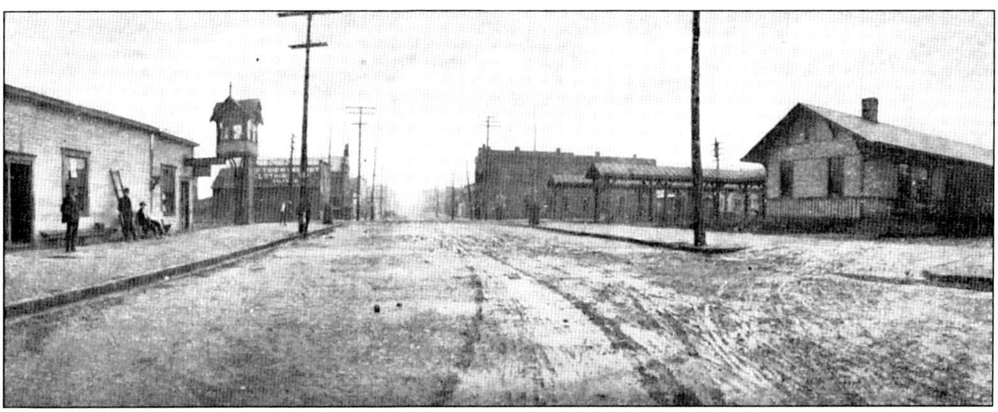

This photograph of Fifteenth Street looking north, toward the railroad tracks, shows the Pennsylvania Railroad station and passenger platform on the east side, and the switching tower on the west side. The Stark Electric Railroad Company tracks are barely visible through the mud. The interurban lines power plant was located on the current Lake Park Boulevard, across from the old Lake Park Chautauqua Picnic Grounds, between Alliance and Sebring. For those without automobiles, the streetcar served as inexpensive transportation to Salem, Canton, and Alliance. One could travel as far as Cleveland, Pittsburgh, and Detroit on the interurban.

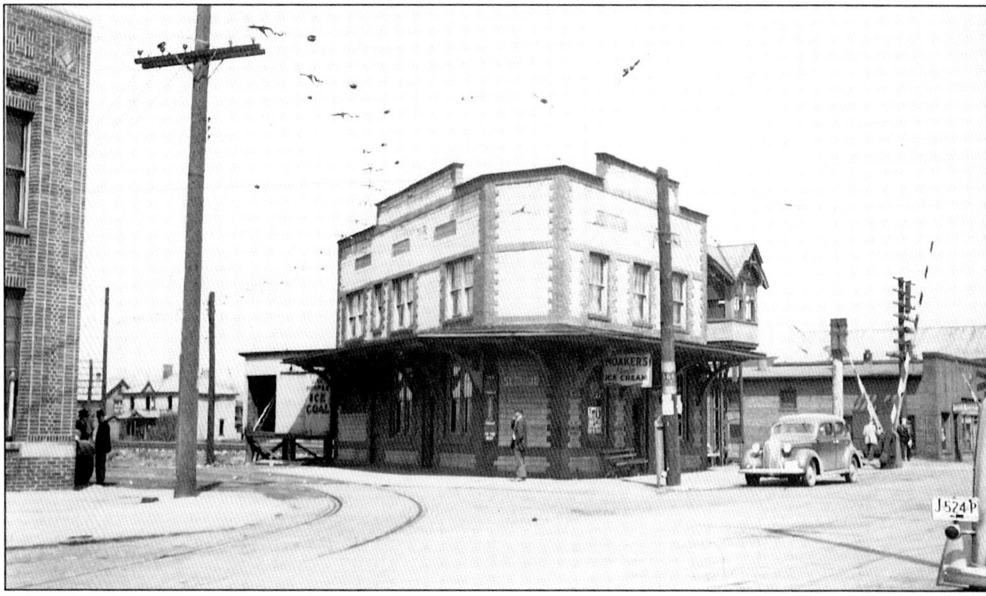

This building was constructed by the Stark Electric Railroad for use as a station. Through the years, other businesses shared the structure, including J.W. Hoopes Ice and Coal Company, which occupied the back portion and promoted its Champion Coal with the motto, "Costs Less Per Season." With the demise of the streetcar in 1939, the bus became the primary form of public transportation. Many refer to it as the old bus station. Inside, the church-like pew seats were a comfort to the patient traveler. One could peruse a magazine or newspaper while enjoying candy or Noaker's Ice Cream, which was offered for sale at the confectionery stand. In later years, the business was owned and operated by the Beadnells. The building was renovated to include a drive-thru business. The two-story brick building once housed the offices of the old Sebring Pottery Company.

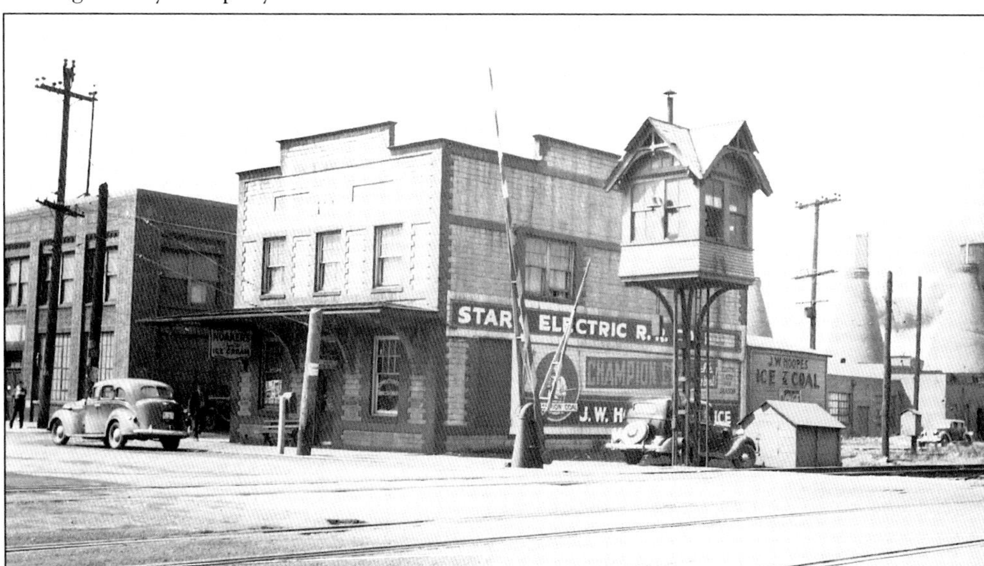

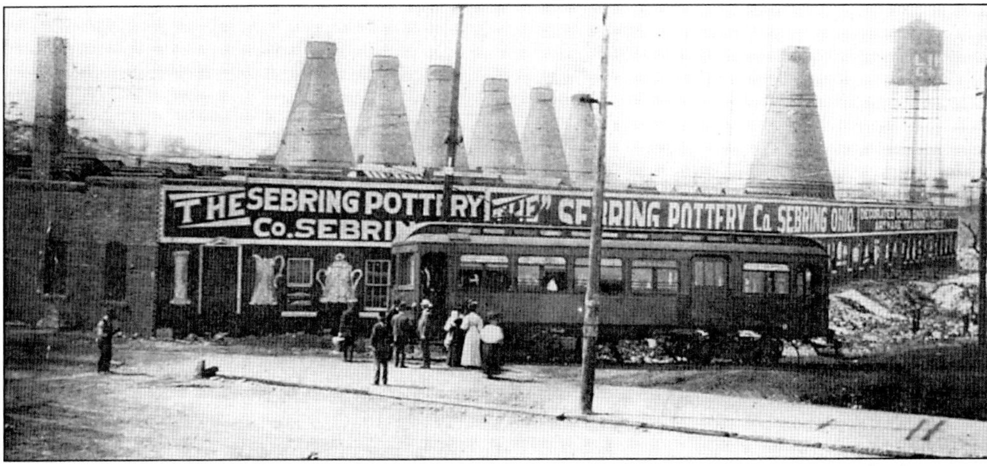

Passengers board the streetcar in front of the Sebring Pottery Company in 1906. The large sign and artwork painted on the building was the most effective billboard available. The water tower for The Sebring Lumber Company can be seen in the background. This card was sold by S.E. McKee, a news dealer, who founded the newsstand business in Sebring just prior to the turn of the century. The building, which housed his business, was constructed in one day, and the carpenters who erected the building slept there that night. This is another example of how fast the growth of this little community was progressing. McKee remained in business until 1910, at which time he sold it to a Mr. Slickman.

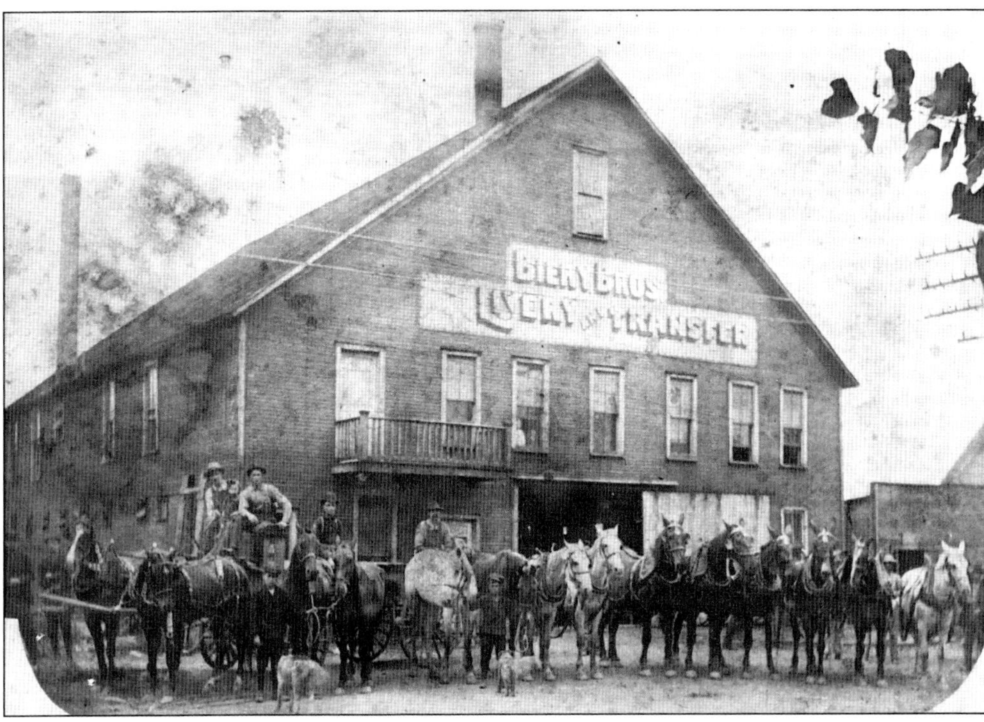

The Biery Brothers Livery Barn was located on West Oregon Avenue between North Fifteenth and North Sixteenth Streets. Prior to the automobile the livery business thrived in Sebring and other communities. The Bierys owned one of the farms purchased by the Sebrings in 1898. Today, a descendant of the Biery family operates the Biery Cheese Company near Louisville.

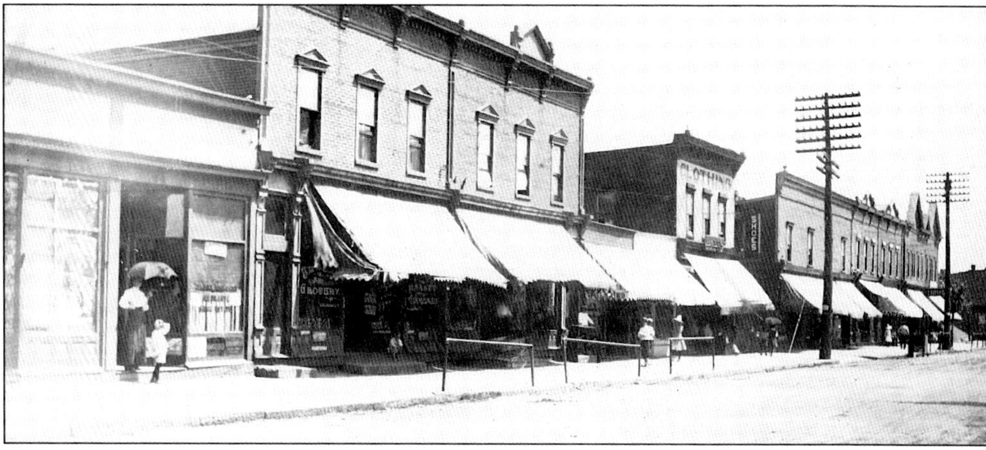

Awnings emerge on this sunny afternoon in Sebring in 1905. This postcard view shows the first block on the east side of South Fifteenth Street. The large canvases obstruct many of the businesses, so a detailed view is limited. The one-story building on the far left is the Sebring Real Estate Company. This building was razed and replaced by the Midland-Buckeye Federal Savings and Loan Association brick structure. The next building housed a grocery and bakery business. Giving the appearance of two buildings, the building has been altered over the years and has been home to Islay's, Lucy's Eat-A-Rama, and Thelma's Diner. The small one-story building was a tailor shop when this picture was taken. In the 1970s, Jim Taylor's barbershop was located here; however, since the 1990s it has been occupied by Mac's Video Store.

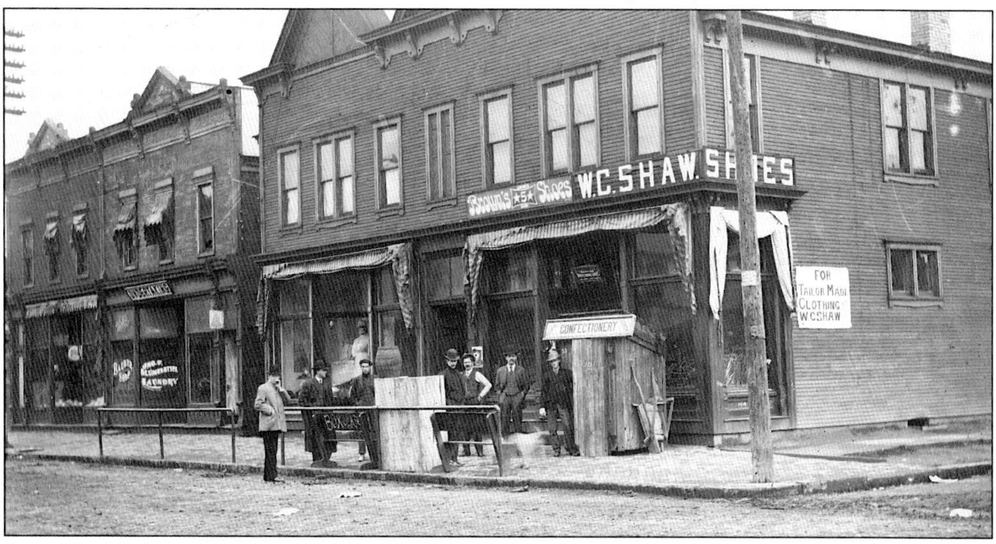

Several of Sebring's most noted businesses are shown in this 1910 photograph of the Geiger Block. Owned by Max Geiger of Alliance, Ohio, it stood on the northeast corner of North Fifteenth Street and Oregon Avenue. The south portion was occupied by W.C. Shaw's Shoes and Tailor-Made Clothing. Occupants of the north end are unknown; however, the window display shows items to be raffled off at the Oliver China Company picnic. The next set of buildings was occupied by a barbershop, John Frederick Blumenstiel's Laundry, and William Mooseman, undertaker (Ashton's 5 & 10 occupies this location today). John Blumenstiel and Carrie M. Weigel were the first couple to be married in Sebring, which took place on December 20, 1900. Mooseman moved to Sebring in April 1910, at which time he opened the village's first undertaking business.

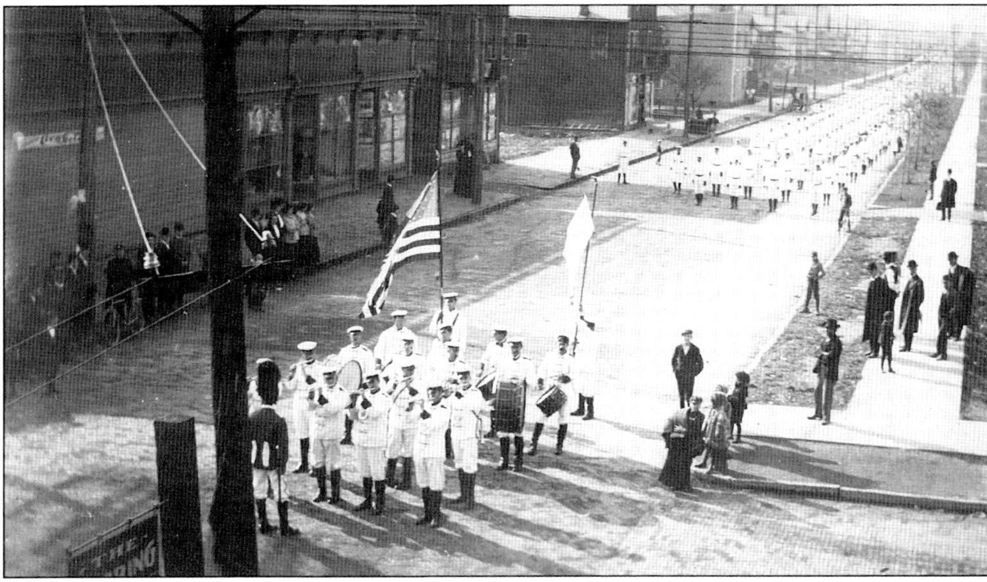

The Taft Club, supporters of William Howard Taft's 1908 presidential campaign, march down Ohio Avenue while the members of the Sebring band perform at the North Fifteenth Street intersection. The empty lot at the far right is where the Sebrings built the community's first financial institution, the Citizens Banking Company (now Bank One). The one-story building on the south side of Ohio Avenue was known at that time as the Stone Block.

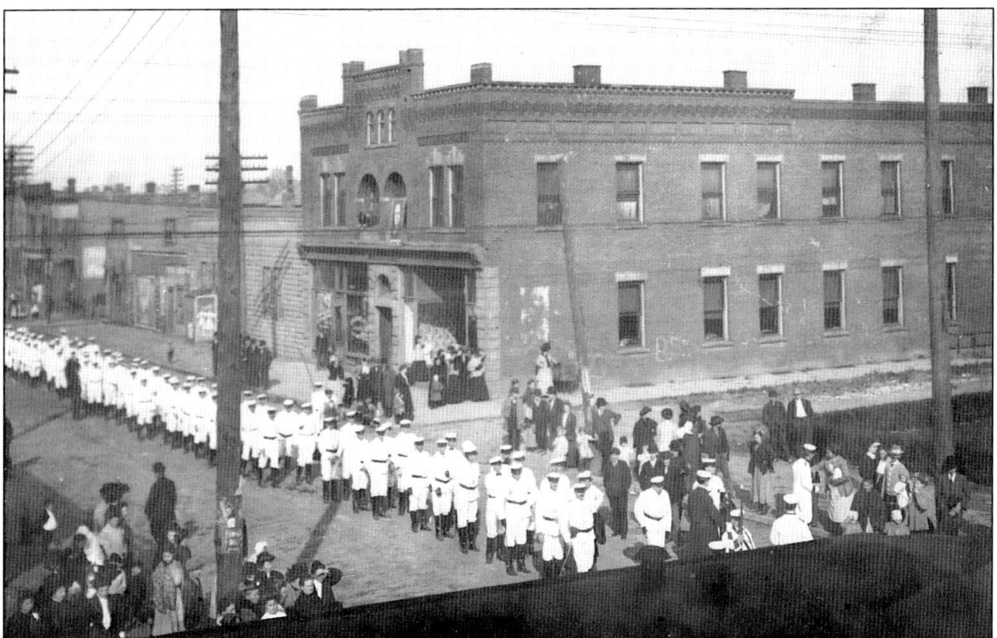

Taken from the top of the switching station, the Taft Club and the community greet William Howard Taft at the North Fifteenth Street crossing. Taft's train can be seen at the bottom of the picture. However, not all of the community supported the Ohio native, and on the second floor of the Katzenstein Building, a picture of Taft's opponent, William Jennings Bryan, is proudly displayed.

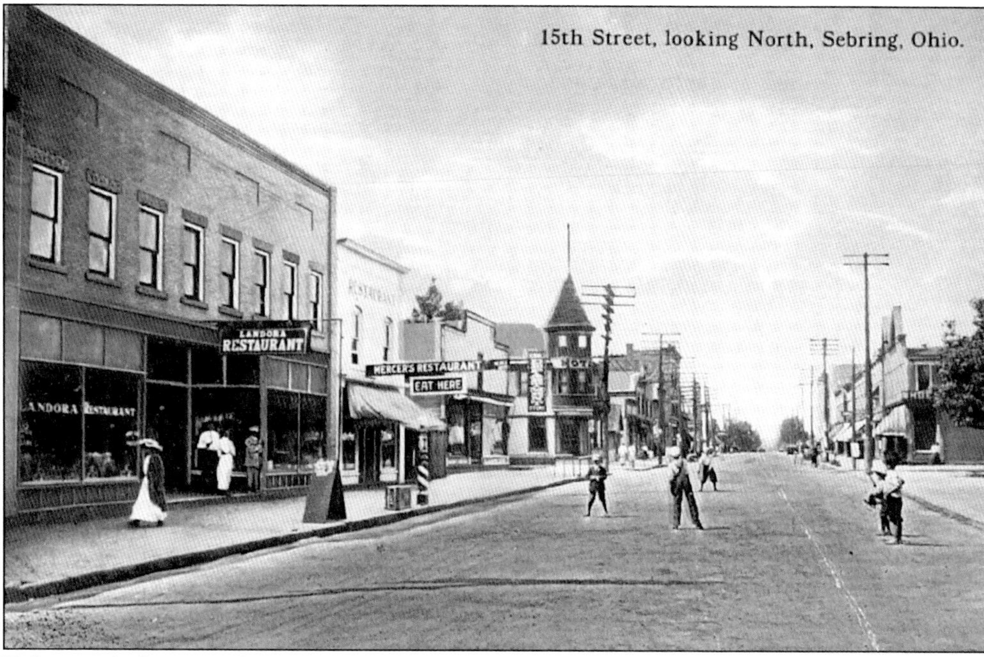

Folks watch from Landora's Restaurant door as children play catch on North Fifteenth Street during a quiet afternoon in the early 1900s. This postcard also captures a view of A.P. Mercer's restaurant, which many would remember years later as Calderone's Tavern. Next door, on the corner of West Oregon Avenue and North Fifteenth Street across from the Sebring Hotel, was Bert Baer's Department Store. The Crystal Lounge occupied this spot in later years. The Landora Restaurant site became the location of Zerbe's Napa Auto Parts Store and is now occupied by Dan's Carpet.

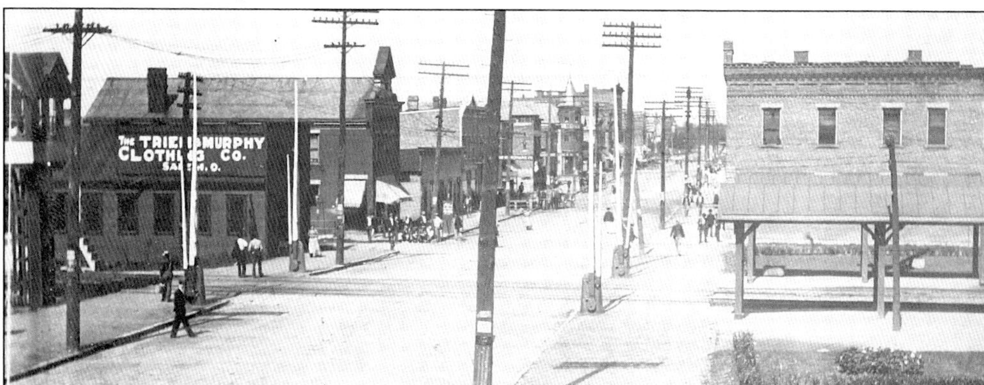

This image depicts another busy day on North Fifteenth Street c. 1908. On the left, directly across the tracks, the effective use of advertising for a Salem clothing store is evident on the frame building. The number of passenger trains that passed through on a daily basis was tremendous. The next building (with the awnings), on the northeast corner of West Pennsylvania Avenue and North Fifteenth Street, is the Williams Brick Block. According to a 1901 edition of the *Sebring News*, L.R. Williams operated the Union Restaurant, which had accommodations for about 30 guests at full occupancy. The building still stands today; however, the front has been altered. Williams came to Sebring from Enon, Pennsylvania, in the spring of 1901.

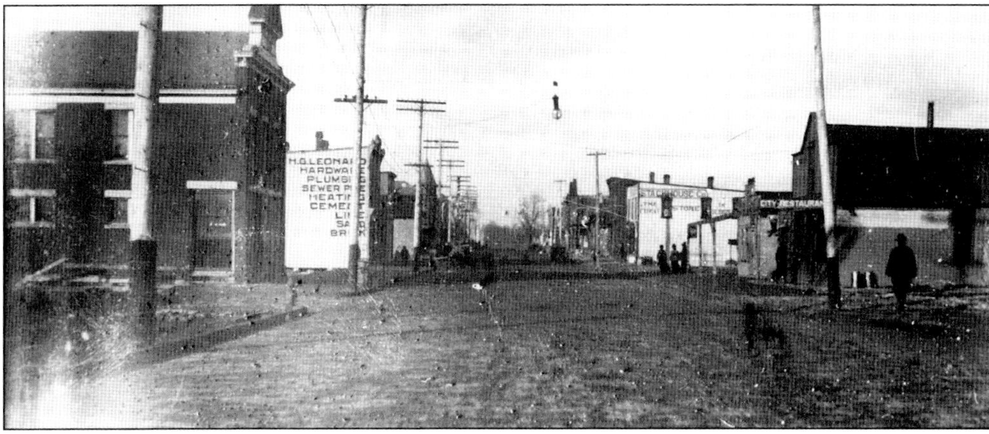

Shown here is one of the earliest photographs of Fifteenth Street. Looking north from the railroad crossing *c.* 1901, the frame structure on the far right is occupied by the Charles Kindler's City Restaurant. This building, and the lot to the south, was owned by Samuel Katzenstein of Alliance. Katzenstein purchased the first lot in Sebring and built the first house. For this, he was denounced by his fellow townsmen of Alliance as a dreamer. Before his house was completed, he had secured a good tenant for a term of years, which assured him an interest on his money of about 15 percent. Then, Samuel purchased more lots. In 1903, he erected a large two-story brick and stone building on the empty lot next to the City Restaurant. Another significant business is The Stackhouse Company on the east side. On October 28, 1899, John Stackhouse opened the first store in Sebring. The grocery and provisions store's first day sales amounted to $6.70. Within a year the building was enlarged and a warehouse was added. By the end of 1901, the sales were approximately $2,000 a month.

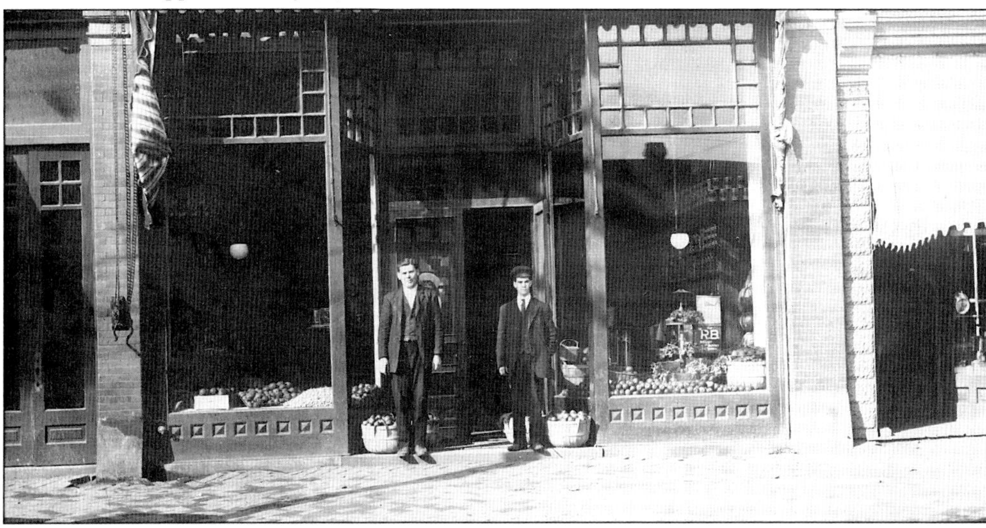

Edward Oliver was proprietor of a large general store in the Norris Block, known to many as the Victoria Building, on North Fifteenth Street. Oliver began his business career in Dennison, Ohio, in the early 1890s. After an economic downfall in Dennison, Oliver heard of the opportunities waiting in the new town of Sebring. On July 1, 1900, he opened his doors offering the community dry goods, notions, groceries, boots, and shoes. With sales exceeding $2,000 a month, he moved down the street into Mr. Norris's brick block in April 1901, increasing his sales room to 25 feet by 90 feet. Pictured are Cal Pettay and Ed Oliver's son Clyde standing outside the store in the Norris Block.

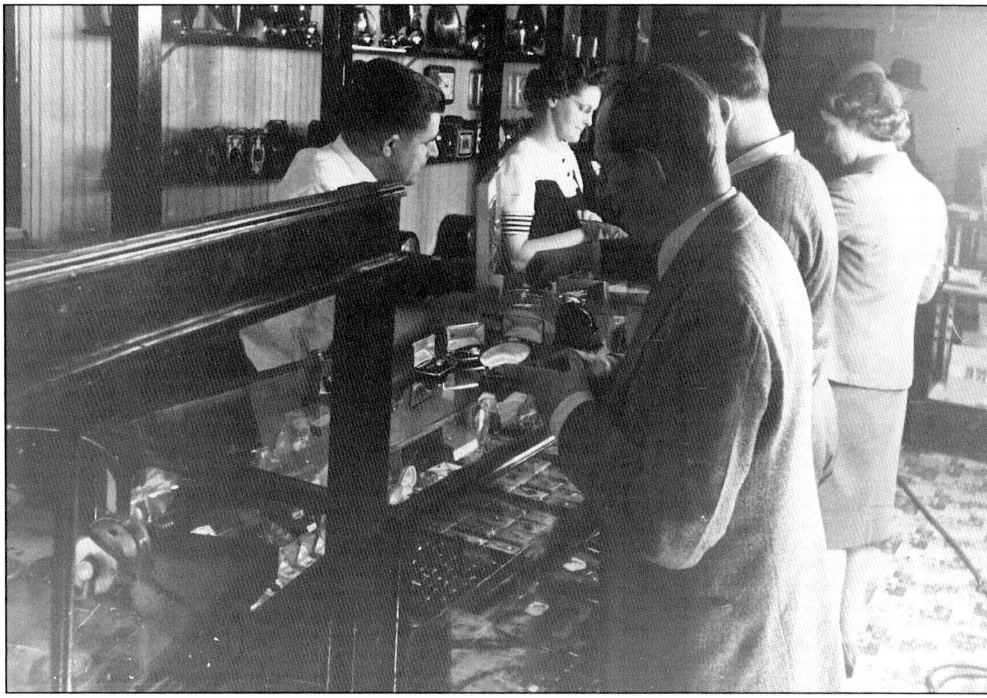

Gilbert Ostermeier and Myrtle Griffith assist customers at the Ostermeier Jewelry Store, which was located at 235 North Fifteenth Street. The store was owned and operated by Gilbert M. Ostermeier. Gilbert and his brother, Henry, started their business in 1920, when they bought out M.I. Kirkman's store. In 1923, Henry bought out his brother's interest and operated until 1926. The history of the jewelry trade in Sebring is somewhat complex. Henry sold to Mr. W. Webb, who then sold to his son-in-law, John Schulie. Gilbert reappears in 1936, when he purchases the Rector Jewelry Store, a predecessor of Schulie. Thus Ostermeier reemerged as the premier jewelry store.

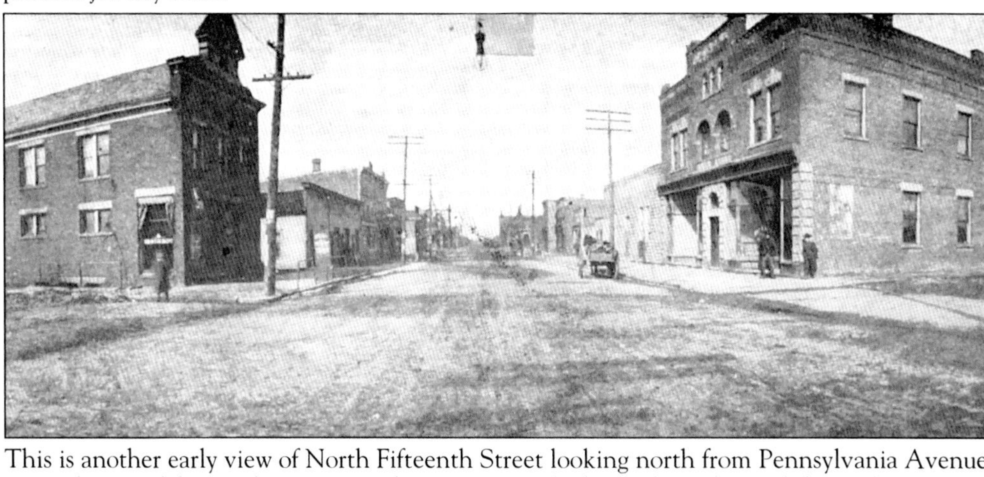

This is another early view of North Fifteenth Street looking north from Pennsylvania Avenue. A good view of the newly constructed Katzenstein Block, on the right, and the Williams Brick Block, on the left, show the architectural detail of both buildings. The Williams building has seen significant changes over the years, while the Katzenstein Building has seen little change over the years. Many will remember when the Allen and Son Furniture Store and Hotel occupied this building.

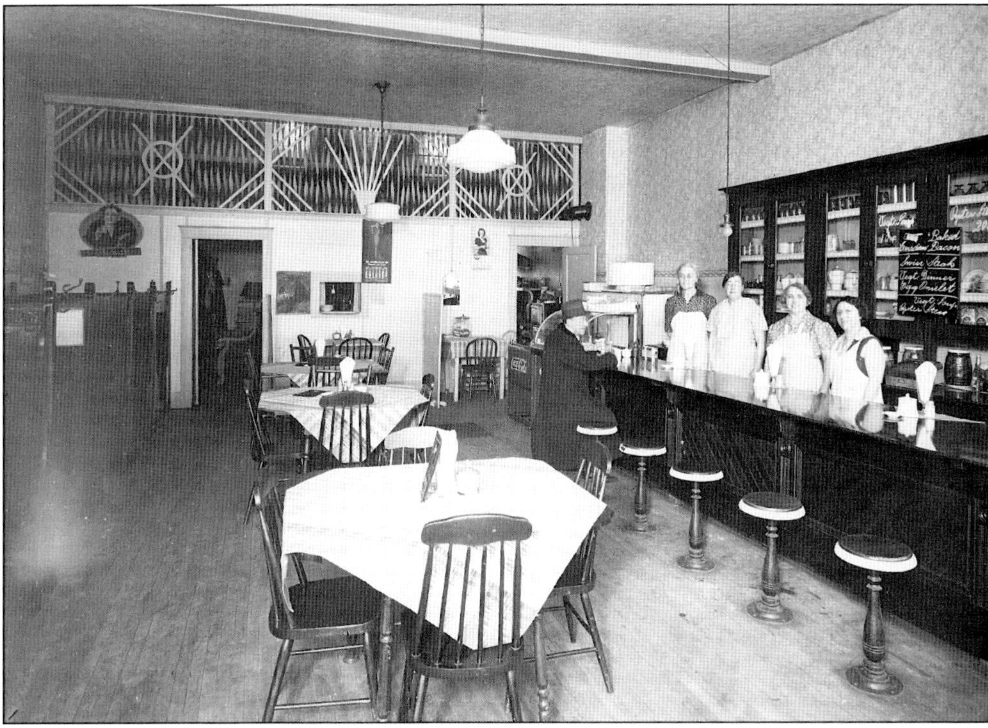

A charming smile greets the hearty appetite of a customer at this quaint restaurant. Over the years, several eating establishments occupied the southwest corner of North Fifteenth Street and Ohio Avenue. Names like the Reitlers, Dick Colvin, Tom Erb, and "Tuck" Turner were all associated with this small establishment. Taken in March 1939, this photograph depicts Annie Stump, the tall woman at the far left.

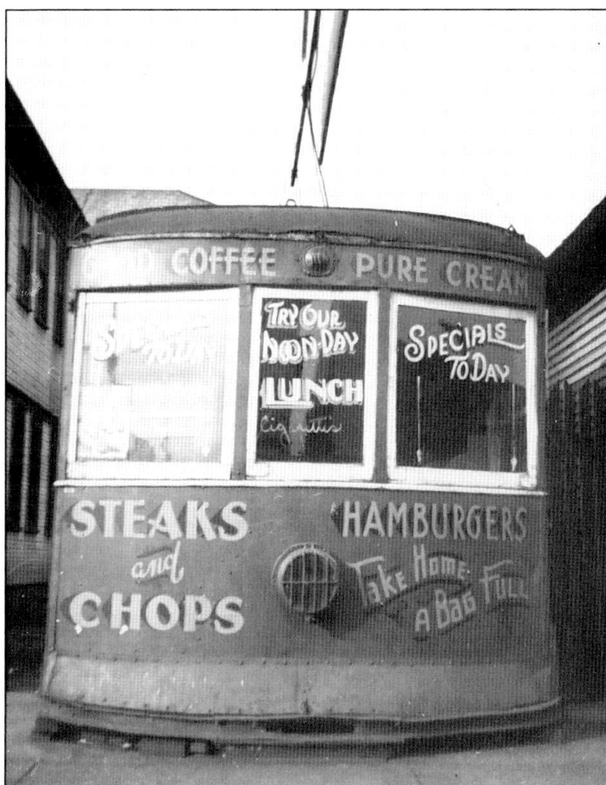

The Diner, located next to the Hotel Sebring, at 213 N. Fifteenth Street, was owned and operated by Irene and Karl Mongelluzzo when this picture was taken on November 19, 1941. The diner was a converted interurban car from the old Stark Electric Railway Company.

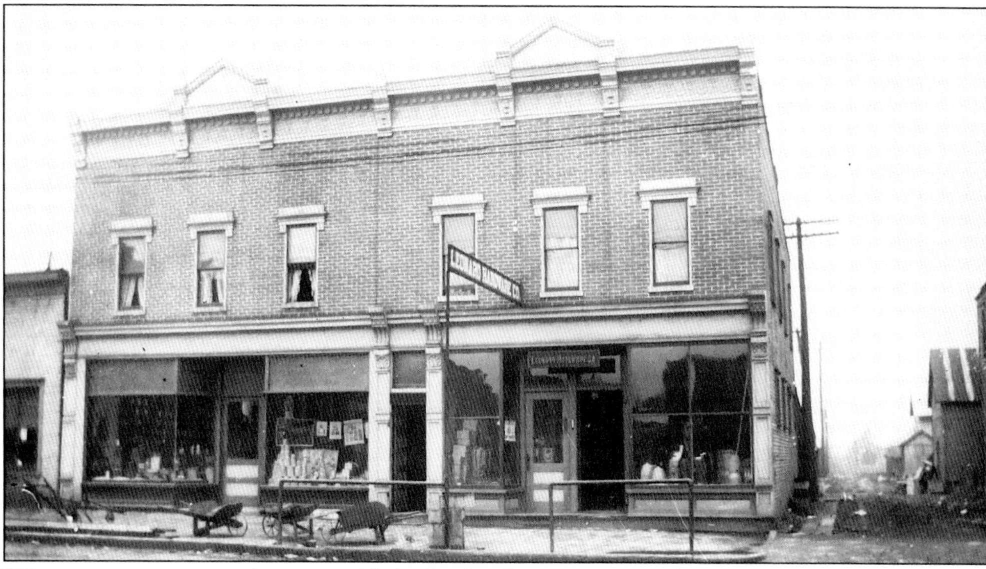

When a community is being established a hardware store can be one of the most profitable business opportunities. This is precisely what H.G. Leonard, who was well established in Salem, Ohio, had in mind when he sent his sales representative, R. Emmet Lee, to Sebring in 1899. Soon after, Leonard purchased a lot on North Fifteenth Street for $1,000. On July 19,1900, when a two-story structure was completed and opened for business. Along with general hardware, Leonard added a line of shelf and builder's hardware, stoves, tin, and granite ware, sewer pipes, slate and felt roofing, and plumbing. Soon after, it was necessary to double the size of his building. In this photograph, you can see the original building (the right portion) and the twin addition. In his first year of business, H.G. Leonard exceeded $50,000 in sales.

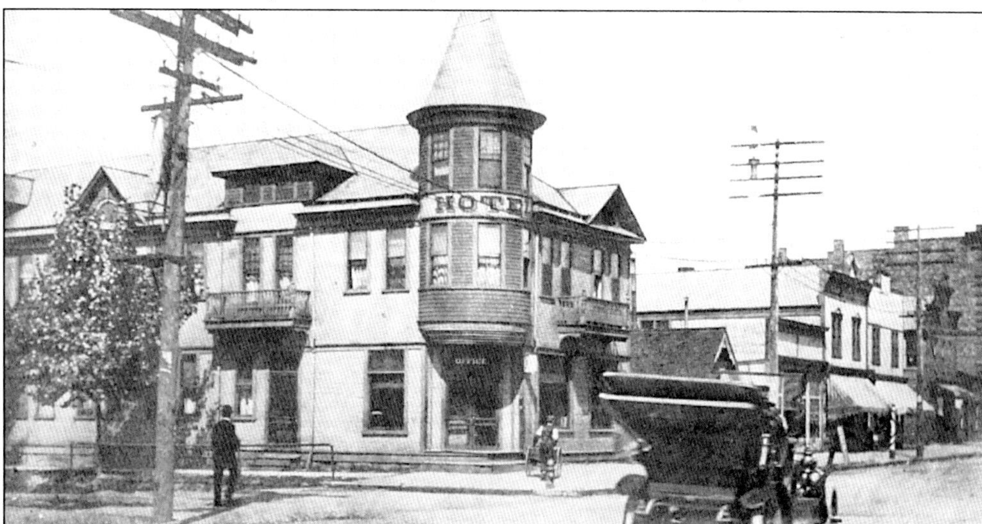

The centerpiece of downtown Sebring was the Hotel Sebring. This architectural beauty, with its Queen Anne tower, left a lasting impression on the many visitors to this community. Though many remember it in the winter of its life, in its day, the hotel accommodated key people in the pottery business. Located on the northwest corner of North Fifteenth Street and Oregon Avenue, the building burned down in the late 1940s. This postcard view shows it at its peak in 1910.

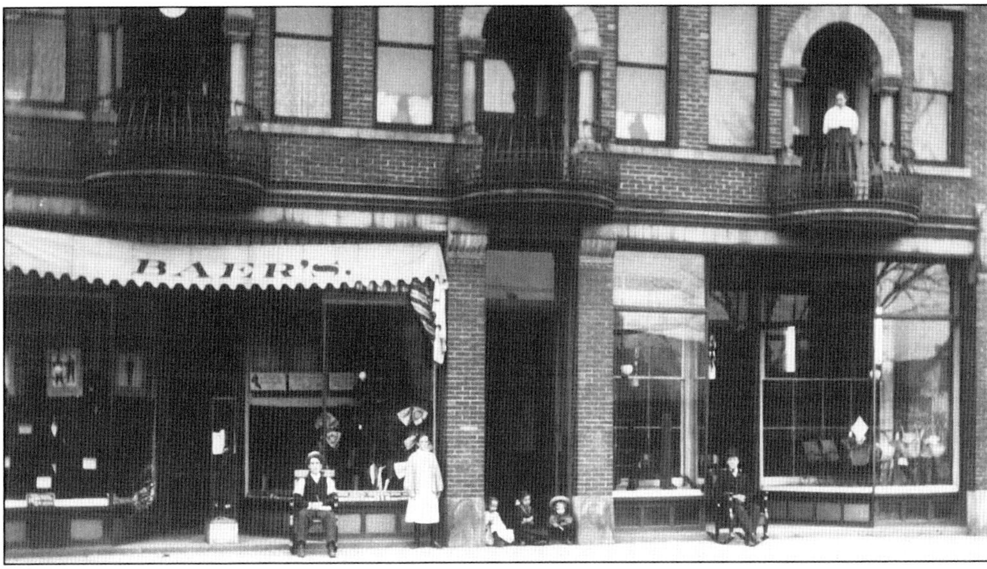

The Mahoning Brick Block was designed by Architect Jacob Myers, who opened an office in Sebring in 1901. This building has changed considerably over the years. Its post-Victorian appearance of stone arches and wrought-iron balconies have been replaced by a simplified brick face. Myers also designed the Methodist Episcopal Church, E.H. Sebring's residence, and O.H. Sebring's residence. In this photograph, we see Baer's Men's Clothing Store, on the right. Another occupant of a portion of this building was the C & P Super Market, owned by Melvin "Pete" Hesser and Cliff Dougherty. Attorney Richard Ross occupies this site today. The right portion of the building housed Eddie's Sport Shop and Billiard Room, which was owned by Eddie Howell. Today, Gromoll's Drug Store occupies this site while the second floor serves as apartments.

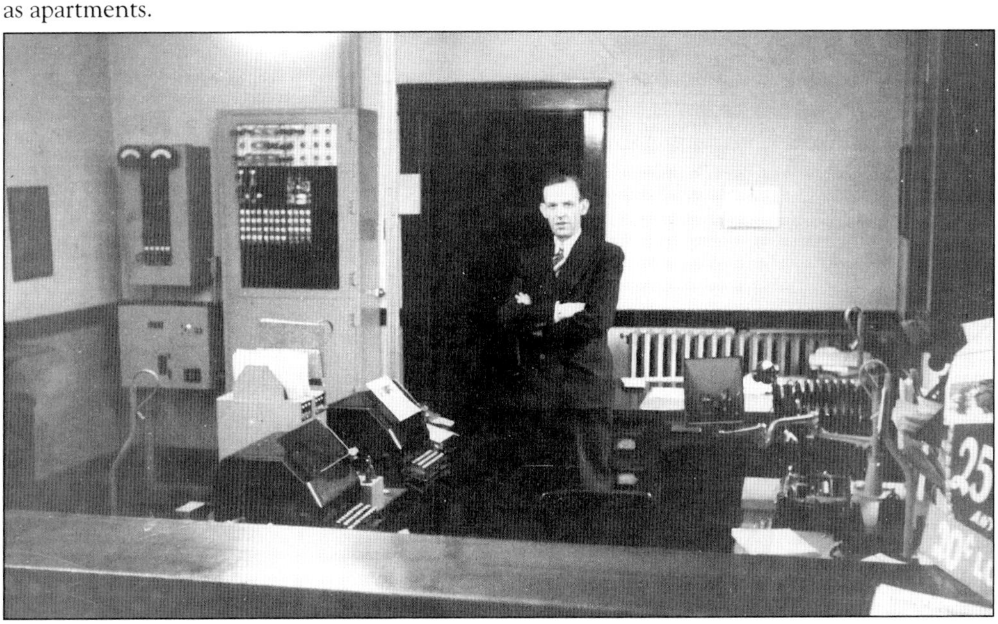

Howard Crewson, manager of the Western Union Telegraph Office, poses in his office at 103 North Fifteenth Street during the late 1930s or early 1940s. Crewson was appointed manager in 1920 and served in that position for 25 years.

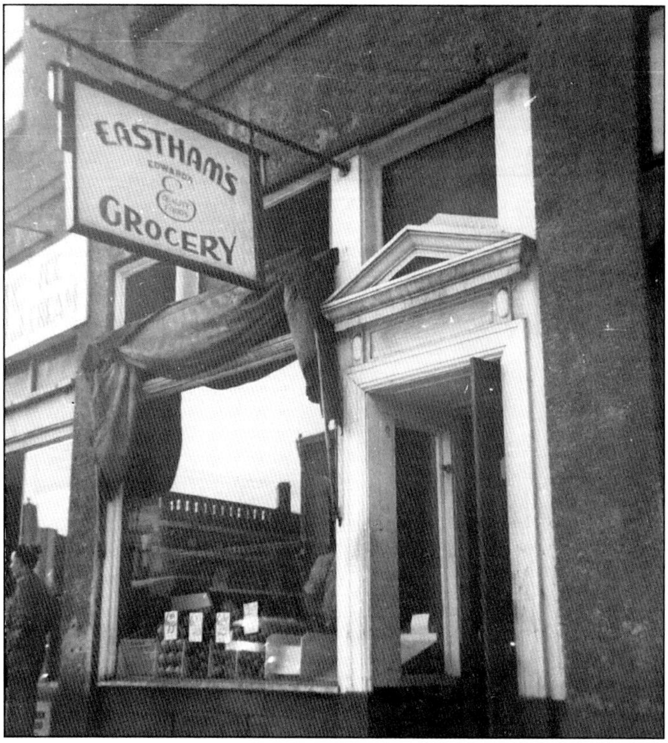

Eastham's Grocery, which began operation in 1940, was owned and operated by Thelma J. and A. Clyde Eastham. Located at 291 North Fifteenth Street, the store remained in operation until Mr. Eastham's death in the early 1960s, when the space was rented to Elsass.

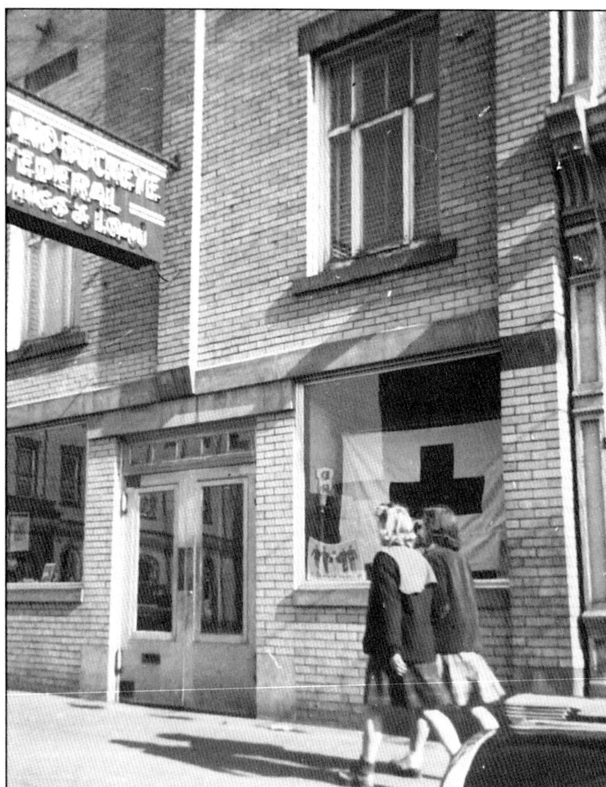

The Midland-Buckeye Federal Savings and Loan Association began as two separate entities. The Buckeye Building and Loan Association was chartered in 1899, with capital stock of $100,000. The first president was Frank A. Sebring, and W.H. Sebring served as secretary. Much of the early development of the community relied on the company for financial backing. Despite the Depression, Buckeye managed to remain open, curtailing withdrawals as much as possible, and keeping foreclosures to a minimum. In the spring of 1938, Buckeye merged with The Midland Savings and Loan Association of Alliance. Construction of this building at 286 North Fifteenth Street soon followed. Midland-Buckeye was a victim of the 1980s savings and loan scandals.

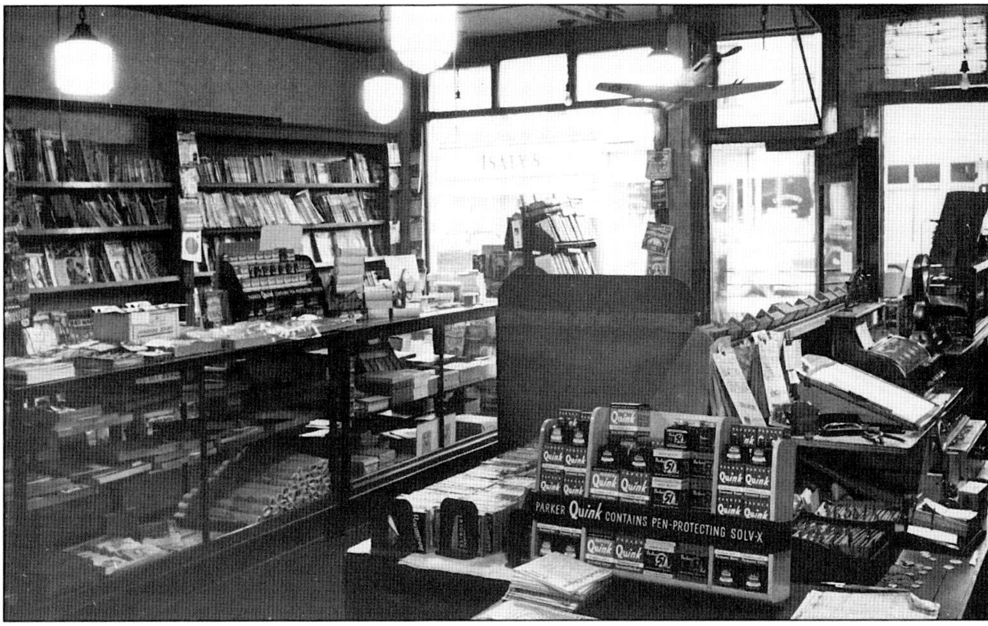

Barbara Stanwyck on the cover of *Motion Picture Magazine*, a 25¢ Pocket Book Mystery by Ellery Queen, or Decca's latest 78 hits were just a few items you could find at Deemer's Newstand on North Fifteenth Street. Snapped on July 21, 1945, from behind the counter, one can see the variety Ralph and Cecil Deemer offered the residents of Sebring. With the war coming to a close, notice the patriotic flair with the model Air Force planes hanging from the ceiling.

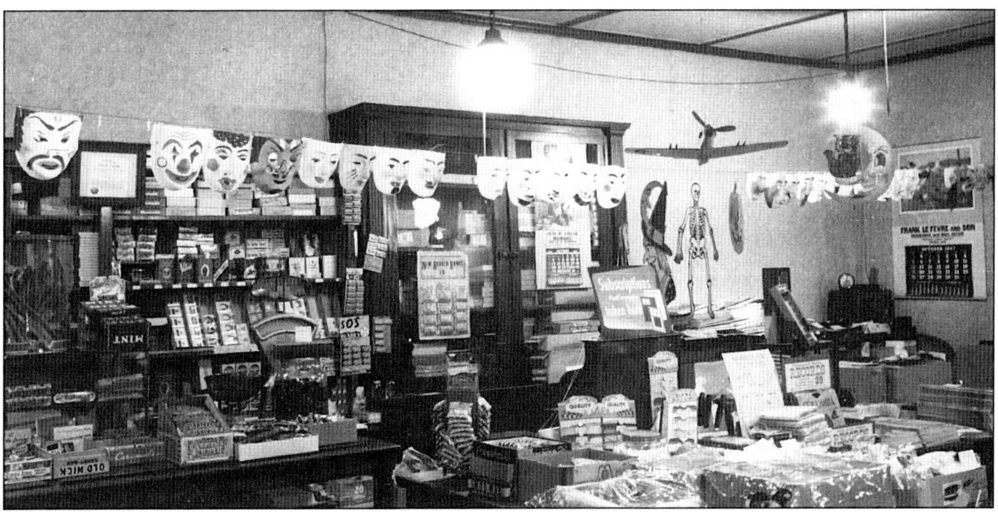

Want to scare your neighbor? Need a great costume for trick or treat? Well, in the 1940s, Deemer's was the place to go, as this was a great hangout spot for skeletons, black cats, and spooky faces. Candy was always in abundance at Halloween. Taken on October 28, 1947, at 12:36 p.m., Deemer's was a mainstay on Fifteenth Street for over 40 years. Note the Frank Le Fevre and Son Insurance and Real Estate calendar hanging on the wall to the right.

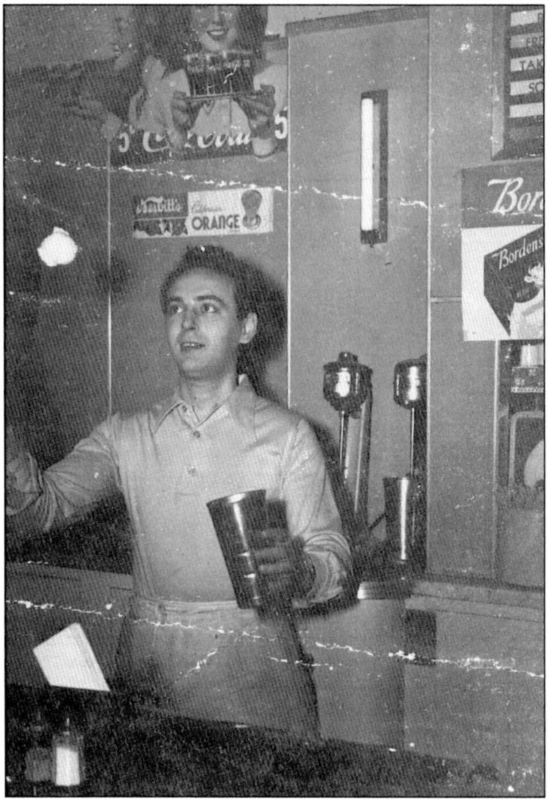

The art of creating a milk shake is demonstrated by Jim Papadeonise at the White Palace Restaurant. Located on the north side of the Strand Theatre, the White Palace was a popular hangout spot in the 1940s.

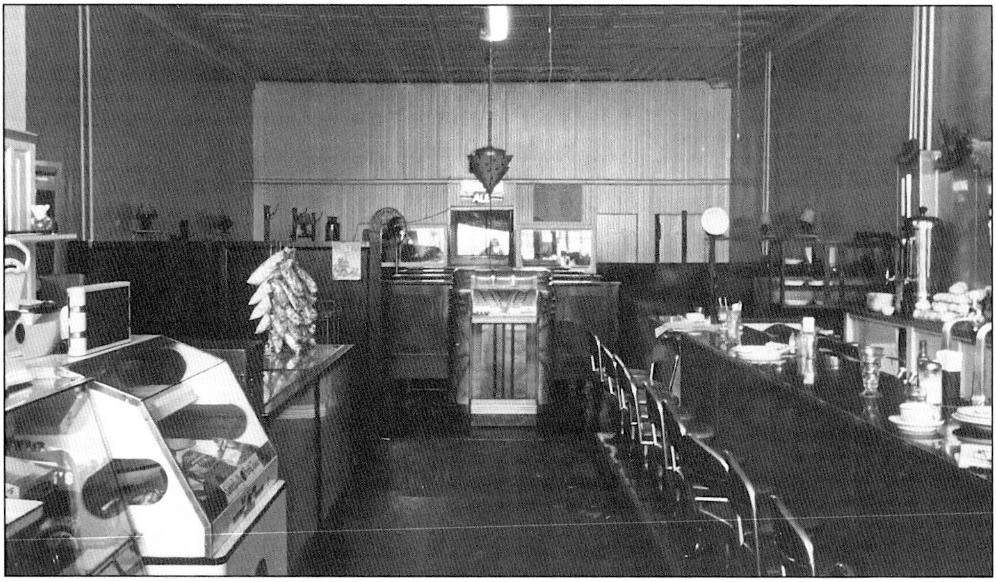

White Palace Restaurant is seen here as it appeared in the 1940s. It was owned and operated by the Papadeonis family.

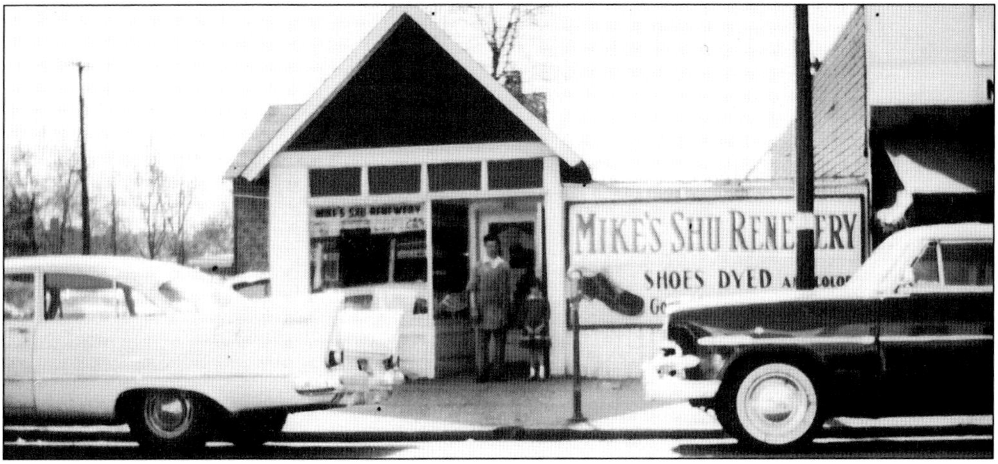

The smell of fresh shoe polish on a fine pair of Florsheim shoes, or new stitching on a trusted pair of work boots are the memories many have of Mike's Shu Renewery on North Fifteenth Street. The small and unassuming building, which stood next to the Hotel Sebring, housed the business that was owned and operated by Karl Scarpetti.

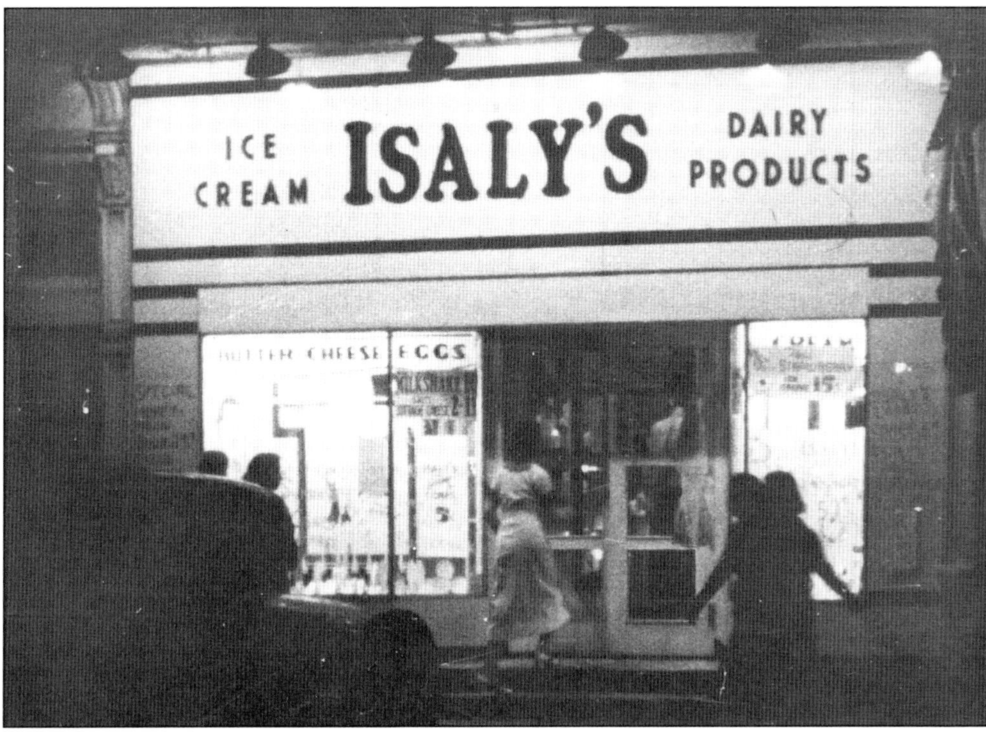

The Isaly Dairy Company, which started in Mansfield, Ohio, was one of the largest and most popular dairy and ice cream producers in the nation. Even though the company no longer exists, Klondike Bars (the trade name and recipe were sold after Isaly's closed) are one of the best selling ice cream products today. At its height of popularity, during the 1930s, 1940s, and 1950s, virtually every town in Ohio, and the surrounding states, had an Isaly's store. This store was known for its Art Deco counters and booths, with streamlined chrome, an Isaly's menu included: sandwiches and fries, sodas, ice cream cones, and shakes. In this photograph, we see customers arriving at the Sebring store on a warm summer evening, probably in the 1940s.

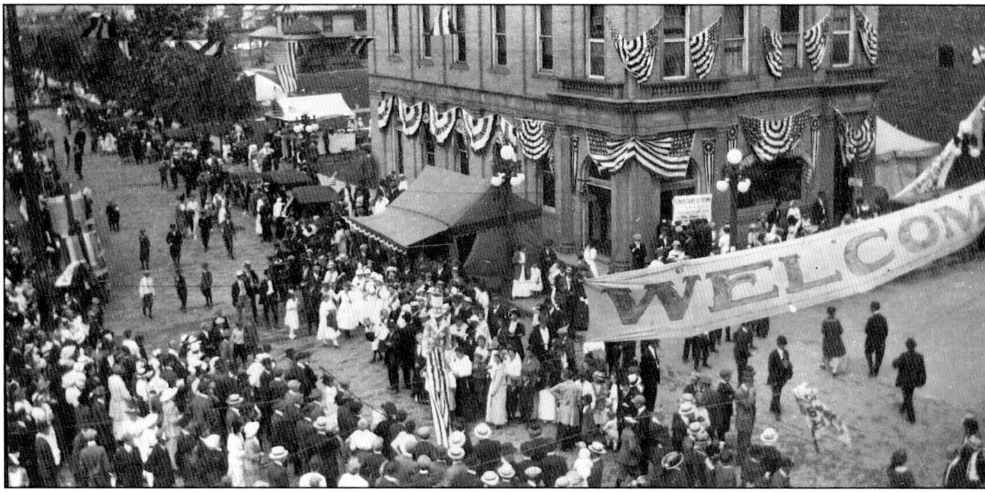

This is opening day of the Citizens Banking Company's new building, in the fall of 1912, on the northwest corner of North Fifteenth Street and Ohio Avenue. The day was filled with carnival-like activities. The sign in front of the Ohio Avenue door of the building stated that your name would be entered into a raffle if you opened a new account. Founded by Oliver. H. Sebring, who served as president, the bank began in a building at 255 North Fifteenth Street around 1900. W.L. Murphy, son-in-law of Oliver H. Sebring, served as secretary. On October 7, 1931, the Citizens Banking Company fell victim to the nation's economic downfall. The financial blow to the community was enormous and the bank would never reopen. Banking was moved to Alliance, during the late 1930s and the War years. In the late 1940s, the Sebring Retail Merchants Association, along with numerous citizens and businesses in the community, raised $100,000 in capital stock. A federal charter was granted on February 7, 1948, and The First National Bank of Sebring was in operation in the old Citizens Building. In the 1970s, they merged with First National City Bank of Alliance. In the 1980s the Alliance bank merged with Bank One.

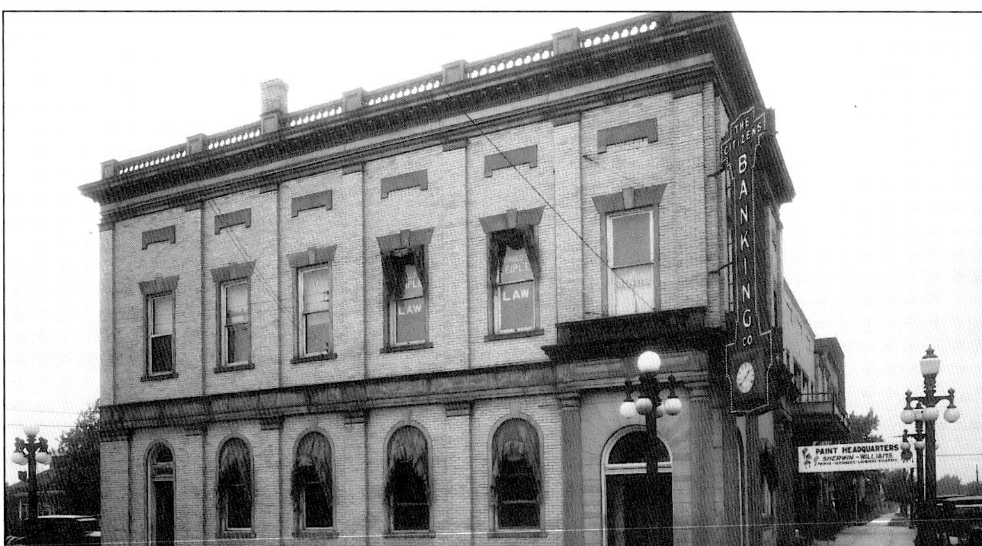

The Citizens Banking Company building is shown here in the mid-1920s. Note the ornate street lamps.

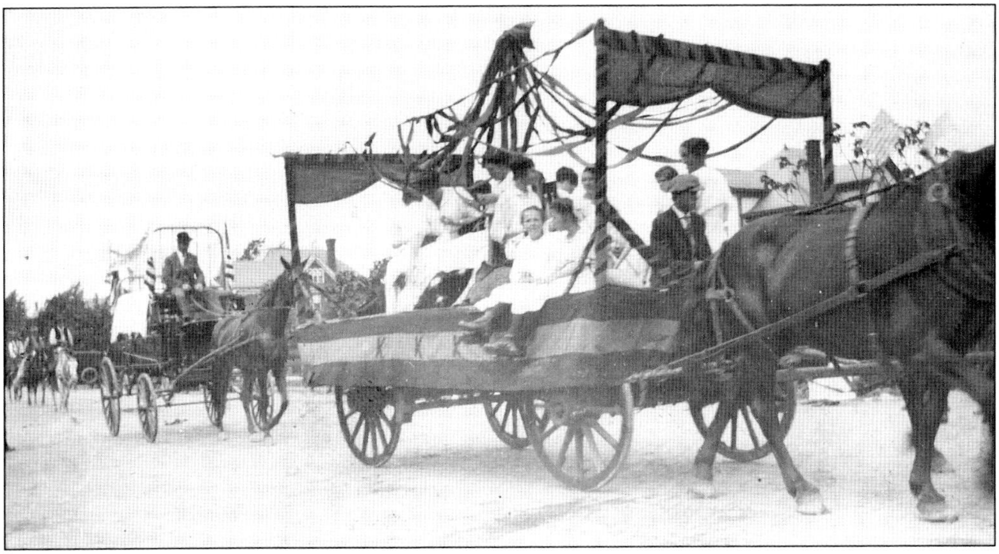

Wagons move down West Ohio Avenue at North Sixteenth Street, during the Harvest Home Festival, in 1912.

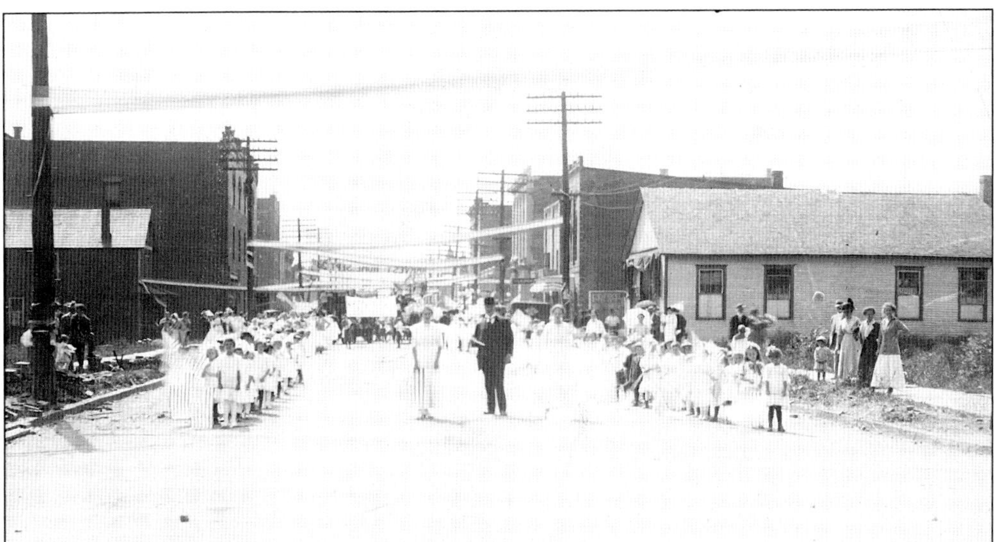

Participants in the September 1912 Harvest Home Festival pose on North Fifteenth Street. The photograph was taken from Maryland Avenue looking south towards Ohio Avenue. The children represent the school system as the banner down the road reads grades seven and eight. The festivals were an important part of the Sebring community for a number of years.

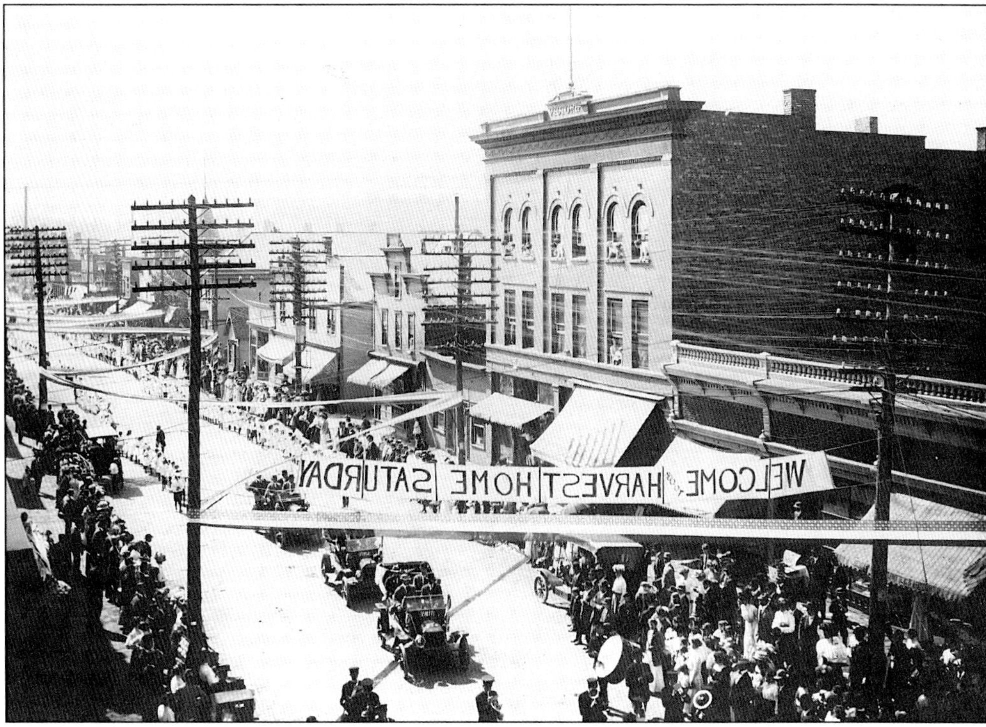

Streamers give North Fifteenth Street a festive look during the 1912 Harvest Home Festival. This view, taken from the roof of the Mahoning Block, by DeWolf Studios, shows the Harvest Home Festival parade. The Sebring family and other distinguished residents participated in the parade.

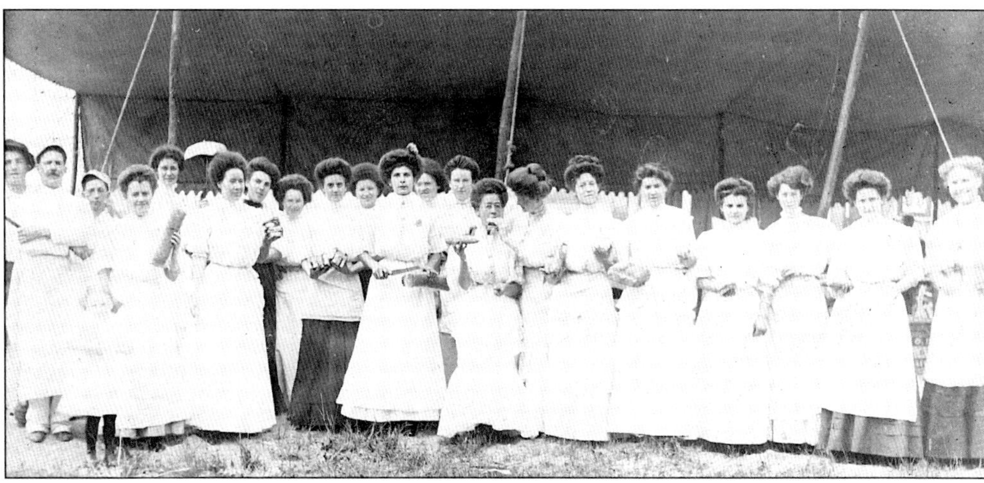

Some of the women of Sebring start the preparations for the Annual Ox Roast during the Harvest Home Festival in October 1908. Your choice "ten cents." The newspaper said it best: "In a vacant lot now occupied by Bank One, a large tent was erected. Here the mingling of food odors that rose to a hungry man's nostrils was enough to make him swoon. A large pit was dug and tubs of butter offered their golden treasure to those eating piping hot ears of sweet corn. Thick succulent sandwiches of roasted ox meat were served."

Five

A Dwelling Place

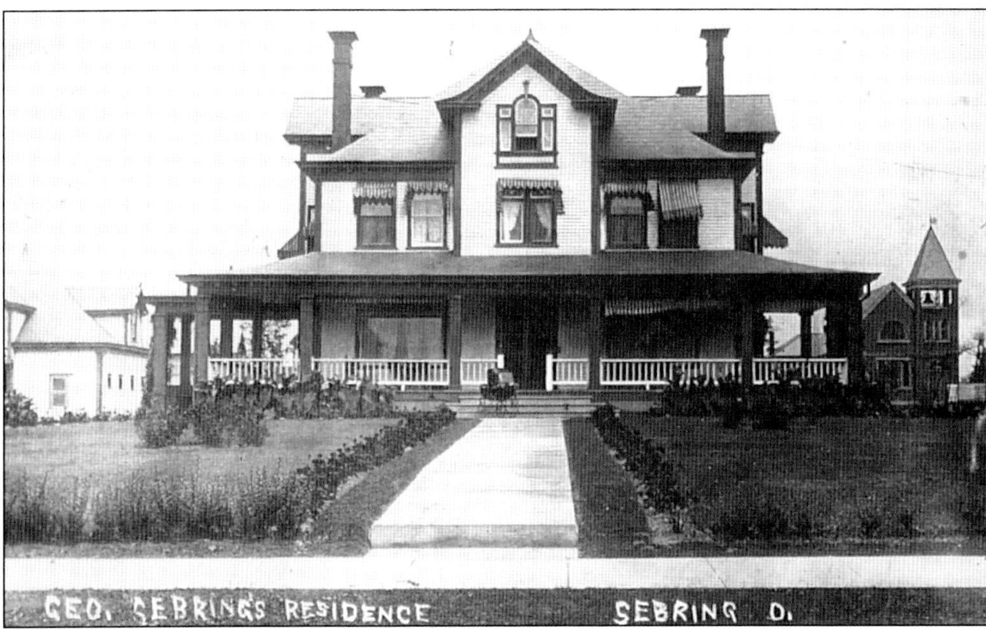

The George E. Sebring residence was the first of the Sebring homes to be built in the village, and construction began in the fall of 1898. The home was located on the northwest corner of West Ohio Avenue and Sixteenth Street, and the cost of construction was estimated to be between $8,000 and $12,000. George E. Sebring was the first insurance agent in Sebring, operating (along with his son H. Orville) one of the first real estate companies, known as Sebring Real Estate. He was responsible for bringing the Strong Enamel Company from Bellaire, Ohio, and in 1911, founded Sebring, Florida. Mr. Sebring divided his time between Ohio and Florida, and he eventually sold this home to his nephew, Charles L. Sebring, and live out the remainder of his life in Florida. He died on January 4, 1927, at the age of 68. He was survived by his wife Cora Harris Sebring and five children: George Eugene Jr., Payne, Dorothy, Orville, and Mrs. Samuel (Ethel) Rose. Note the carriage house, on the left, and the First United Presbyterian Church, on the right.

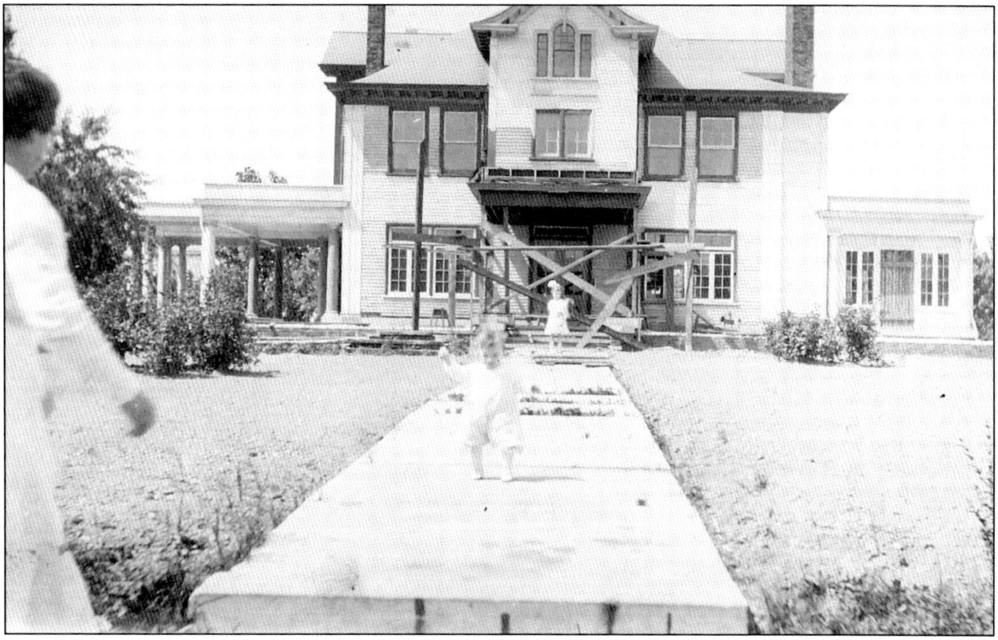

After Charles Leigh Sebring, son of Frank, purchased his Uncle George's home, he altered and expanded the house considerably. Married three times, Charles's first wife, Jesse Morgan, died during childbirth. He married his second wife, Conradine Uran, on January 25, 1911, in Alliance. It was at this time that they moved into this residence. After the death of Conradine in 1965, Charles married Marion Headland. Charles was sales manager of the Edwin Knowles China Company of Newell, West Virginia. In 1946, he and Conradine moved to Sebring, Florida, where they became prominent in the citrus business. Charles had three daughters, Mrs. Allen Duane (Barbara) Gage, Mrs. Roy (Josephine) Smail, and Mrs. Don (Evelyn) Beddoe. Mr. Beddoe was a well-recognized actor in over 300 movie and television productions in Hollywood. His appearances include, *The Best Years of Our Lives*, *Pillow Talk*, and *A Star is Born*.

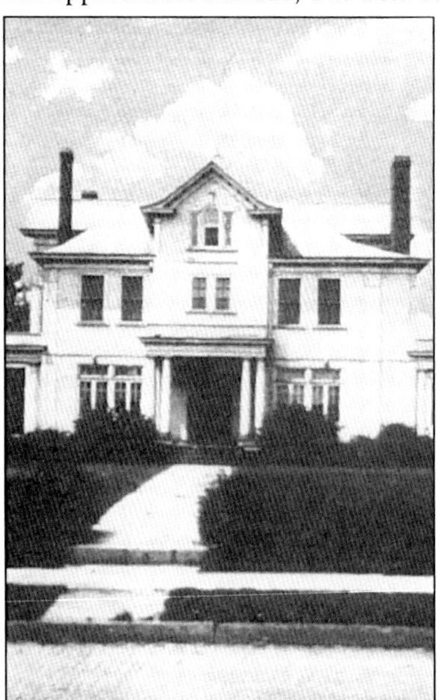

This 1920s postcard shows the C.L. Sebring home as most older Sebring residents would remember it. After Charles and his wife Conradine moved to West Virginia, the house was purchased by William V. Oliver. In 1934, "Vern" Oliver was responsible for purchase of the Saxon China Company building from bondholders and organizing the French-Saxon China Company. He remained head of the firm until his death in 1963. He was a leader in the pottery industry, serving as president of the U.S. Potters Association. His widow remained in the home until her death. In the 1970s, the contents and fixtures of the house were sold at auction and the house was torn down. The C.L. Sebring manor is located on this site today.

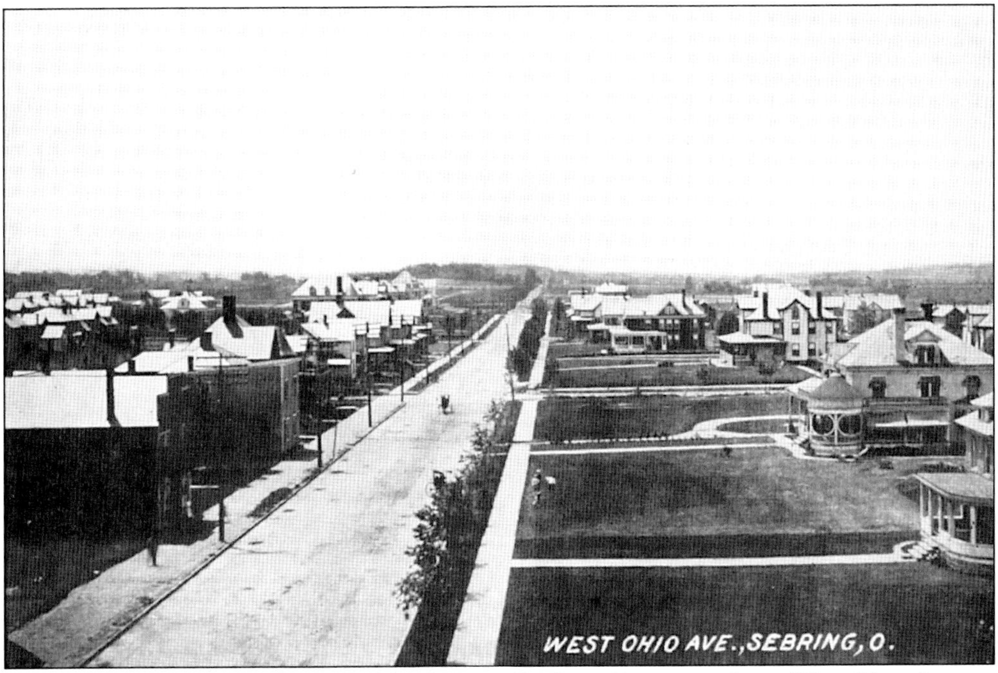

This postcard view, from the roof of the Citizens Banking Company, shows West Ohio Avenue with its pristine yards and carefully pruned hedges. On the right, the house with the gazebo front porch is the Charles L. Sebring residence, which was Frank A. Sebring's first home. Across Sixteenth Street is the George E. Sebring residence and the late Will Sebring's home, which is now Dean's Funeral Home.

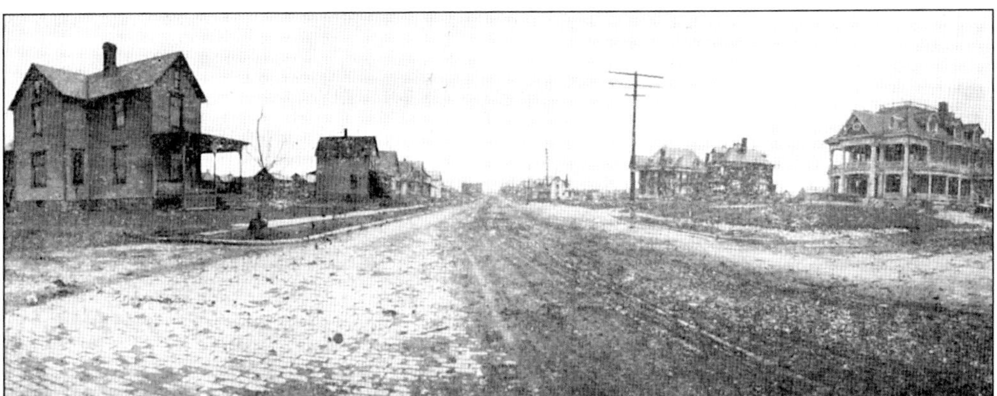

This early view of West Ohio Avenue, looking east, shows the transformation of the street from dirt and mud to brick. On the north side, the curbing and brick have been installed. On the south side, roadwork has not been completed for the newly constructed homes of Frank A. Sebring, Will and Anne Sebring Murphy, and Oliver H. Sebring. S.E. McKee had installed electricity to the Sebring family homes by this time.

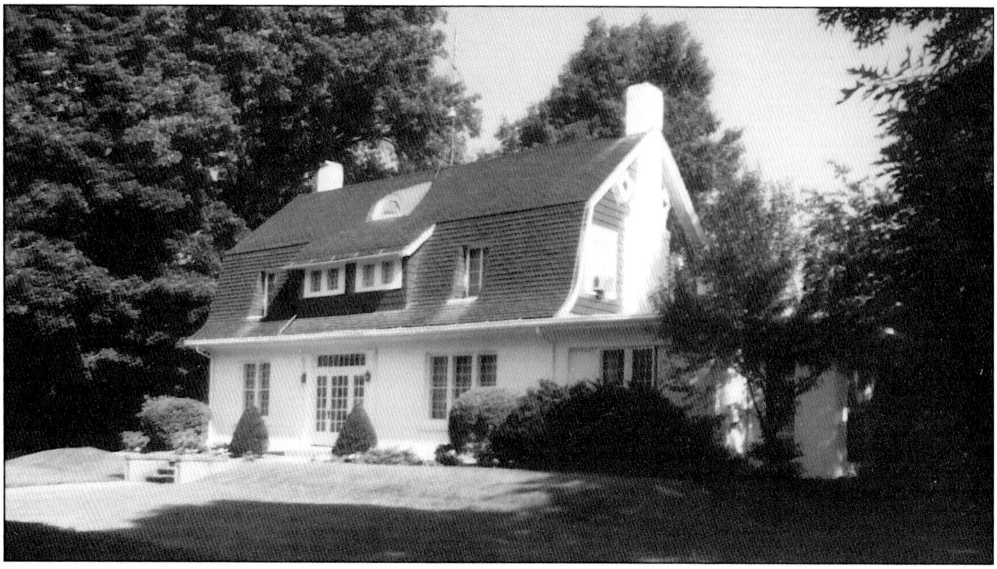

This photograph depicts the Willard I. and Helen Sebring Gahris residence at 456 West Ohio Avenue. Though it is not one of the largest homes on the street, it has a sense of elegance and grandeur and is not overbearing or pretentious. The stucco home is typical of the style built by the second and third generations of wealthy industrialist families in the early teens. Mrs. Gahris was the daughter of Mr. and Mrs. Frank A. Sebring. Unfortunately, she will always be remembered as the hostess for the "Welcome Home" dinner for Colonel Charles C. Weybrecht at the Lakeside Country Club at Myers Lake in Canton, Ohio. Weybrecht, along with Mrs. Gahris and several other prominent people, were victims of botulism from canned ripe olives in August 1919. Mrs. Gahris was known for her golfing skills and just weeks before her death won top prize at the club's annual outing. Her husband was active in his father-in-law's business, the Sebring Pottery Company. He died unexpectedly in the early 1920s en route to New York on business. The Gahris's only child, Gretchen, lived with her mother's parents. She married J. Harrison Keller and lived in this home for a number of years. It was purchased by Roger and Marilyn (Eastham) Johnston in 1966. They sold the home in 1998 to the Slusser Family.

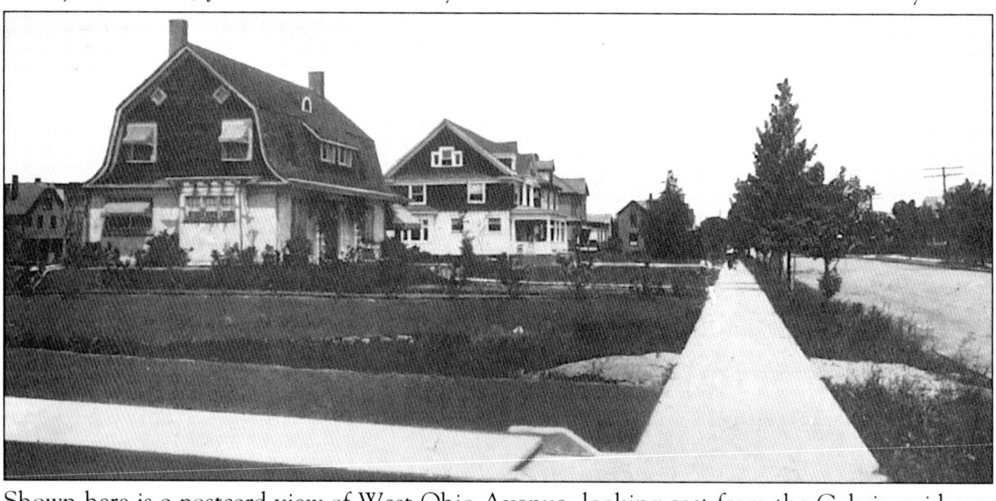

Shown here is a postcard view of West Ohio Avenue, looking east from the Gahris residence in the teens. The view of the west side of the house shows the gambrel style roof, which was prominent in the era between 1910 and 1920.

Considered the largest and the grandest of the homes in Sebring, Oliver H. Sebring's residence was designed by architect Jacob Myers. It was located on the southwest corner of West Ohio Avenue and Sixteenth Street. The exterior was altered several times. In this photograph, prior to 1902, the front porch and the porte-cochere were not built yet. Oldest of the six brothers, Oliver established the Citizen Banking Company, The Sebring Manufacturing Corporation, and was co-owner (with his son Bert) of the Sebring Cooperage Company. Mr. Sebring's business interests extended outside Sebring. He was a director and vice president of the Knowles, Taylor, and Knowles Pottery of East Liverpool and vice-president of the Louis H. Porter Company of Chicago. Oliver and his family were also active participants in the Sebring campground revivals.

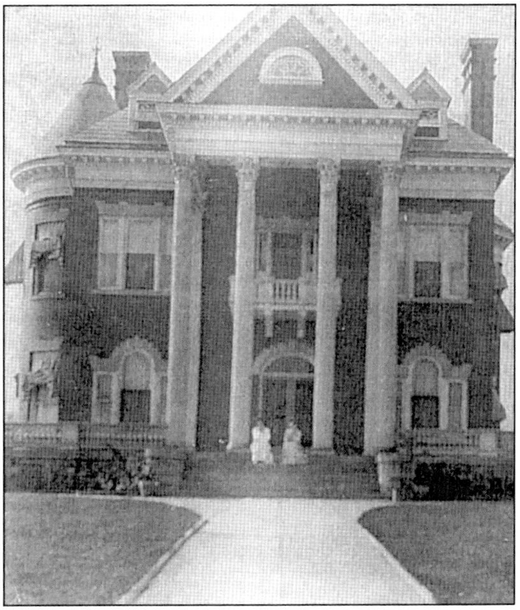

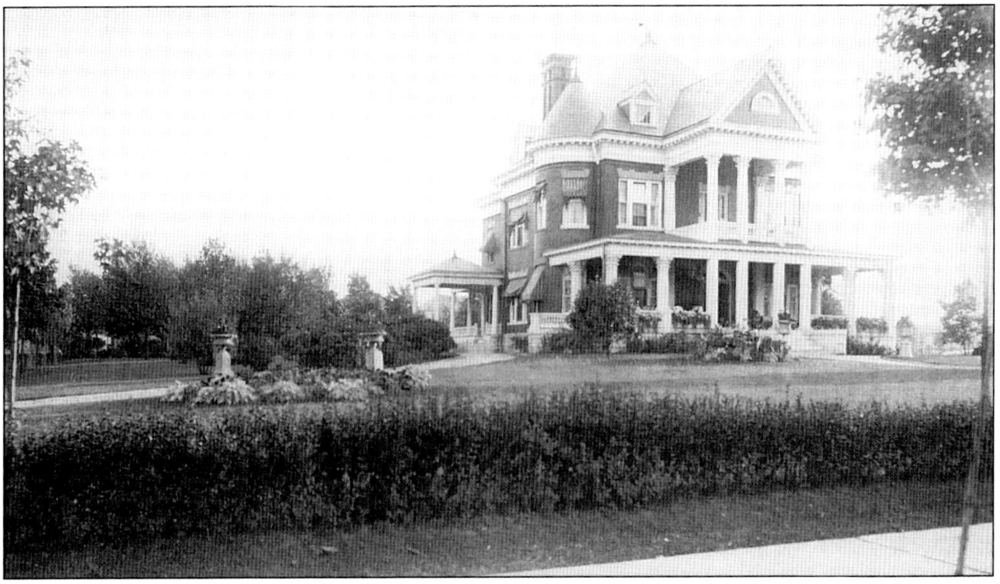

This is a view of the O.H. Sebring estate after the addition of the front porch and the porte-cochere. With thirty rooms and seven bathrooms, the cost to build this home was estimated to be $75,000. The beautiful landscaping complements this wonderful estate. The typical park-like setting with the large urns and hedges were commonplace during the Victorian and post-Victorian (Edwardian) era. This gave the family the opportunity of privacy, even though the lots were not enormous.

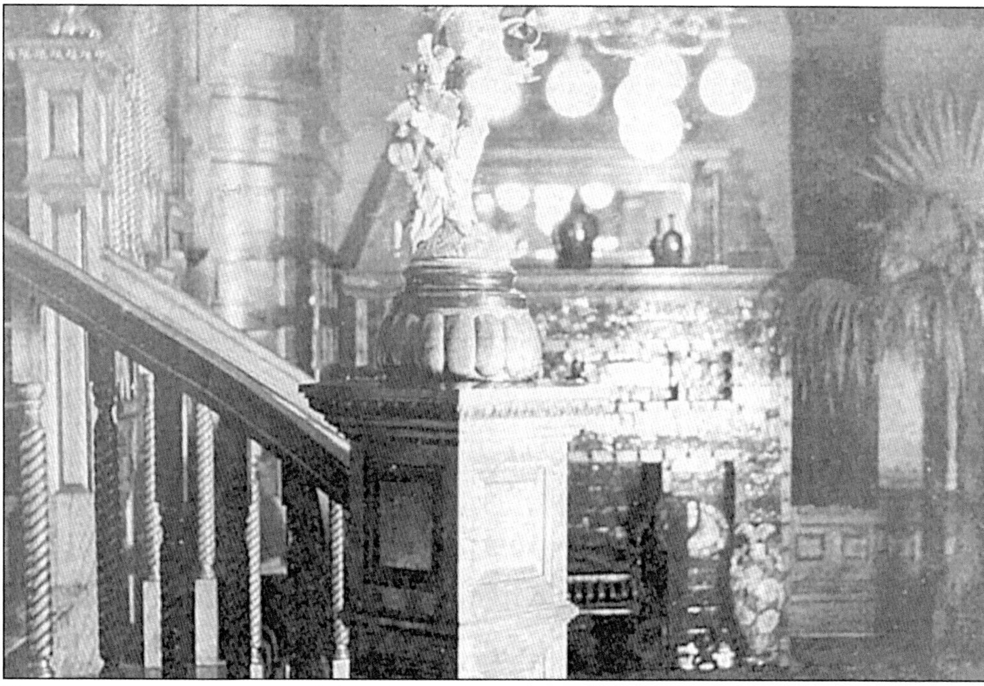

This rare interior view provided by Betty Grove, granddaughter of O.H. Sebring, was taken from the staircase looking toward the receiving hall. The semi-circular room was on the east side of the home (part of the circular tower), which can be seen in the exterior photographs. Note the ornate lighting fixture on the newel post and the beautiful statues between the arches leading into the room. As always, ferns and palms were a significant part of the interior decorating. Their delicate leaves were a nice contrast to the heavy, but wonderfully crafted, woodwork.

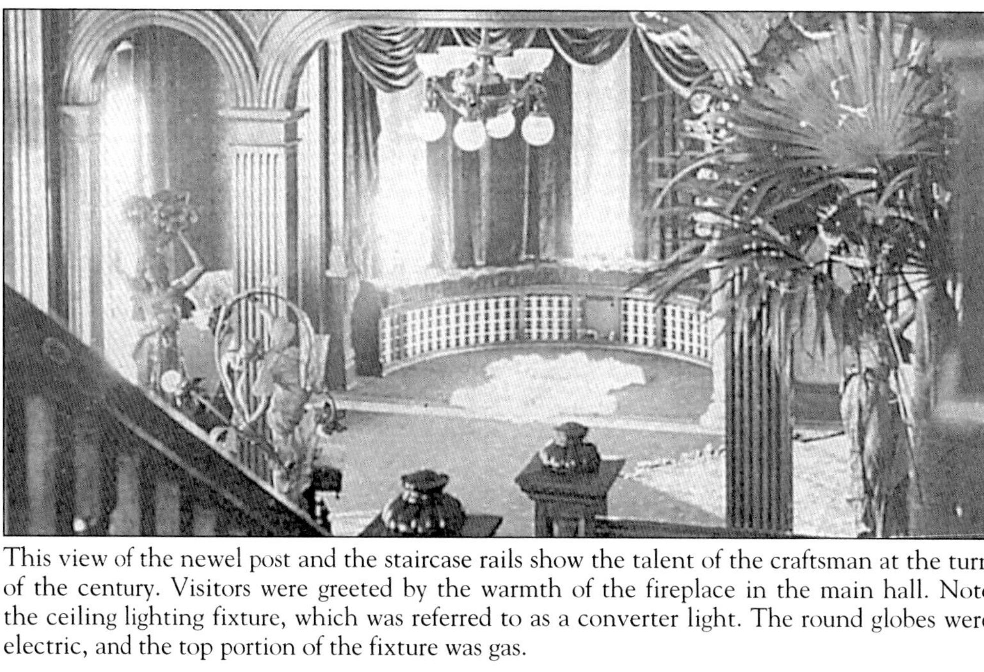

This view of the newel post and the staircase rails show the talent of the craftsman at the turn of the century. Visitors were greeted by the warmth of the fireplace in the main hall. Note the ceiling lighting fixture, which was referred to as a converter light. The round globes were electric, and the top portion of the fixture was gas.

Just prior to his death on July 24, 1929, Oliver H. Sebring remodeled the house. According to his granddaughter, Betty Grove, the home was virtually gutted. Rooms were enlarged, the fireplaces were removed or changed, and summer sleeping rooms and dressing rooms were added over the porte-cochere. Over the front porch, a large sunroom was added, where Mrs. Sebring kept her canaries. The total cost of remodeling was estimated to be $200,000. In the late 1930s, the home was converted to apartments by Dr. and Mrs. A.M. (Kathleen Sebring) Overlander. Kathleen was the granddaughter of Oliver. During Thanksgiving evening dinner in 1943, fire broke out and rapidly spread to the attic, where the wood burned down inside the brick veneer shell. The first alarm was sounded at 5:55 p.m., and the fire was brought under control by 8:30 p.m. with the help of the Alliance Fire Department. This photograph shows the aftermath of the fire. Note the enclosed porch over the front.

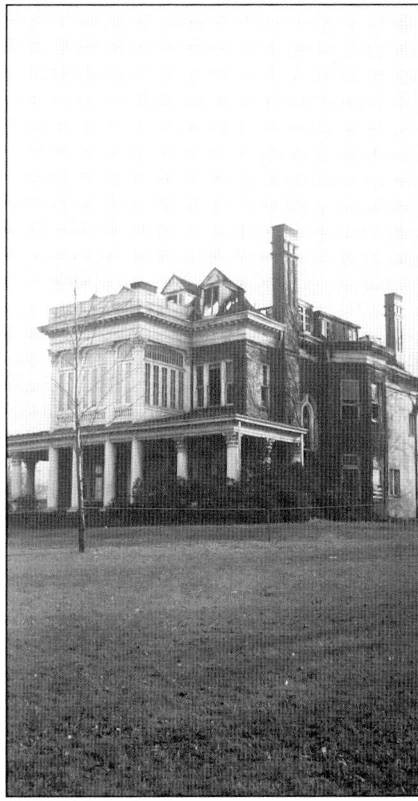

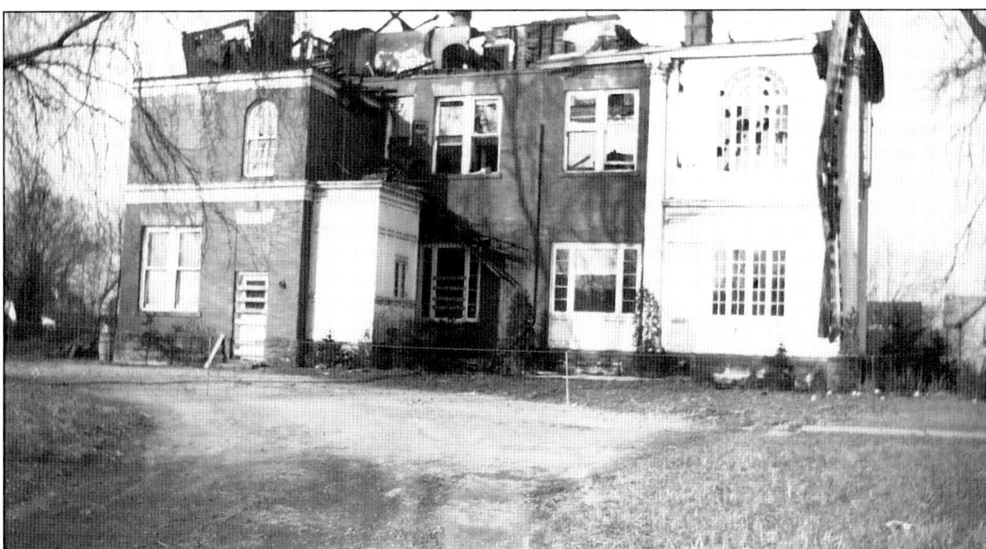

In a few hours, the history and grandeur of Sebring's most beautiful home was wiped away. This photograph of the back of the home shows the empty shell a few days after the devastating Thanksgiving Day fire. The home was torn down soon after.

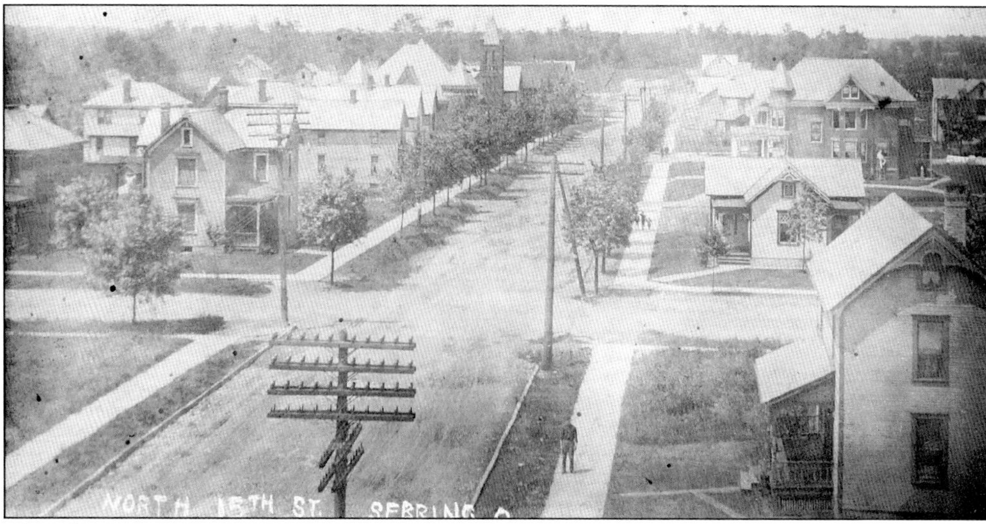

This photo postcard was taken from the roof of the Mahoning Building in 1907. Looking north, down North Fifteenth Street, Maryland Avenue is visible. The home on the northwest corner is the residence of Sebring's first postmaster, Dick Albright. On the east side, between Maryland and Indiana Avenues, the Fred Sebring residence is the brick structure with the Queen Anne tower. Also note that the Methodist Church is visible in the photograph.

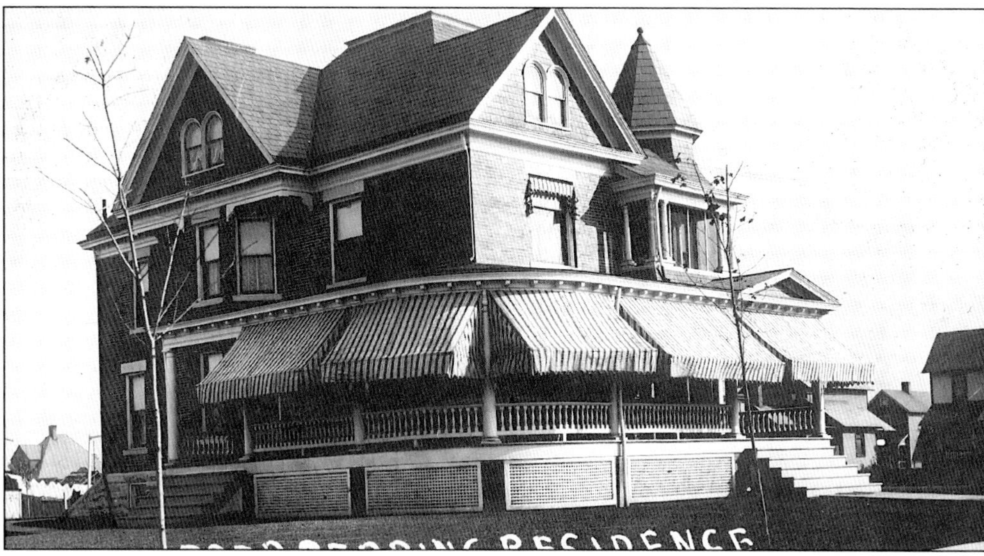

The Fred Sebring residence is located at 438 North Fifteenth Street. The only brother who did not build on West Ohio Avenue, Fred was head of the Limoges China Company and founded the Saxon China Company. This home is very similar to the Will Sebring residence, which is now the Dean Funeral Home, since the same architectural details can be noted in both houses. Fred Sebring died on December 13, 1925, of a heart attack. He had just returned from an extensive visit to Sebring, Florida, and was discussing the trip with his wife Kathryn when he was stricken. The home was purchased by Druggist Lewis A. Bandy and remained his residence until his death in the 1940s. The home was restored by the Risbecks in the late 1980s early 1990s. The home was purchased, in the fall of 1995, by Rachel and Trevor Cannell, who have continued the restoration. Mr. Cannell is assistant director of Pharmacy at Alliance Community Hospital.

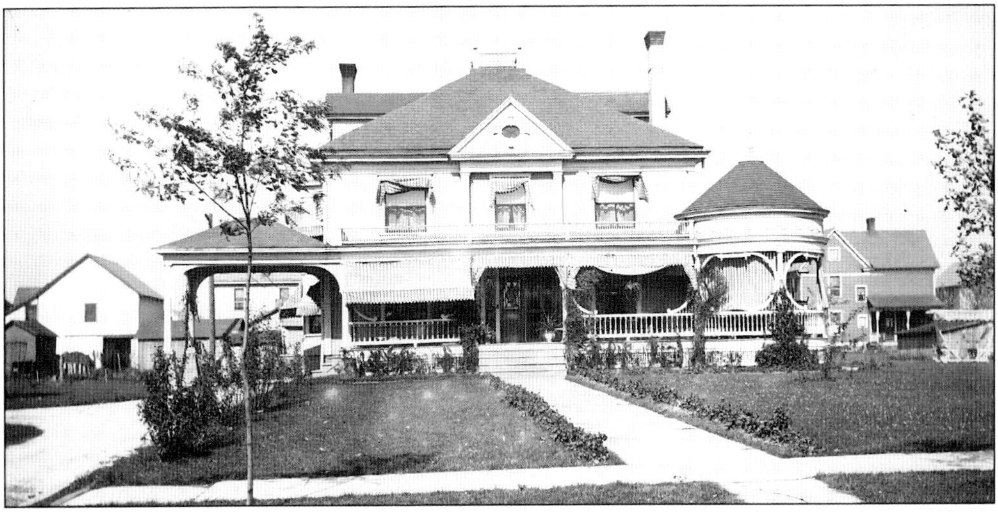

Before the palatial residence at the corner of West Ohio Avenue and 18th Street was built for Frank A. Sebring, he lived in this house on the north side of West Ohio Avenue between 15th and 16th Streets. Built in 1900, it was the second Sebring family residence to be built in the new community. When the residence was built, it had a box-like appearance to it. The extensive front porch with the circular corner and the porte-cochere were added. After F.A. Sebring's new home was completed, his nephew Charles L. Sebring purchased the home after his marriage to Jesse Morgan. Charles moved after his wife, Jesse, died during the birth of their child Evelyn in 1906. In later years, Howard Pinkerton resided in this home, which has since been torn down.

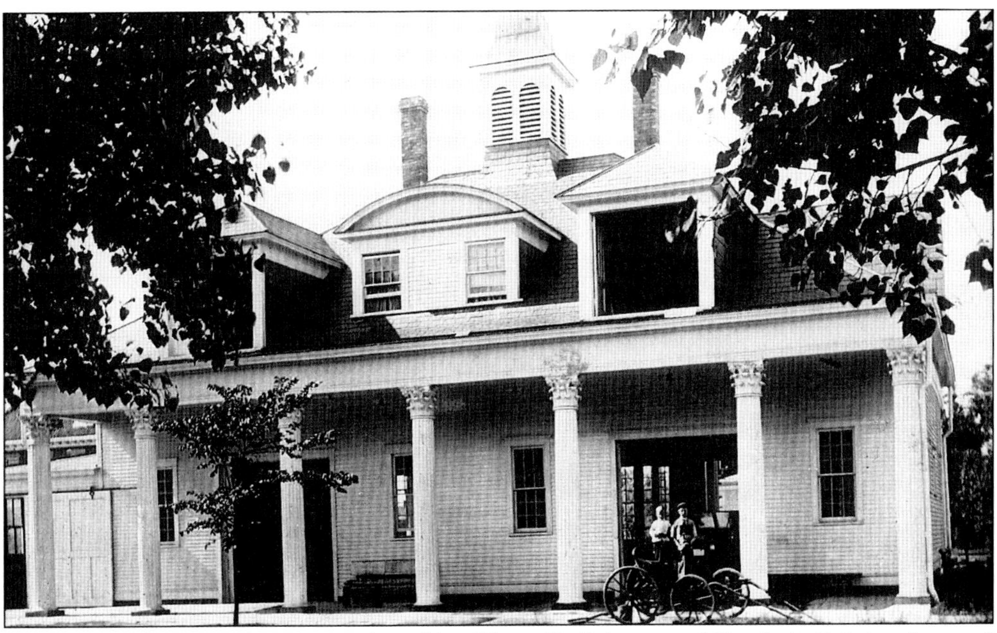

This beautiful carriage house was shared by Oliver H. Sebring and Frank A. Sebring. Located behind the W.L. Murphy residence, between North Seventeenth and Eighteenth Streets and West Ohio and Oregon Avenues, the grandeur and style of the carriage house was in line with the lovely homes built by the families.

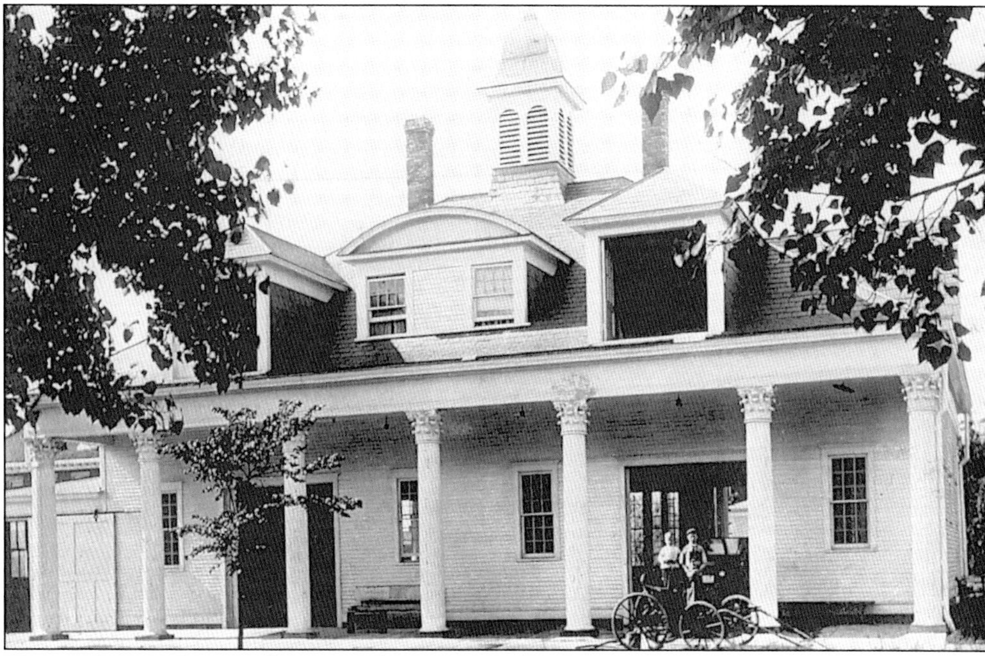

The residence of Mr. and Mrs. William L. Murphy is shown in this *c.* 1908 postcard. Annie Murphy was the daughter of Oliver H. Sebring and was instrumental in the development of the Sebring Campground meetings. She was the writer of the popular hymn "Constantly Abiding," which is still published in church hymnals throughout the world. In the late 1930s, she moved to Burbank, California, where her sisters Pearl Taylor, Hazel Cliff, and Wilda Sebring lived. Annie died in March 1942. Will Murphy, who died in the early 1930s, was head cashier of the Citizens Banking Company, founded by his father-in-law, and was also involved in various aspects of the pottery business. They were the parents of one child, who was adopted. His name was Edwin T. Murphy, and he died in 1968.

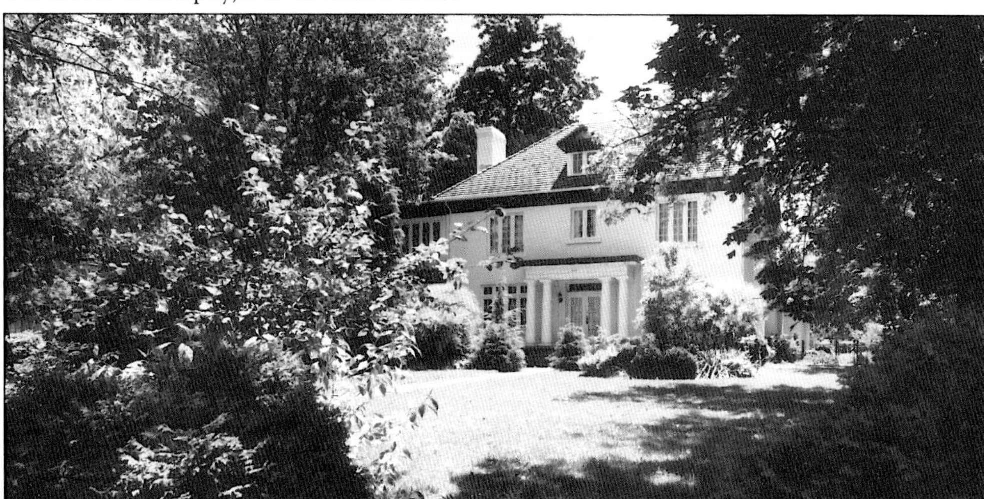

Perhaps the greatest house transformation in Sebring's history is the W.L. Murphy home. Pictured as it looks today, the home was enlarged and remodeled probably in the 1920s and is currently owned by Henry DeMuth. Other owners of the home have included the Marlin Watkins family and the Paul Schreckengost family.

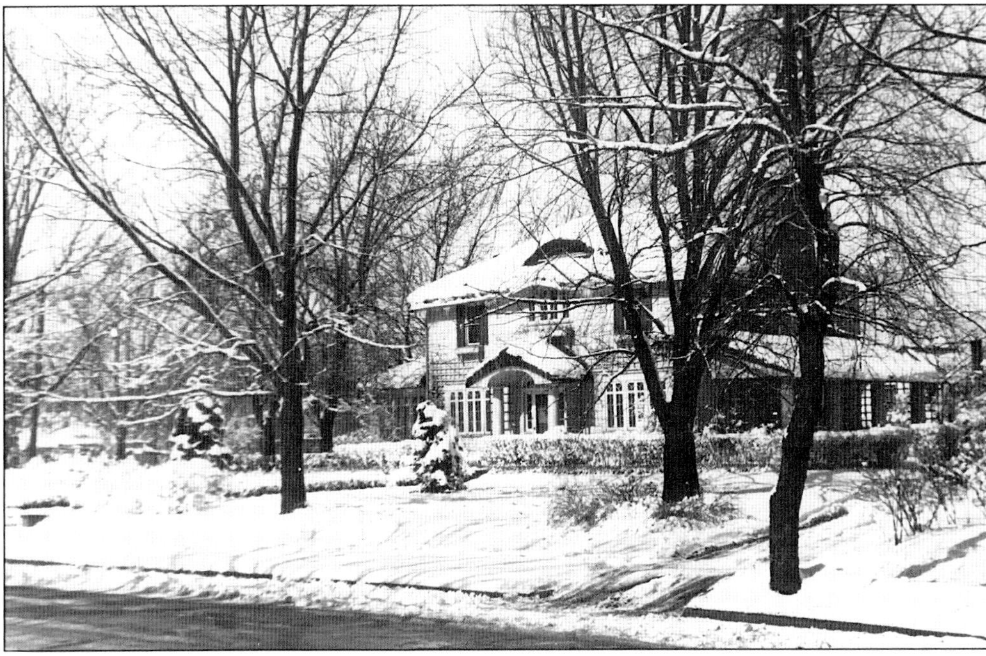

A warm fireplace and a cup of hot cocoa would have been appropriate on this snowy day in the 1940s. The residence of Mr. and Mrs. Ray Y.(Hazel Sebring) Cliff is located at the northwest corner of North Eighteenth Street and West Ohio Avenue. Hazel was the daughter of Oliver H. Sebring. Mr. Cliff was manager of the Saxon China Company. The home was purchased by John B. Briggs, a founder of Royal China Incorporated.

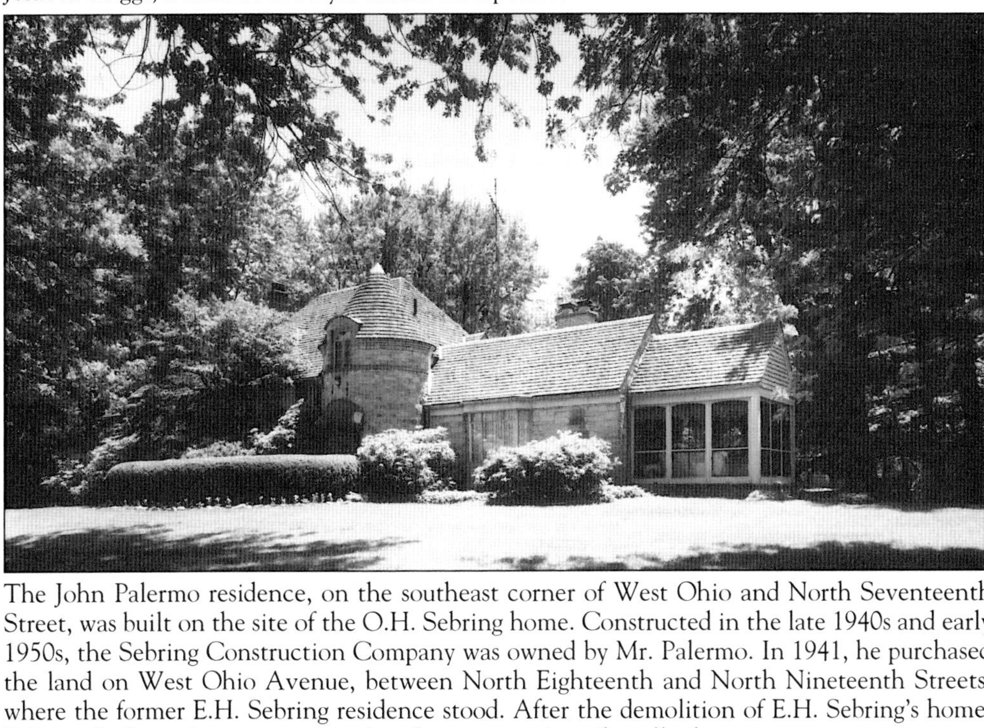

The John Palermo residence, on the southeast corner of West Ohio and North Seventeenth Street, was built on the site of the O.H. Sebring home. Constructed in the late 1940s and early 1950s, the Sebring Construction Company was owned by Mr. Palermo. In 1941, he purchased the land on West Ohio Avenue, between North Eighteenth and North Nineteenth Streets, where the former E.H. Sebring residence stood. After the demolition of E.H. Sebring's home, Palermo laid out the property into lots for construction of smaller homes.

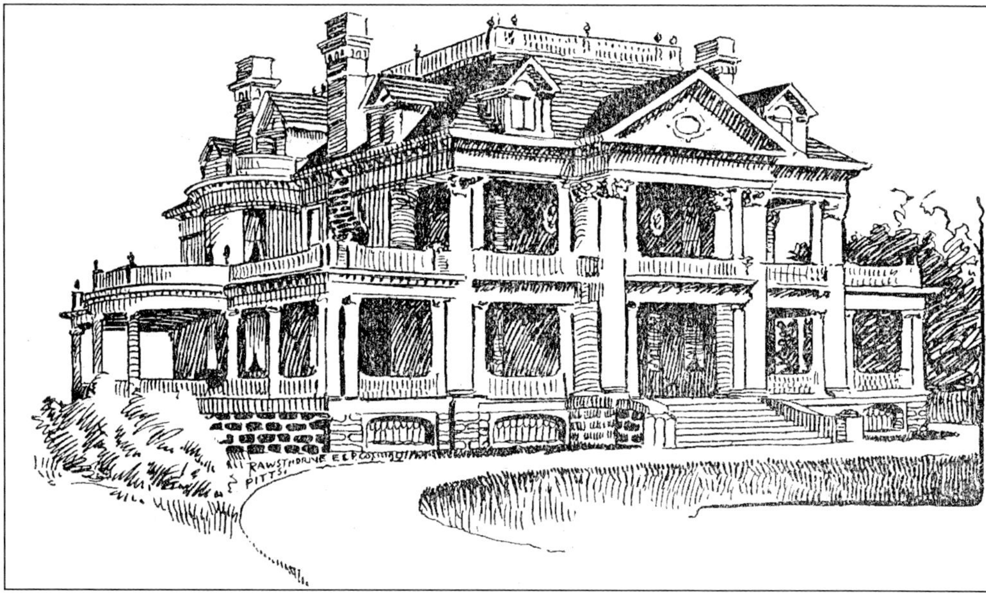

The Frank A. Sebring residence is the last of the Sebring family's pillared mansions on West Ohio Avenue. Designed by Rawsthorne of Pittsburgh, the home was built of Italian glazed bricks and was completed in 1902. Frank was the founder of the Sebring Pottery Company and the Limoges China Company. He was also associated with the Salem China Company, The Owen China Company of Minerva, and the Bradshaw Company of Niles. He moved the Niles plant to Alliance and operated it under the name Leigh Pottery Company. Mr. Sebring was very active in the development of Sebring. Through his involvement with the F.A. Sebring Realty Company and the West End Realty Company, hundreds of houses were built in the community. Mr. Sebring died on November 23, 1936.

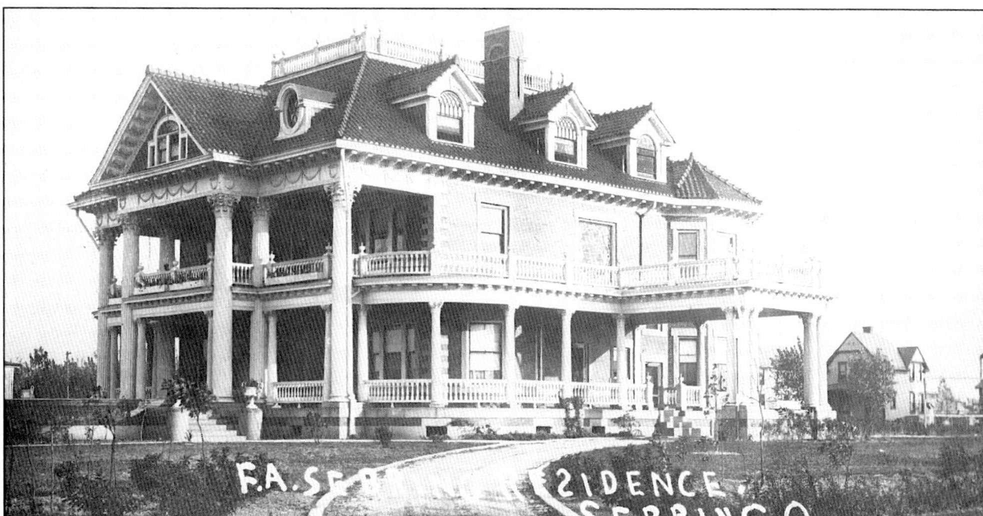

Through the efforts of Mrs. J. Lynne Biery, the grandeur of Frank A. Sebring's home will come alive again and will be preserved for future generations. In 1999, the home, which is on the National Register of Historic Places, will undergo major restoration to create a country inn. The ballroom on the top floor will be restored, the gardens will come alive again for the enjoyment of guests, and the flavor of Sebring's historic past will live on for decades to come.

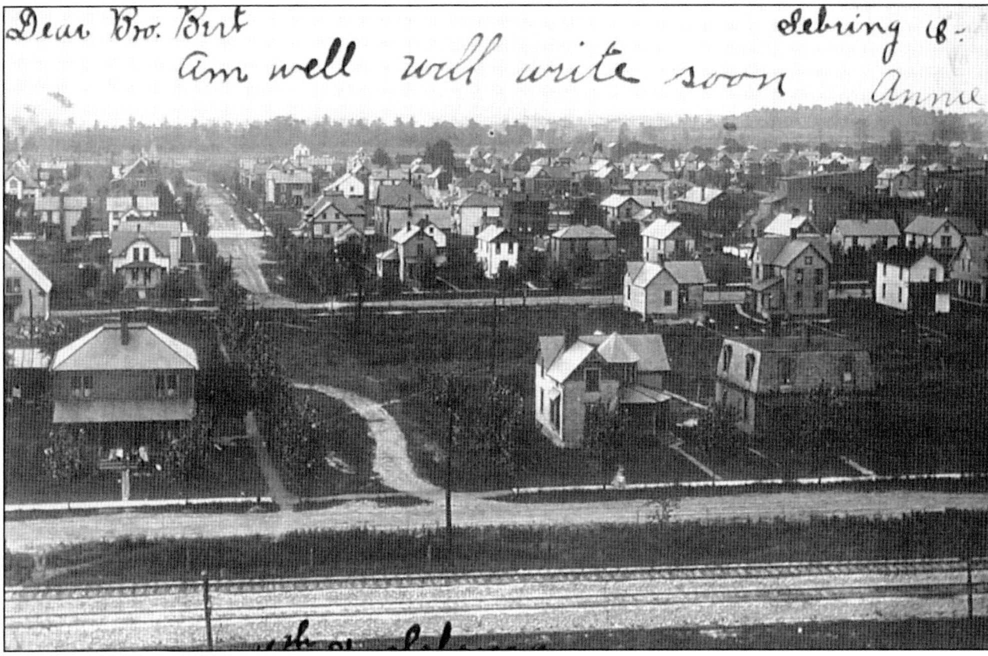

This aerial view from the Sebring Lumber Company's water tower is looking north toward the residential area. The first street running horizontally is Pennsylvania Avenue, the second is Oregon Avenue, and the street running vertically is North Sixteenth Street. Some buildings of note are the First United Presbyterian Church (toward the back on the left) and the back of Mr. and Mrs. George E. Sebring Sr.'s home at North Sixteenth Street and West Ohio Avenue.

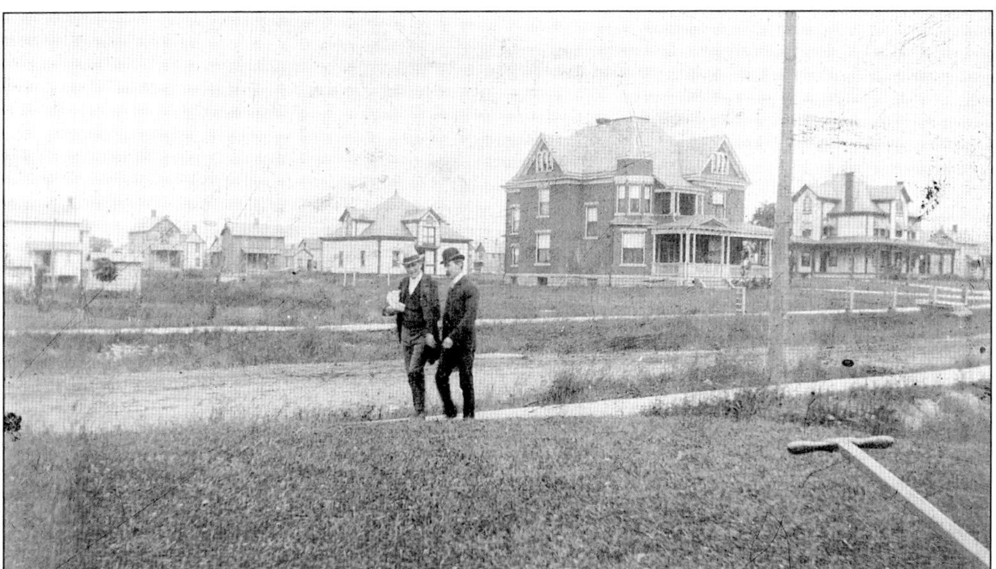

William L. Murphy and Reverend H.C. Morrison stroll down West Ohio Avenue on September 4, 1902. The photograph was taken by Charles J. Albright, who was married to Emma Sebring, Mrs. Murphy's aunt. The homes in the background are the Will Sebring residence and George E. Sebring Jr. residence.

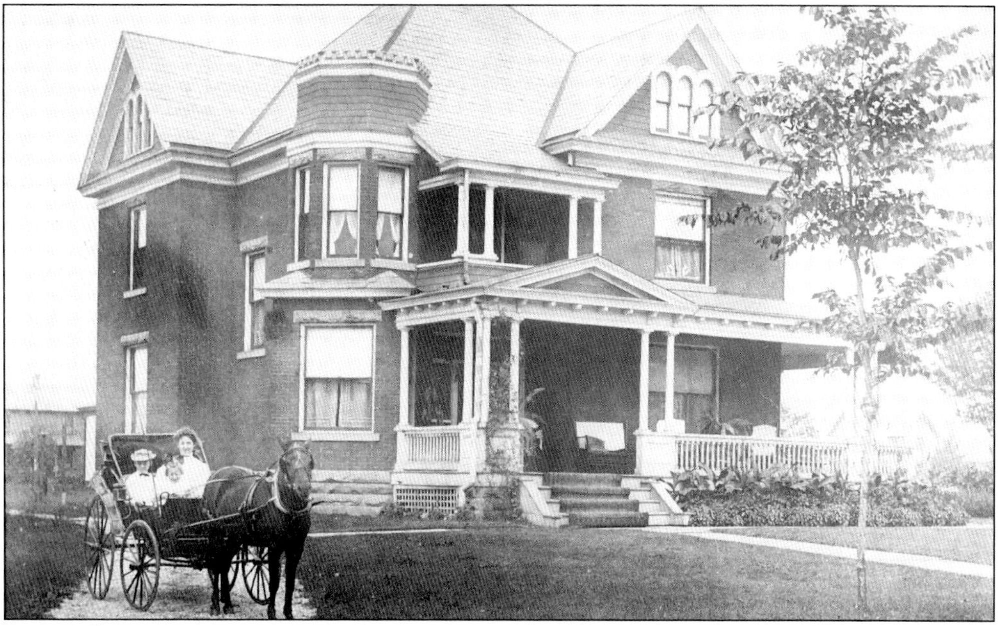

Mrs. Will H. (Eva Huston) Sebring and her children, Earl E. and Virginia, stop the buggy in the driveway of their residence long enough to have this picture snapped in 1907. Mrs. Sebring's late husband, Will, was treasurer of the Sebring Pottery Company, Limoges China Company, and the Sebring Land Company. His death occurred on Friday, December 9, 1904. According to an article in the *Sebring News*, "he (Will) was walking across the railroad tracks when he was struck by the No. 15, a west bound express that was going approximately 70 miles per hour. Due to a hearing impairment, Mr. Sebring misjudged the distance of the train. Soon after the accident, George Windle's attention was attracted by the groans of someone by the mail catching apparatus. Sebring was removed to the Katzenstein Block, and Dr. Jones and Dr. Klingensmith of Sebring, and Dr. Tressell of Alliance were summoned. After examination, they found that the lower part of his back had been crushed and broken, concluding that death was inevitable. Mr. Sebring regained consciousness, recognizing those about him and remained so up to within a half-hour of his demise. He gave no expression as to the manner of the accident but told them he was about to die and that he had 'poor luck.' "

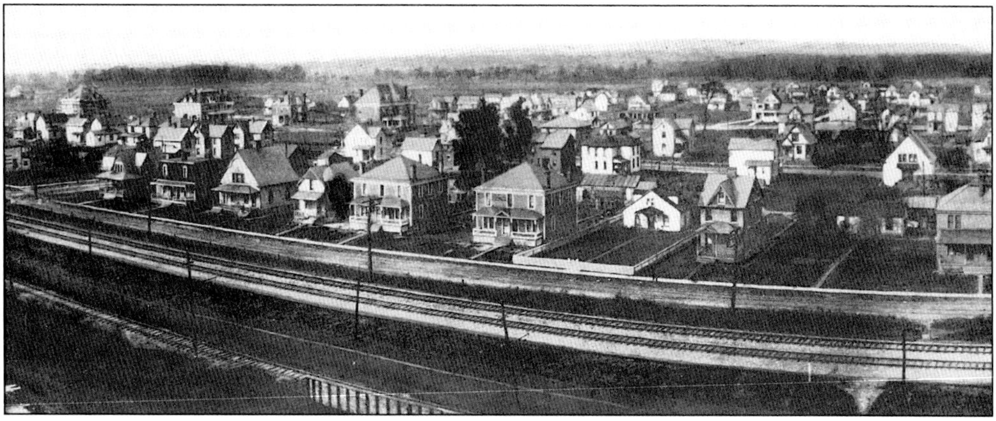

This postcard view looks toward the northwest from the lumber company's water tower. At this time, the residential area ended around North Eighteenth Street. E.H. Sebring's residence was just to the west of what is now North Eighteenth Street and West Ohio Avenue.

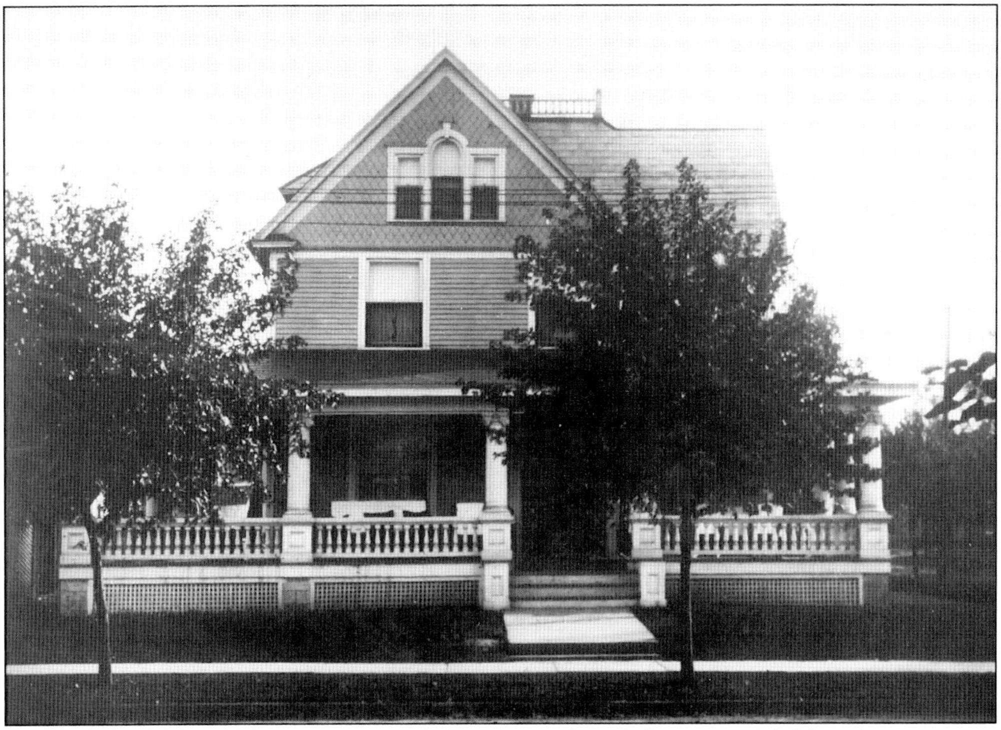

Shown here is the James and Emma (Sebring) Barclay residence at 295 Ohio Avenue. Mrs. Barclay was the daughter of George and Elizabeth Larkins Sebring Sr. Her first husband, Charles Albright, along with three other prominent citizens, was killed in October 1910, when their car was struck by a streetcar at Naylor's Crossing. Albright was manager of the Limoges China Company and was one of the incorporators of the Carrollton Pottery Company.

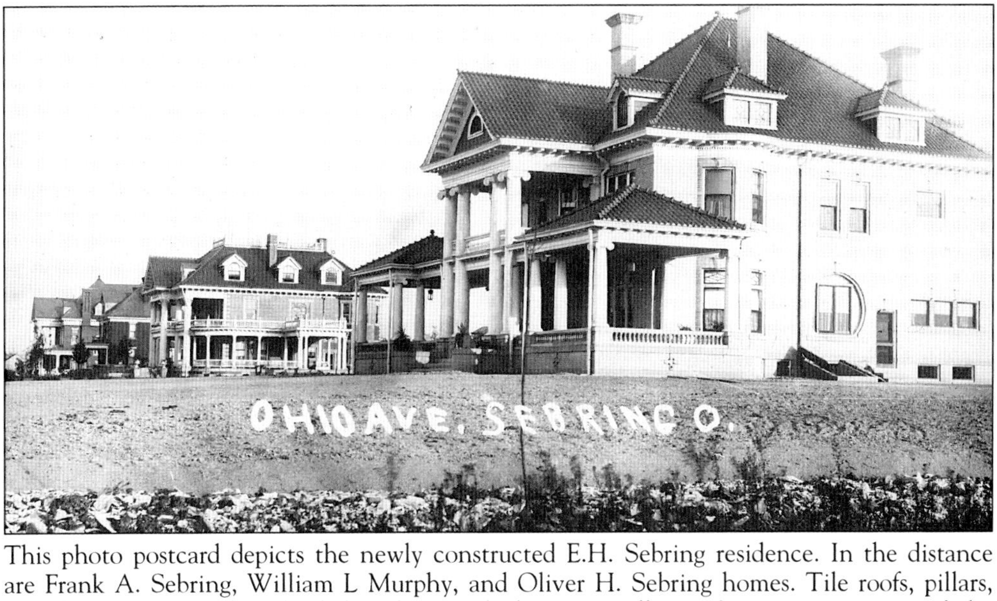

This photo postcard depicts the newly constructed E.H. Sebring residence. In the distance are Frank A. Sebring, William L Murphy, and Oliver H. Sebring homes. Tile roofs, pillars, glazed bricks, as well as leaded and stained glass were all significant components of the Sebring mansions.

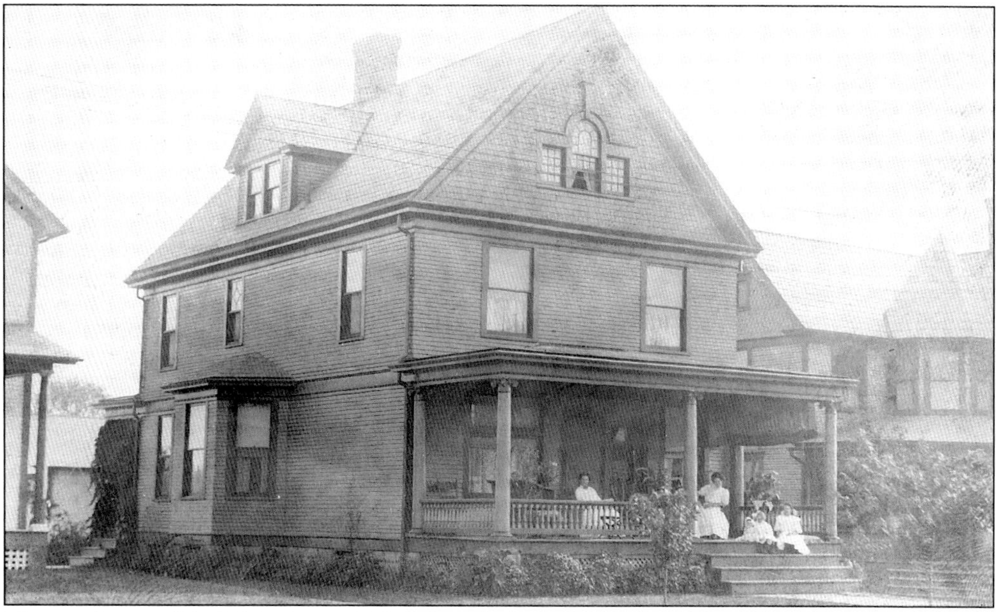

The residence of Earl J.Taylor, at 235 West Ohio Avenue, is represented in this photograph.

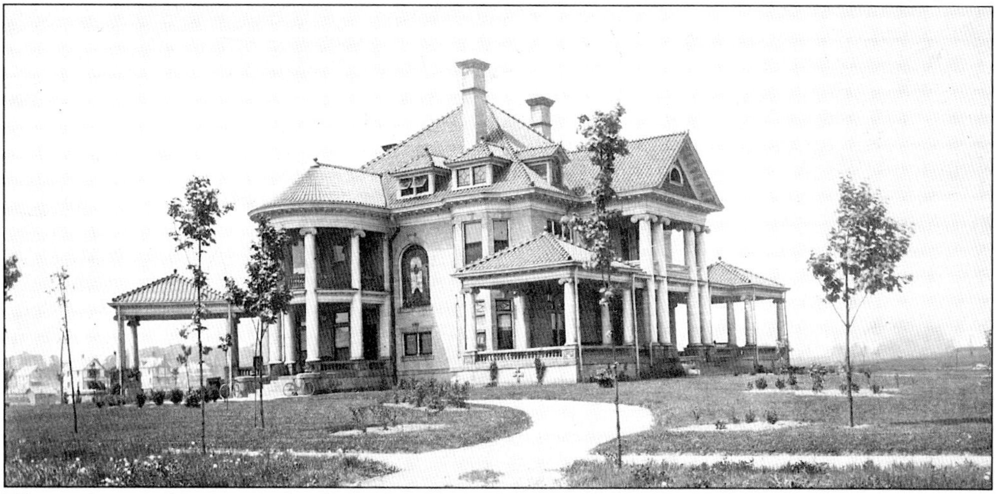

Ellsworth H. Sebring was the last survivor of the eight Sebring Brothers. He was one of the founders of the Sebring Pottery Company in East Liverpool, Ohio. In 1895, Ellsworth and his brother Oliver organized the French China Company in East Liverpool. In 1901, E.H. Sebring moved to Sebring with his family, and in 1911, he purchased the Oliver China Company and renamed it The E.H. Sebring China Company, which he operated successfully until the Depression forced it to close in 1931. Mr. Sebring moved to Sebring, Florida, where he grew citrus fruit. His home was designed by architect Jacob Myers. This view shows the east side of the home with its large stained-glass window, which extended from the middle of the first floor to the top of the second floor. Though the prevailing custom in the early part of this century was to lock up parlors and living rooms, using them only for special occasions, Mr. and Mrs. E.H. Sebring and their seven children chose to "live" in their home. Informality was the keynote in the daily life of this family. Boiled shirts and rustling party dresses seldom made their appearance here, but children with shirt-tails hanging out and rumpled hair might have been seen frequently running through the halls in a playful game of hide-and-seek.

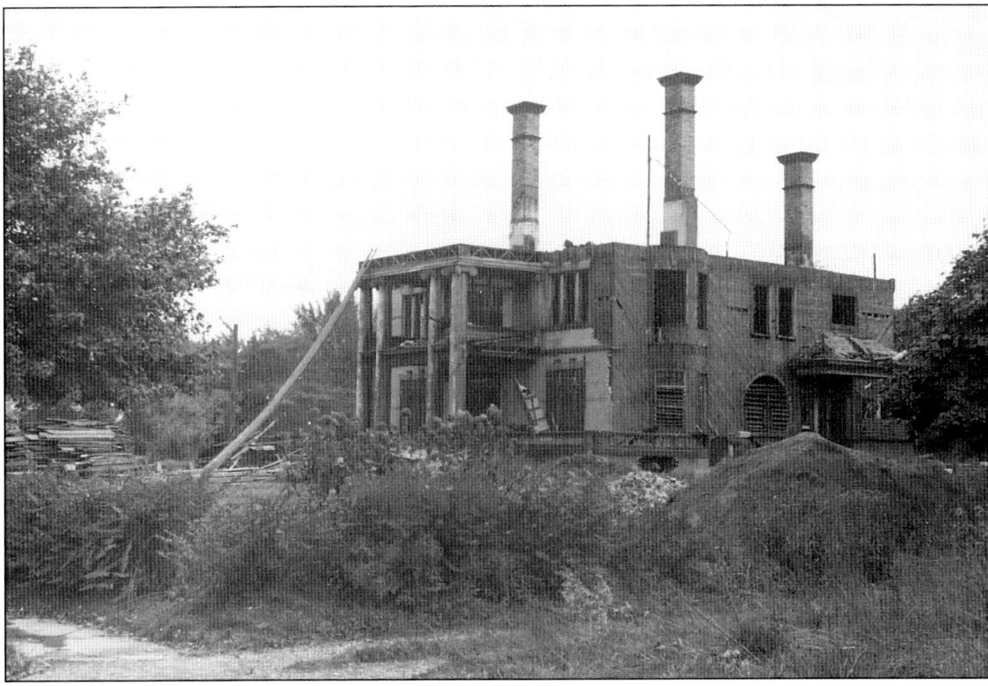

After Ellsworth's death on February 1, 1937, Youngstown Home Savings and Loan held the mortgage on the mansion, which served as a rooming house for two years. On July 31, 1940, the county sold it for taxes at auction to James Palermo. Occupying 350-foot frontage on Oregon and Ohio Avenues, the house stood on two-thirds of a city block. Mr. Palermo's plan to divide the property into lots was underway.

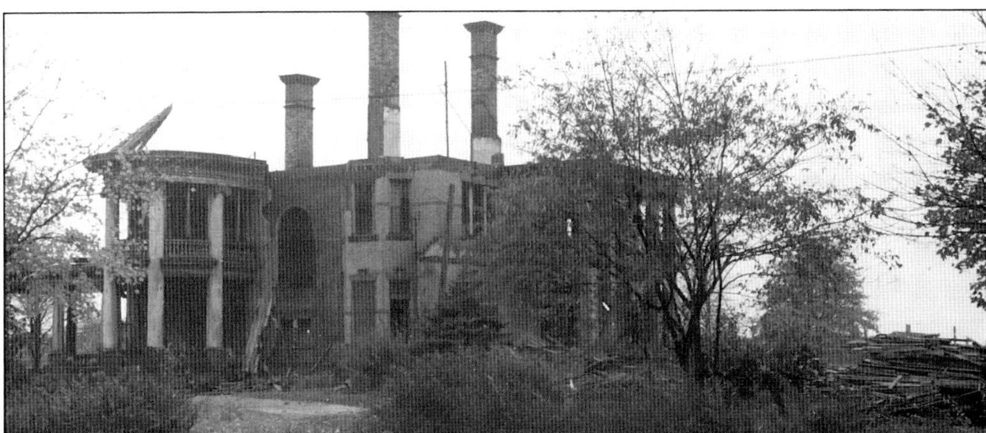

Stripped of its former glory, E.H. Sebring's home fell prey to the wrecking ball in the fall of 1940, rapidly becoming a phantom of its once stately self. Crumbling before the strokes of the demolition crews, the manse, whose halls once echoed with the laughter of many children (now skeleton-like in this photograph), served as a playground for sparrows. Built during an architectural transition period, the home's eclectic style was common for the period. One Sebring family member said, "It was a glorious pile of gingerbread." Oak, maple, mahogany, and a variety of other expensive woods were used in the construction of the interior, while expansive oriental rugs covered its polished floors. The stone alone in the building cost $6,500.

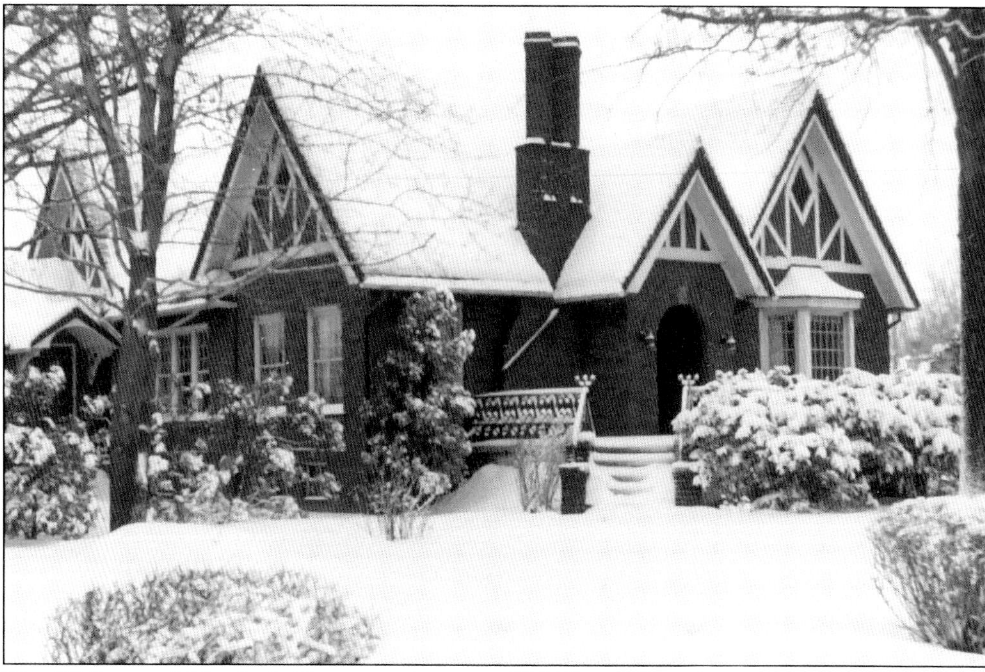

The Wilbur and Elizabeth Dimit residence at 506 West Ohio Avenue is shown here as it appeared in the 1980s. Mr. Dimit and his brothers operated Dimit Brothers Photography Studio in Alliance. Many memories of school and home were captured on a Dimit camera for nearly 60 years. Mr. Dimit was also a member of the Sebring Board of Education.

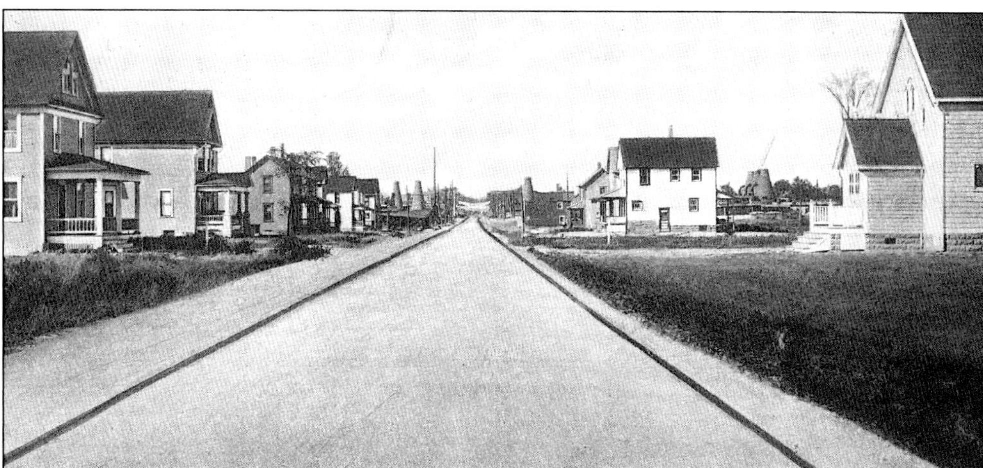

As the pottery industry grew in Sebring, so did its neighborhoods. Pleasant Heights was one such area that the Sebrings planned in the early years. Located south of the potteries on South Fifteenth Street and the adjoining streets, this postcard view shows the area looking north down South Fifteenth Street. On the right is St. Anne's Catholic Church. This hand-colored photograph was taken during one of the Harvest Home Festivals. In the far distance, the streamers wind across North Fifteenth Street. That is probably why the neighborhood is deserted.

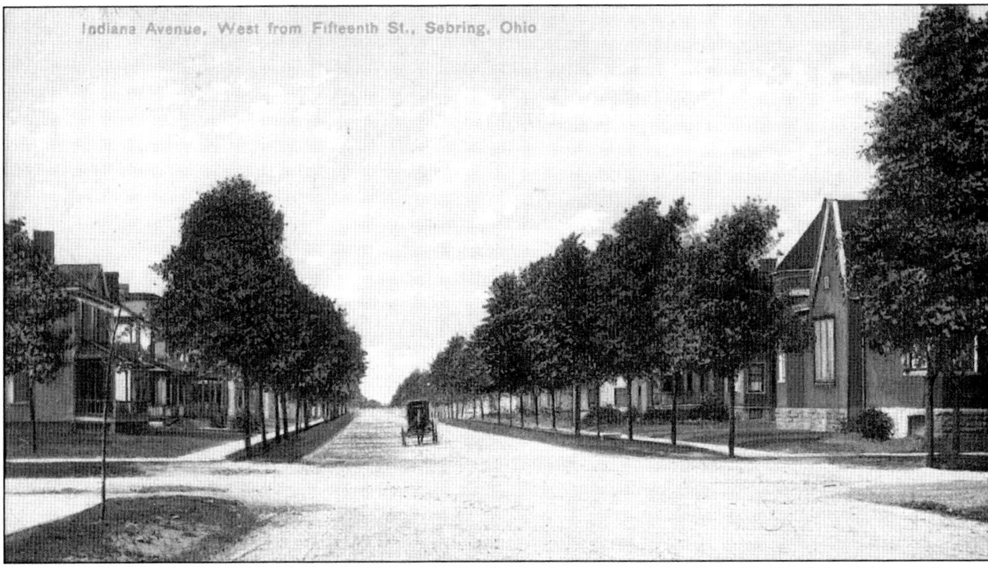

A dusty West Indiana Avenue is the focus of this 1907 postcard published by Heacock and Bortz of Sebring. Printed in Quarto-Chrome, the two photographs on this page were made in Germany. Taken at the intersection of North Fifteenth Street, the Methodist Episcopal Church can be seen on the right. The street eventually became brick (unfortunately it has been paved over in recent years), and the trees lining the neighborhood provided cool shade on hot summer days.

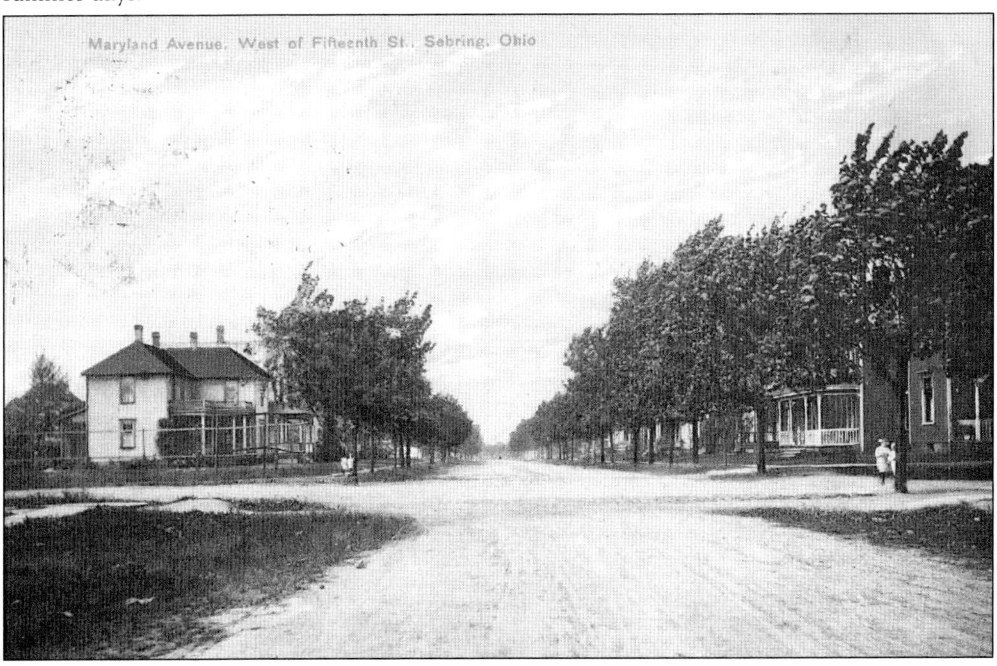

Like the picture at top, this postcard view of West Maryland Avenue from North Fifteenth Street was taken on a breezy summer afternoon. Notice the strong southern breeze against the mighty oaks. The home that was eventually built on the empty lot, on the southwest corner, was the home of Pearl and Ed Coleman. Robert and Margaret Franke resided there for many years, and today, it is the Christiani dental office.

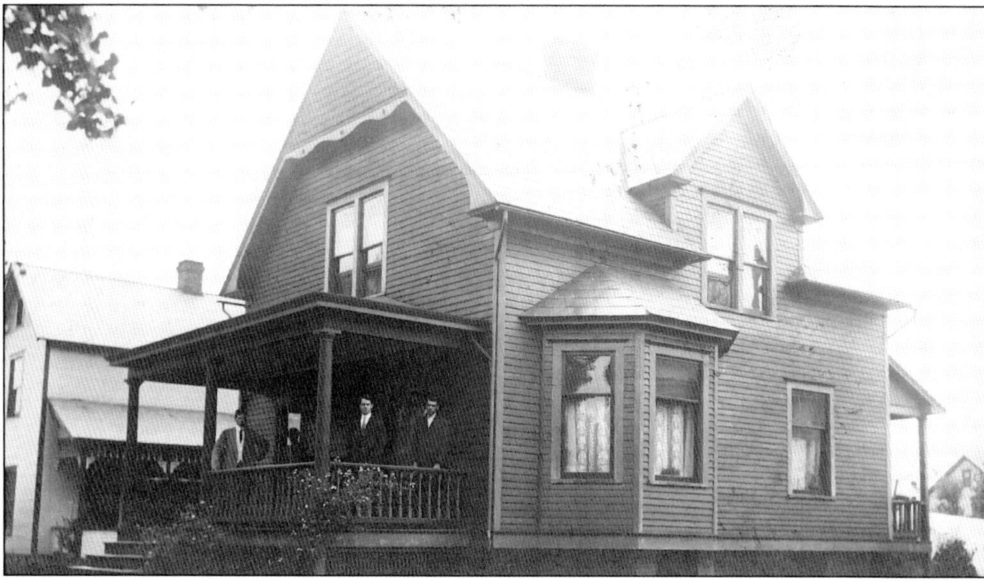

Clyde Oliver and friends pose on the front porch of his home on West Oregon Avenue. He was the proprietor of a grocery store on North Fifteenth Street for many years.

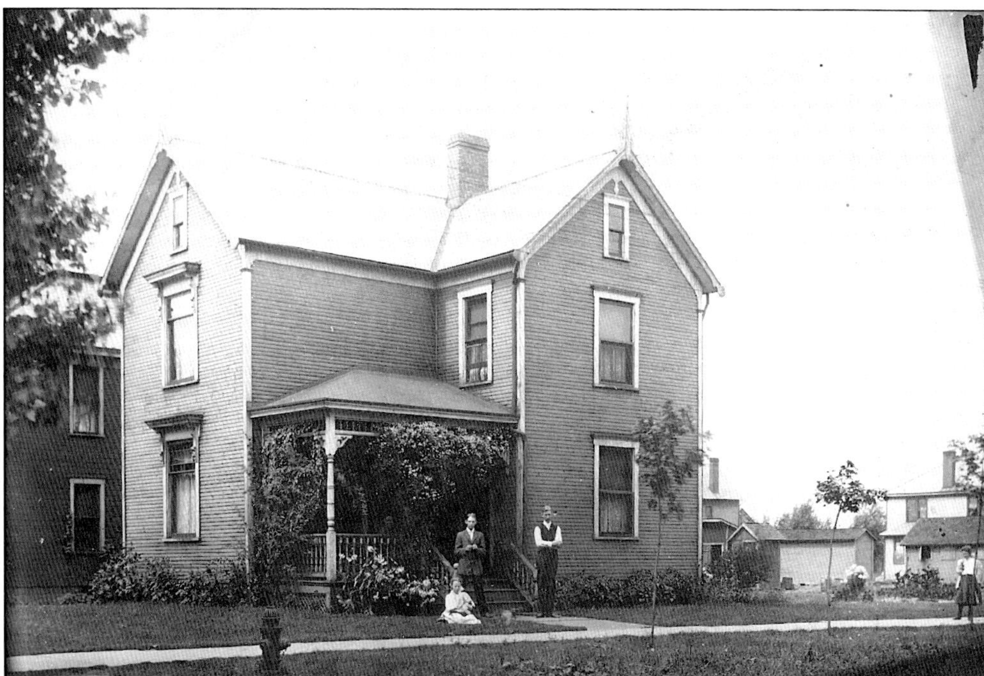

This home stands on the northwest corner of West Maryland Avenue and North Fifteenth Street. It is significant in the community's history because it was the home of Dick Albright, Sebring's first postmaster. Pictured are Ruth Norris Robinson (sitting on the lawn), Bill Norris, and Frank N. Norris. This picture was taken about 1906.

Six

Public Service
Community and Country

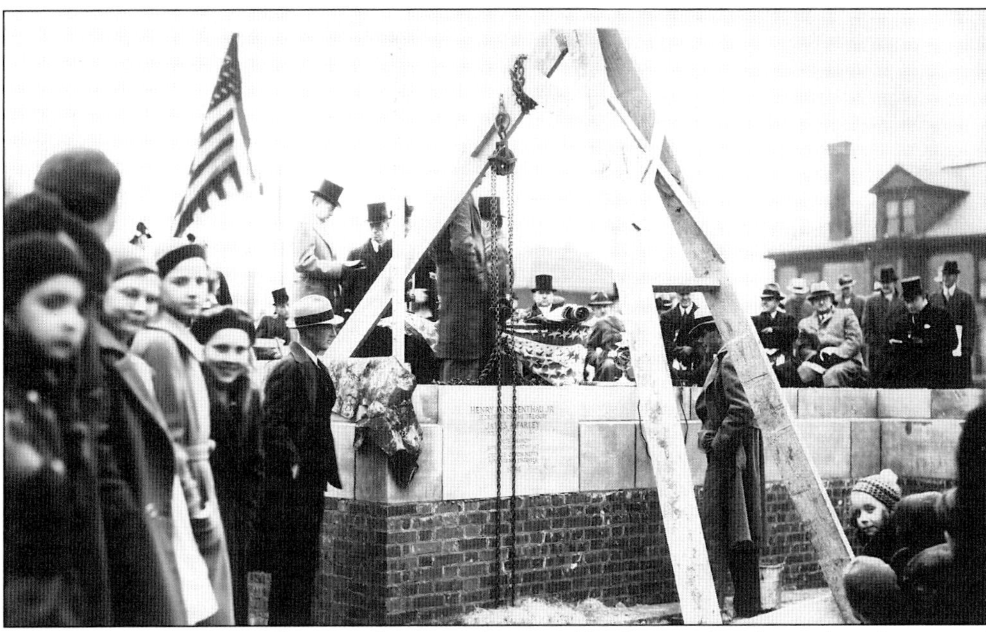

The necessity for a post office in Sebring can be traced back to its founding, when the original location was in a small frame structure on North Fifteenth Street and the first postmaster was Dick Albright. Around 1930, the United States Postal Service promised the community a federal building; however, do to the Depression, nearly four years passed before it became a reality. Land was purchased on the northeast corner of W. Ohio Avenue and North Sixteenth Street, and on Armistice Day, November 11, 1934, the cornerstone laying ceremonies were conducted by the Grand Lodge of Ohio, F. & A.M. In 1930, Samuel Eardley was appointed postmaster, and in 1923, Paul Linke was appointed assistant postmaster. It was during their term that this building was constructed.

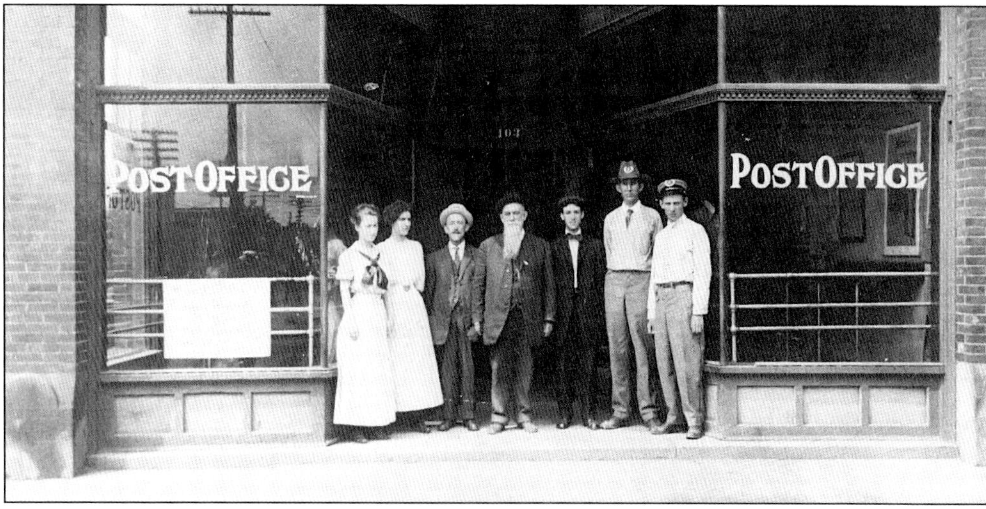

By 1909, the small frame structure on North Fifteenth Street became inadequate because the community of Sebring was growing at such a fast rate. Space was made available in the Mahoning Block, on the northeast corner of East Ohio Avenue and North Fifteenth Street, where Attorney Richard Ross's office is located today. Pictured in this 1912 photograph, left to right, are as follows: Ella Larkins Surls; Bess Daniels Lytle; William Larkins, assistant postmaster; Henry Larkins, postmaster; Bert Elliot; William Paxson; and William Norris, mail carriers. Mr. Paxson and Mr. Norris were the first mail carriers in Sebring and were appointed to the position on March 1, 1912.

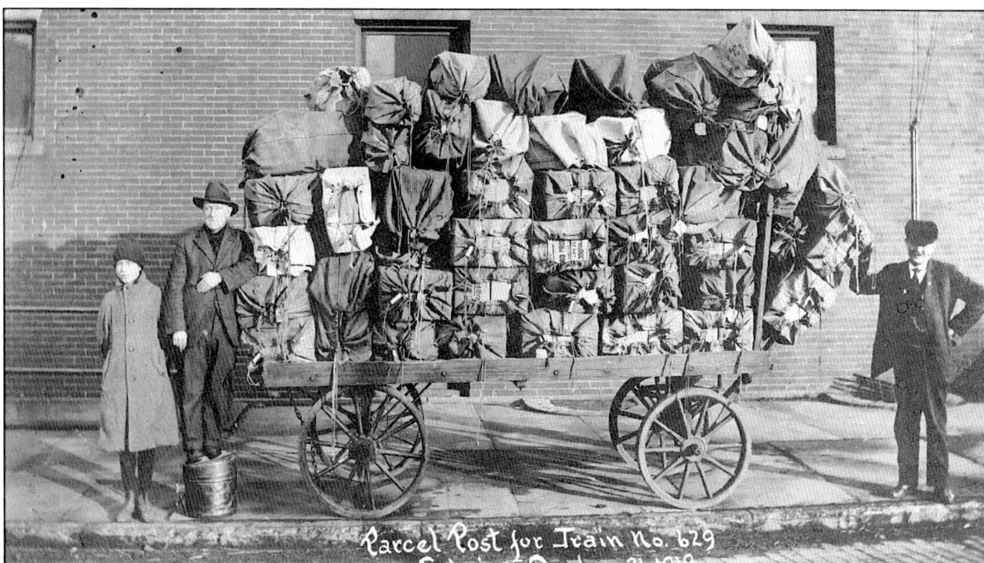

Three months after Sebring was established, total receipts for the post office were $26.61. This included stamps, newspaper wrappers, envelopes, postal cards, and one special delivery stamp. By the end of 1901, sales increased to $1,010.98. Large shipments of parcel post by the local potteries soon outdated the new location in the Mahoning Block because it was virtually impossible to handle the packages in such a small area. Pictured above is an example of the number of parcels leaving Sebring. As stated on the picture, this wagon load is waiting for the No. 629 train on January 21, 1919.

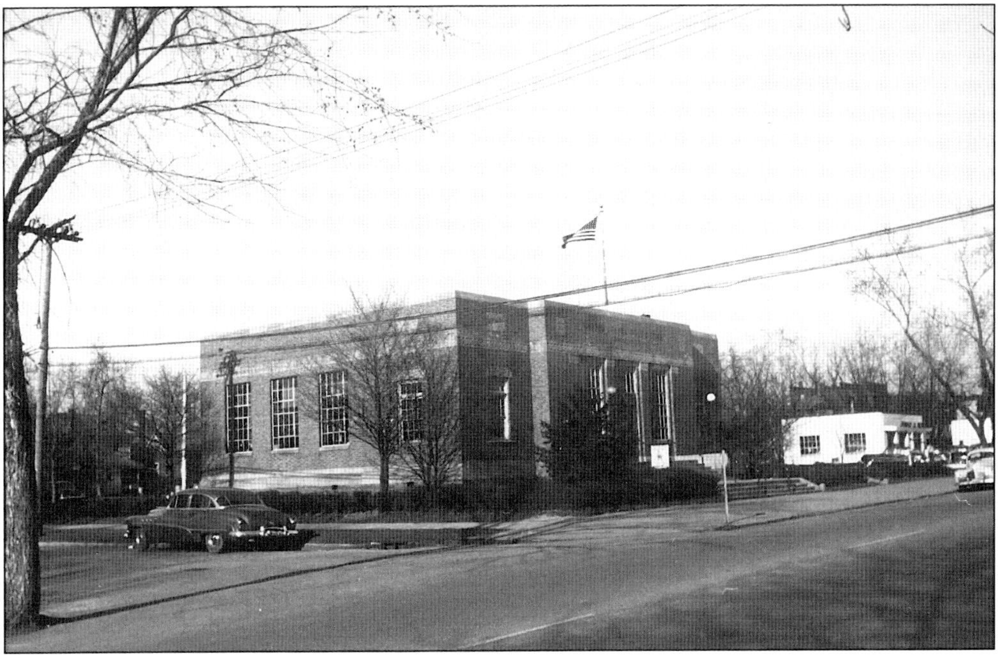

The present post office building is shown here as it appeared in the late 1940s. A significant event occurred on July 1, 1949, when the local post office was advanced from a second class to a first class post office.

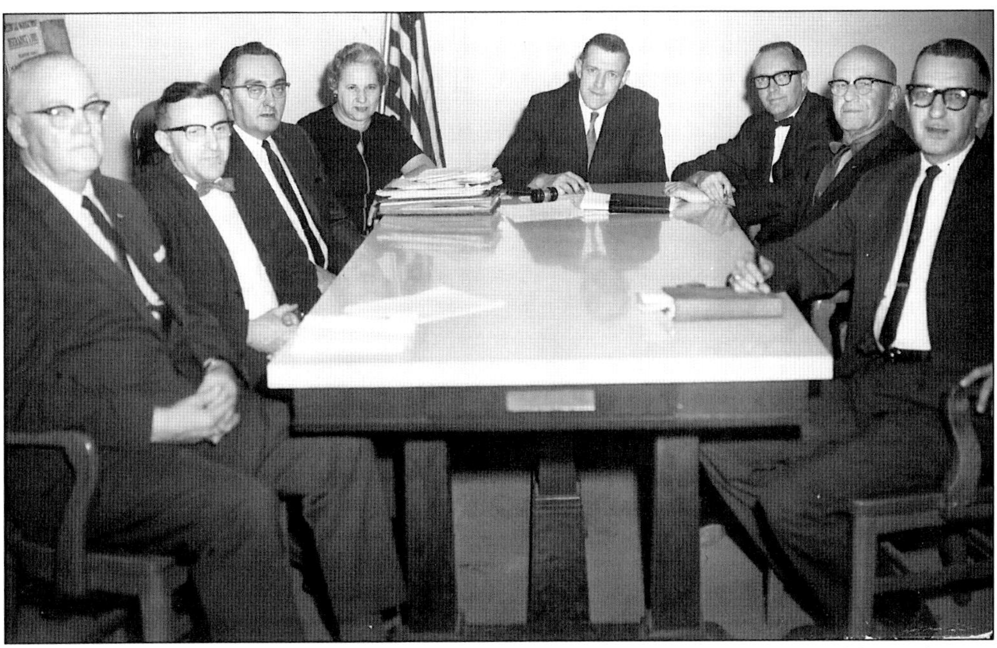

Members of the Sebring Village Council pose in council chambers in the building adjacent to the village hall on November 11, 1966. Pictured are, left to right, as follows: Joe Mills, Ray Elliot, John Fahnert, Helen Erb, Mayor Joseph Harp, James Burch, Frank Buehler, and Joseph Ludwig.

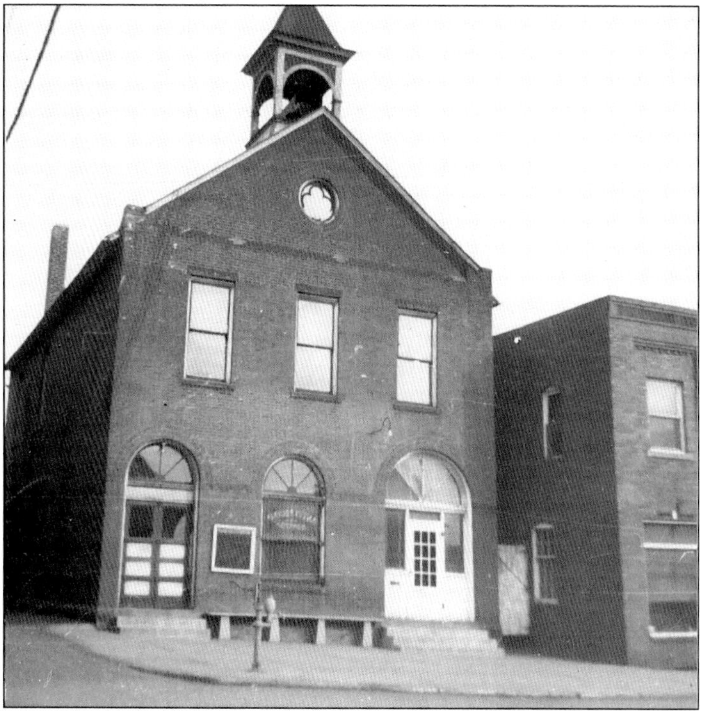

Shown here is the village hall as it appeared on November 19, 1941. Built in 1901, the structure was originally designed to have a tower on the east portion; however, alterations were made to the architect's design.

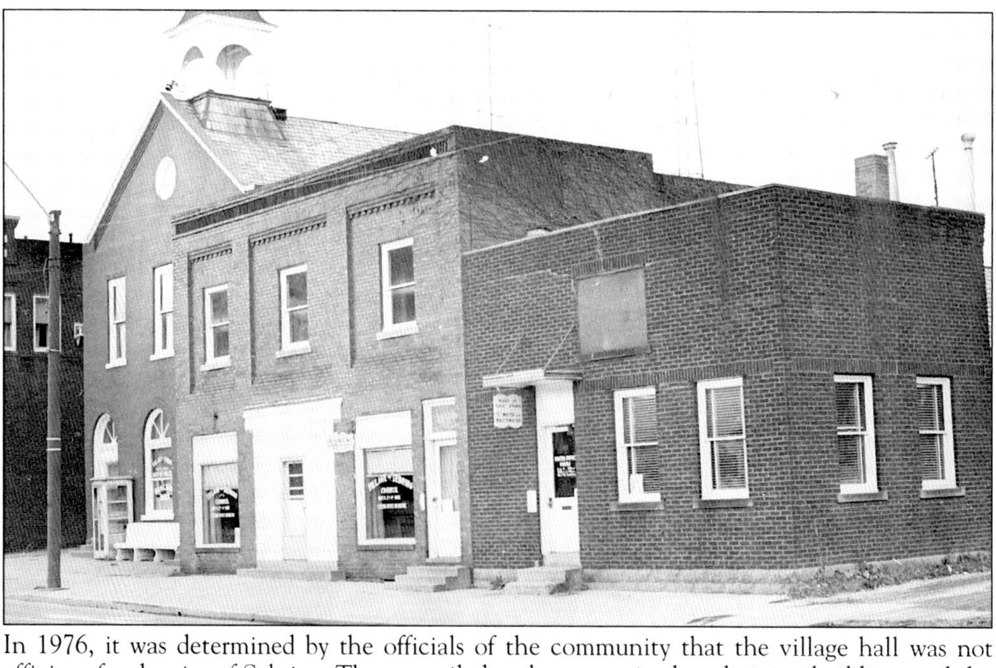

In 1976, it was determined by the officials of the community that the village hall was not efficient for the size of Sebring. The council chambers were in the adjoining building, and the water department offices were housed in another area. It was felt that the consolidation of all departments and the police station was the best solution. The three buildings pictured were all occupied by the village, and their demolition began soon after this picture was taken.

Demolition of the old village hall was well underway in this 1976 snapshot.

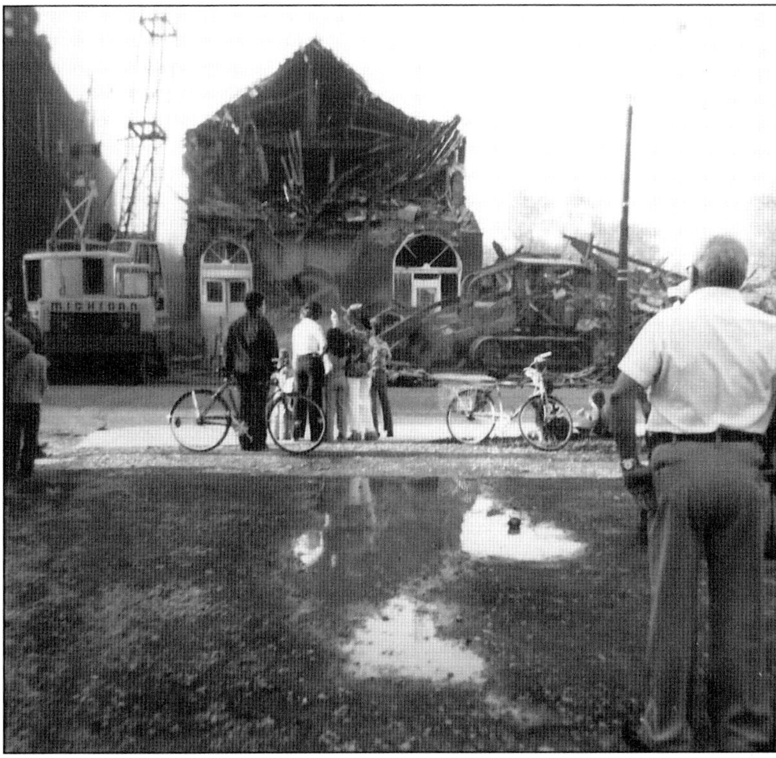

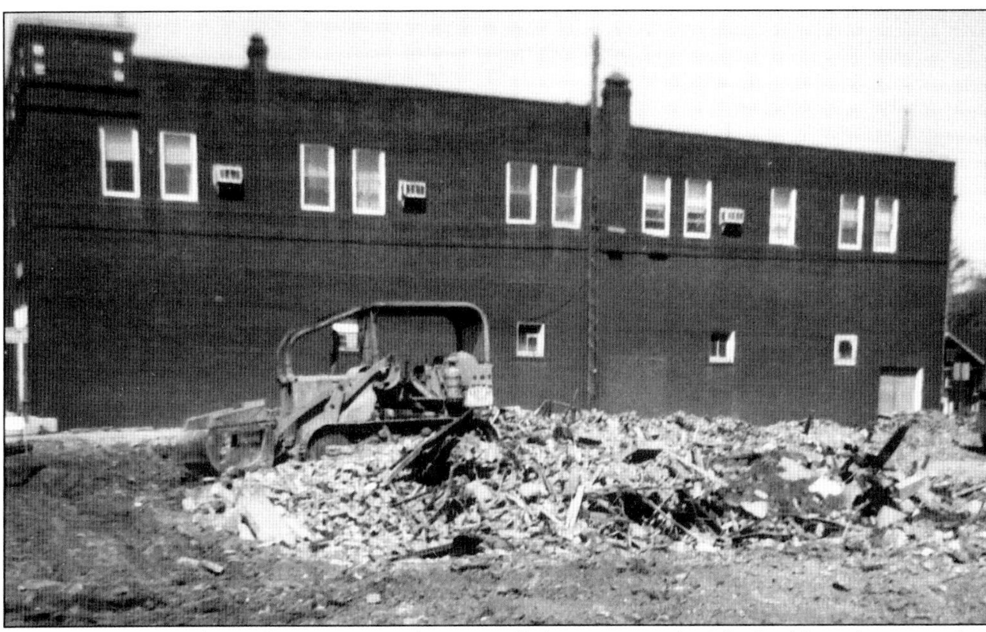

A pile of bricks and wood on an empty lot were all that remained of the building that served its community for 75 years. In 1977, the new municipal hall was constructed with suitable offices for the village's officials, a council chamber, as well as police headquarters. One symbol remains from the past. The town pump is still located in front of the current building, but according to water department officials, it is not hooked up.

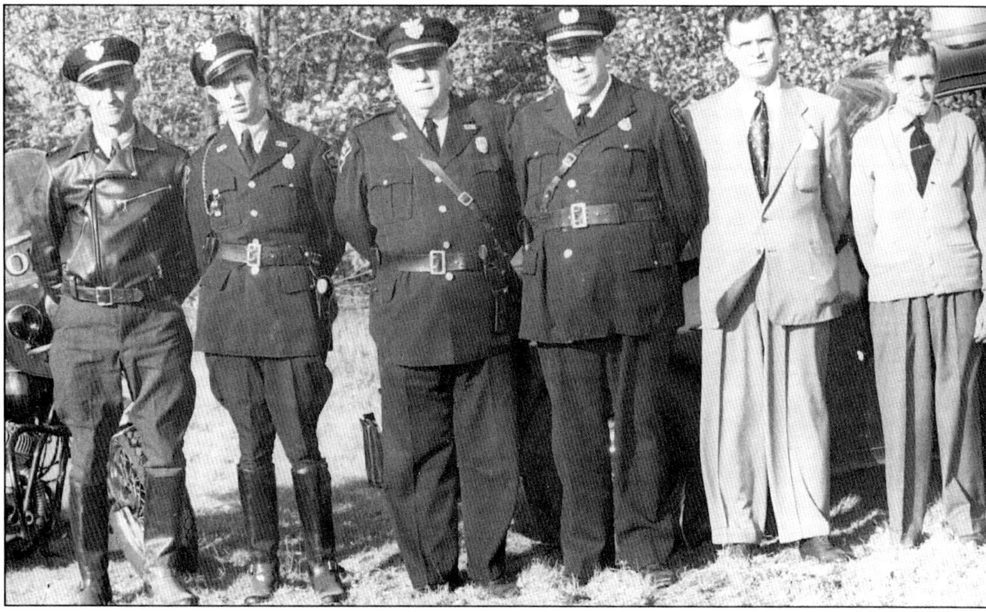

Law enforcement is a key component to the success of any community, and Sebring has been blessed by the dedication of its police force. Pictured in this 1940s photograph, from left to right, are Arthur Eells, Paul Gednetz, Wilbert Parr, Police Chief James Marshall, Mayor William Unger, and Radio Clerk Steve Leighton.

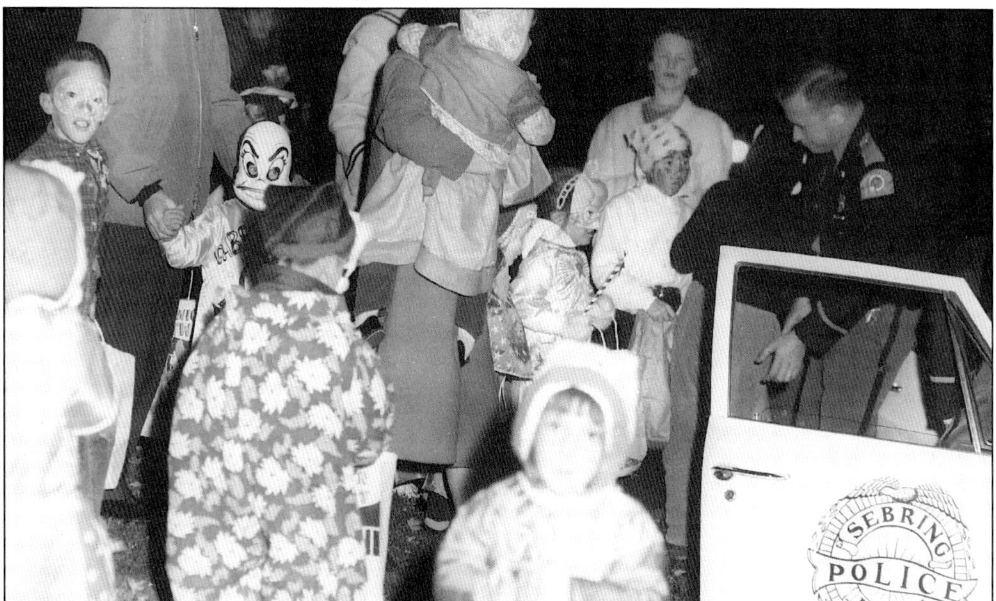

Police officers provide treats to the children of the community on Halloween night in the 1960s. The police force of Sebring has always been involved in community activities. In 1985, the Sebring Police Association was established as a nonprofit organization dedicated to "working towards the common goal of creating and engaging in activities exclusively for charitable, religious, scientific, literary, or educational purposes for the primary benefit of the residents of the city of Sebring, focusing mainly towards the children of the community."

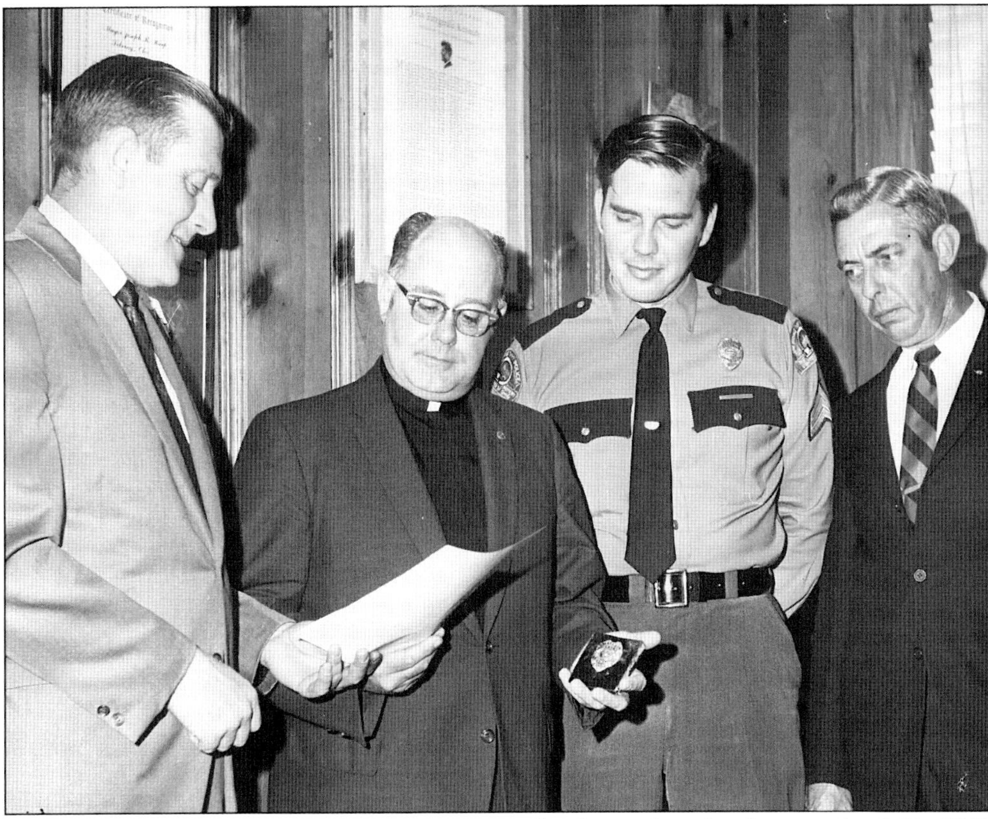

The Reverend C.O. Armstrong was sworn in as the first police chaplain on April 29, 1969, by Mayor Joseph R. Harp (on the far left). His badge of authority was presented from the department by Sgt. David E. Abney (second from right). Police Chief Paul F. Gednetz can be seen on the far right.

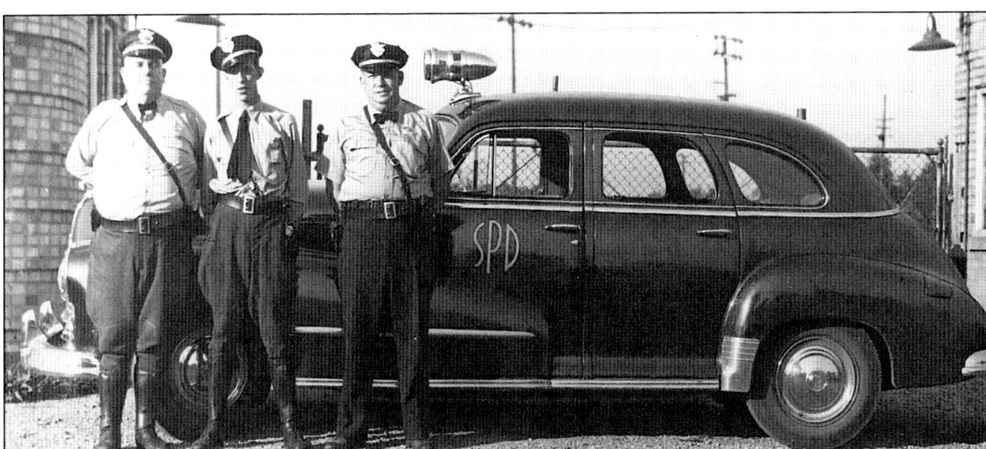

Members of the Sebring Police Department posed in front of a cruiser in 1949 and are shown here, from left to right, as follows: Wilbert Parr, Paul Gednetz, and James Marshall.

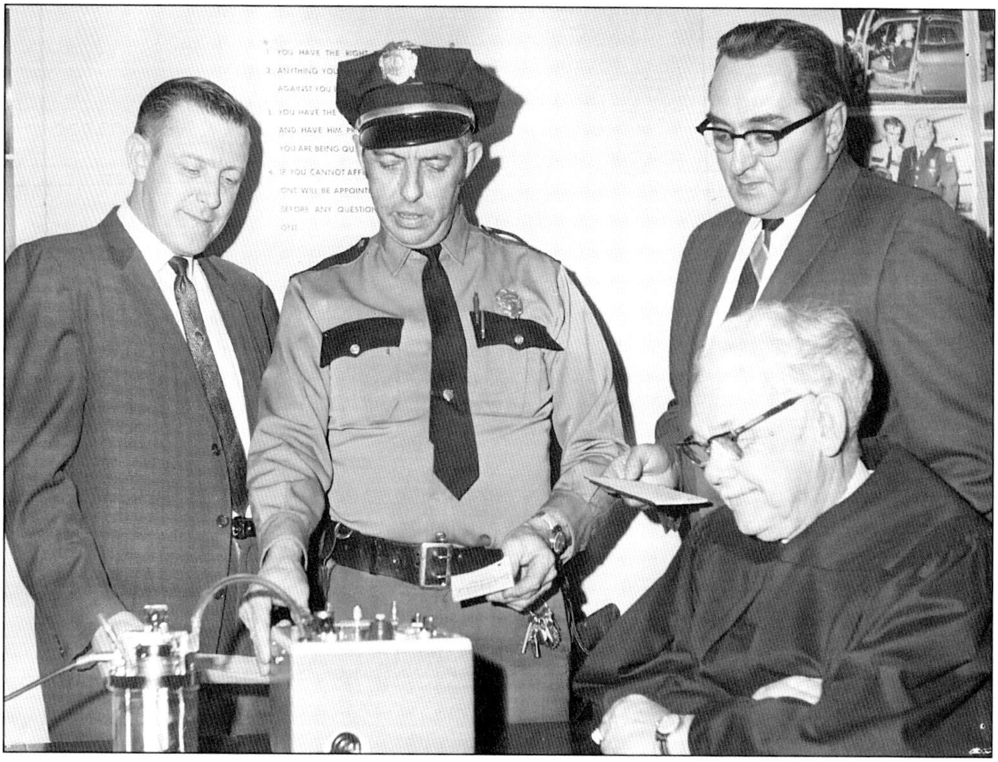

The Sebring Police Department purchases a new Breathalyzer in the late 1960s. Pictured from left to right are the following: Mayor Joseph Harp, Police Chief Paul F. Gednetz, Councilman John Fahnert, and County Court Judge John A. Reddy.

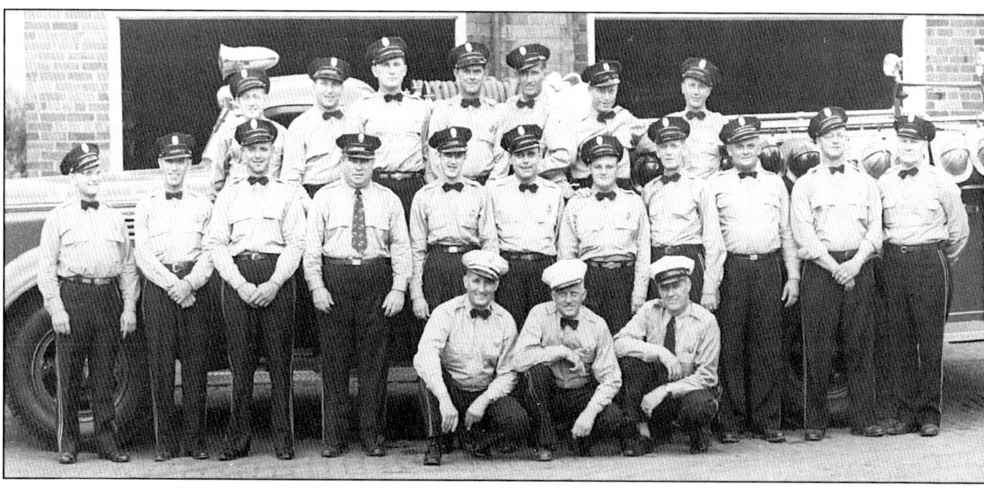

Members of the Sebring Fire Department pose in front of the old station in the alley behind the old village hall in 1949. Members shown here, from left to right, are as follows: (front row) Chief John Watson, Assistant Chief Herbert Vogt, and Lieutenant D. Cameron; (second row) George Halverstadt, Sal Trainer, William Mercer, Russ Sanders, Richard Sanders, Ed Parr, Dale Larkins, Herb Johnston, R. Barnett, Charles Mercer, and Jim Jordan; (back row) George Goodballet, Earl Simpson, George Brimlow, R. Bratton, Art Eells, Johnny Meir, and E. Eaton.

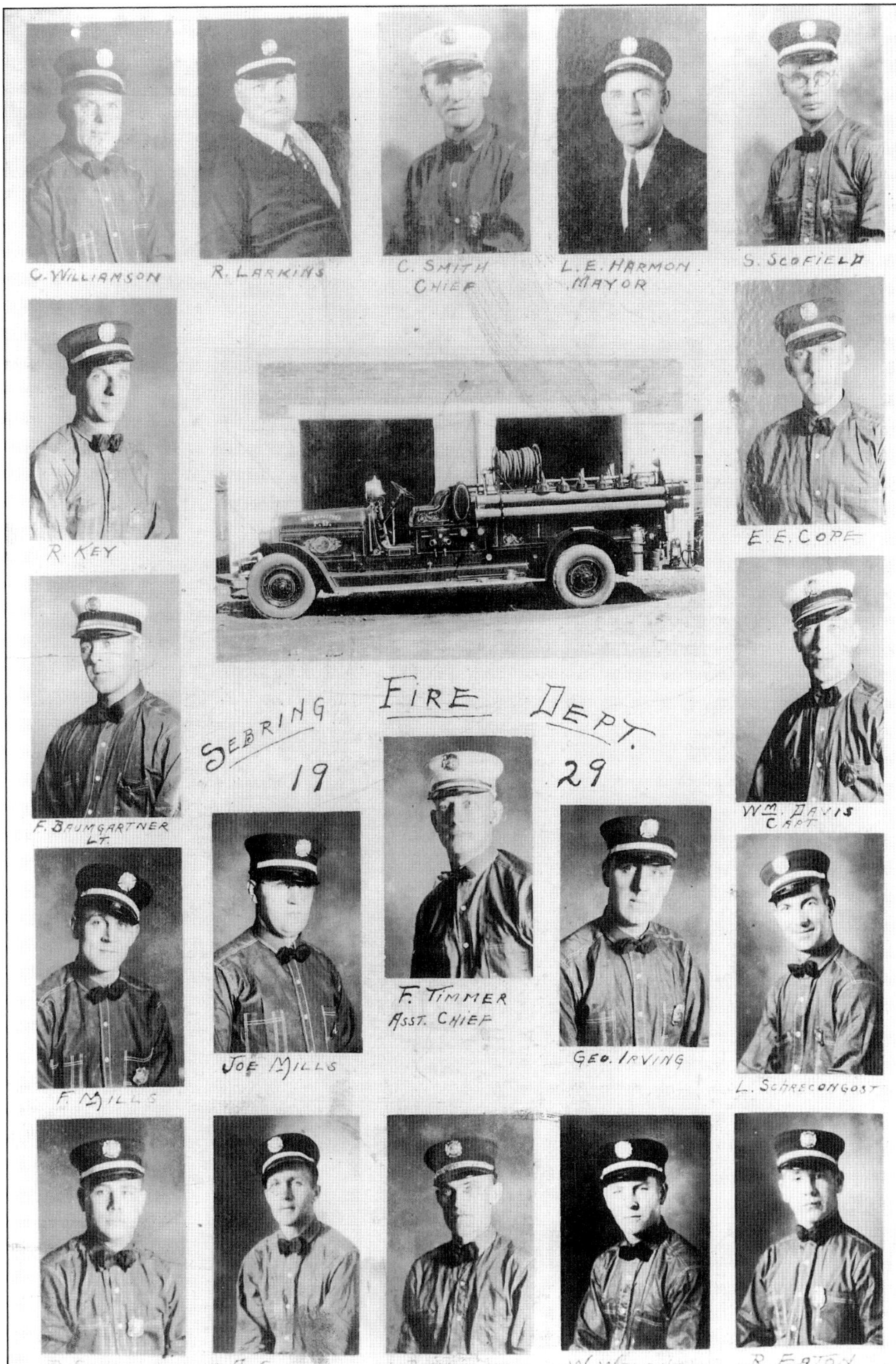

The Sebring Fire Department teamed up with Mayor L.E. Harmon for this 1929 photograph.

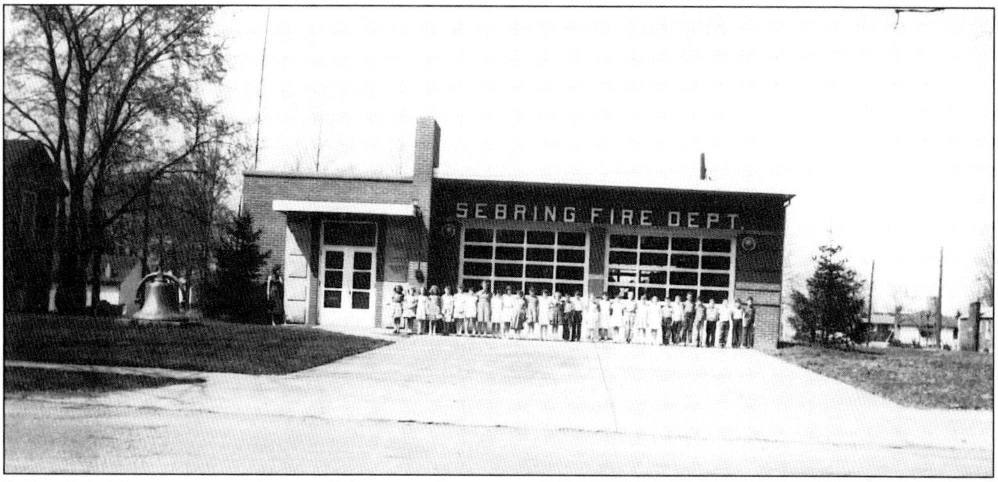

Schoolchildren pose in front of the new fire station on East Ohio Avenue in 1952. Designed by Alliance architect Richard Zuber (he also designed the First United Presbyterian Church), the fire station was built by L.J. Clark. Several additions have been added over the years, including the kitchen to the rear of the building, and, in 1969, the bay was enlarged to fit the new snorkel.

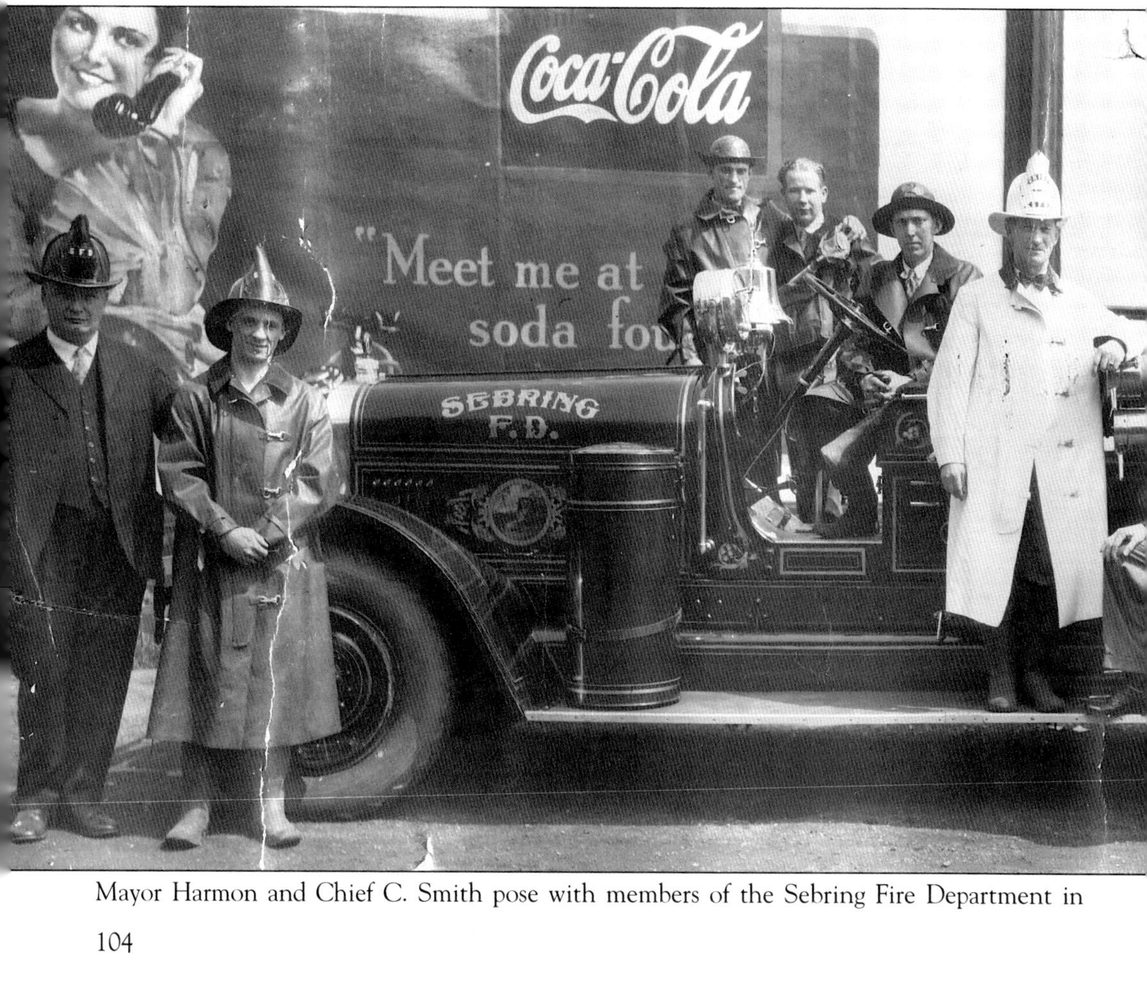

Mayor Harmon and Chief C. Smith pose with members of the Sebring Fire Department in

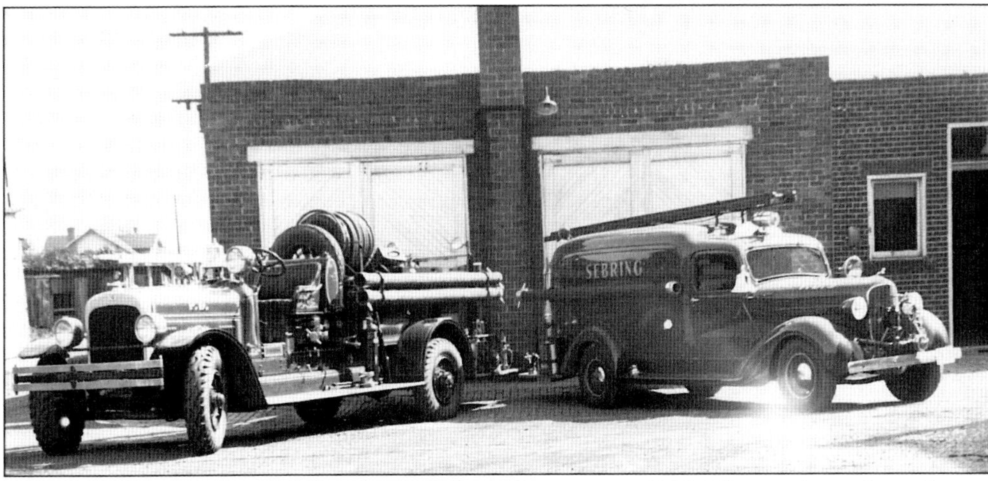

The fire trucks are positioned in front of the old station in 1938. The truck on the right was referred to as a mini-pumper. One of the major fires the department faced in the early years was at the Ohio Avenue Motor Company in January 1931, on the corner of West Ohio Avenue and North Sixteenth Street. Forty-two automobiles were destroyed at a loss of $70,000.

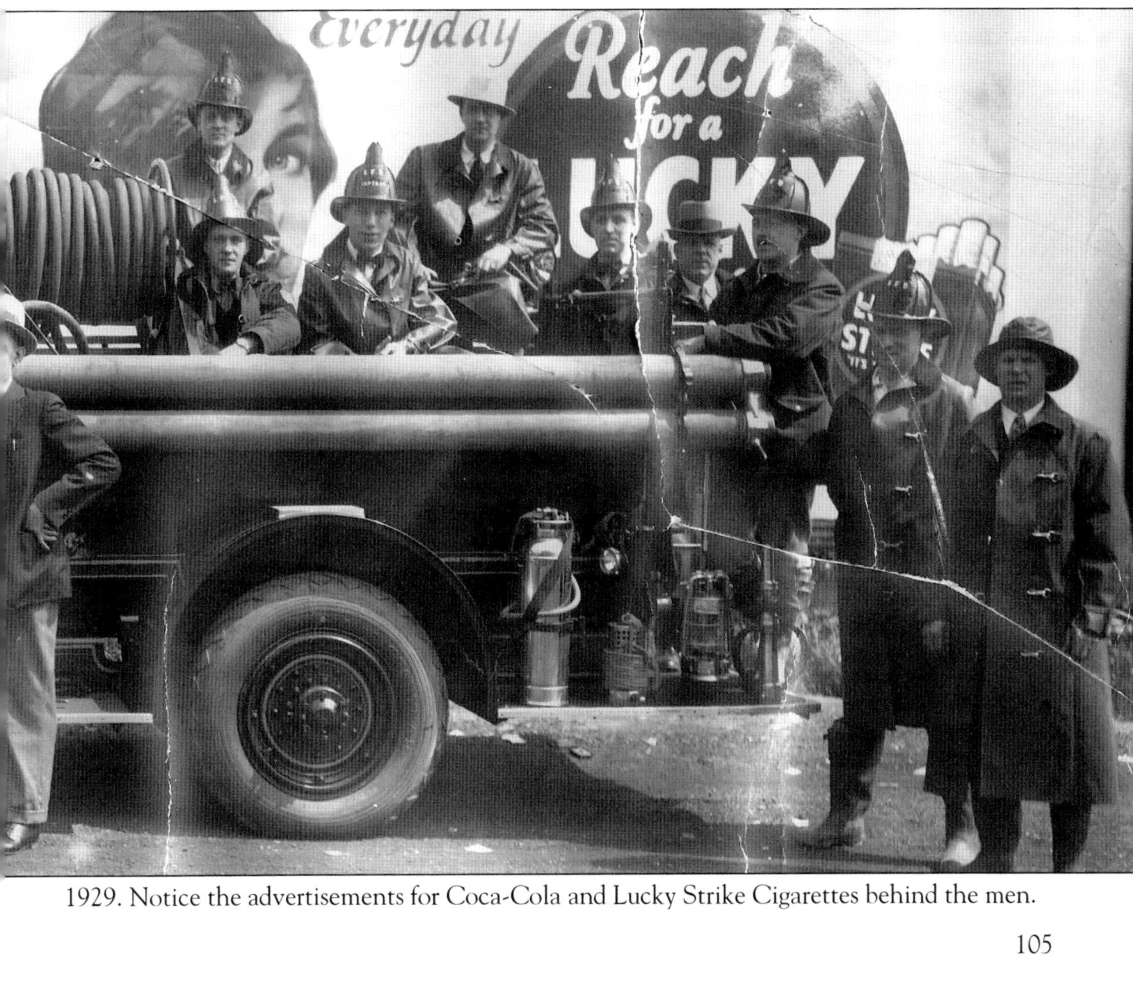

1929. Notice the advertisements for Coca-Cola and Lucky Strike Cigarettes behind the men.

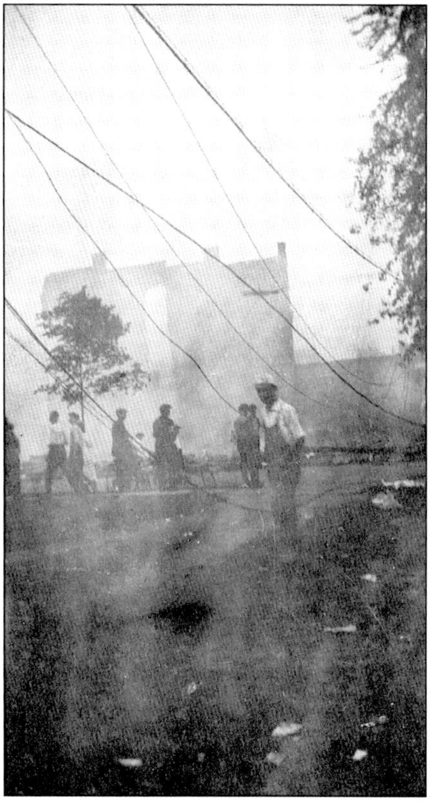

This snapshot shows the devastation of the July 24, 1920 fire, which broke out in a Chinese laundry on West Ohio Avenue. This fire destroyed the Victoria Block, Knight Building, and the *Sebring Times* Building on North Fifteenth Street, which housed businesses and apartments. Unfortunately, the line between the pumping station and the stand pipe was broken, leaving the fire department defenseless. The heat was so intense that the plate glass windows on the east side of North Fifteenth Street cracked. The loss was estimated to be in excess of $80,000.

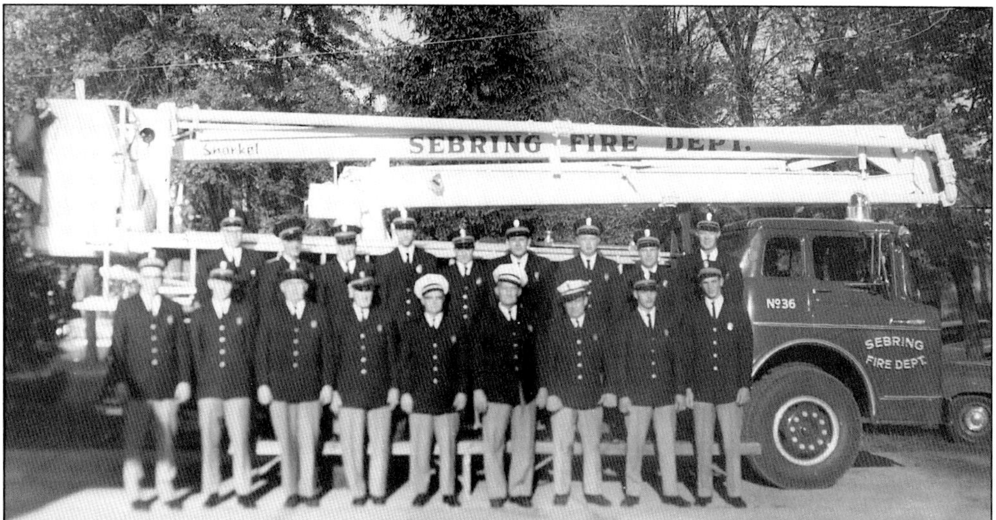

The firemen pose in front of their new 1969 Pierce 55-foot snorkel, which was equipped with a 1,000-gallon pumper. The fire department was a fully self-sufficient operation for many years. The annual Firemen's Festival with its rides and parade has been a major fund-raiser for the department, and the auxiliary has also been instrumental in fund-raising. Over the years, other events, like the Harvest Home Festival and concession stands at Lake Park, have helped to maintain the department. Do to the rising cost, a levy was passed to purchase the most recent truck.

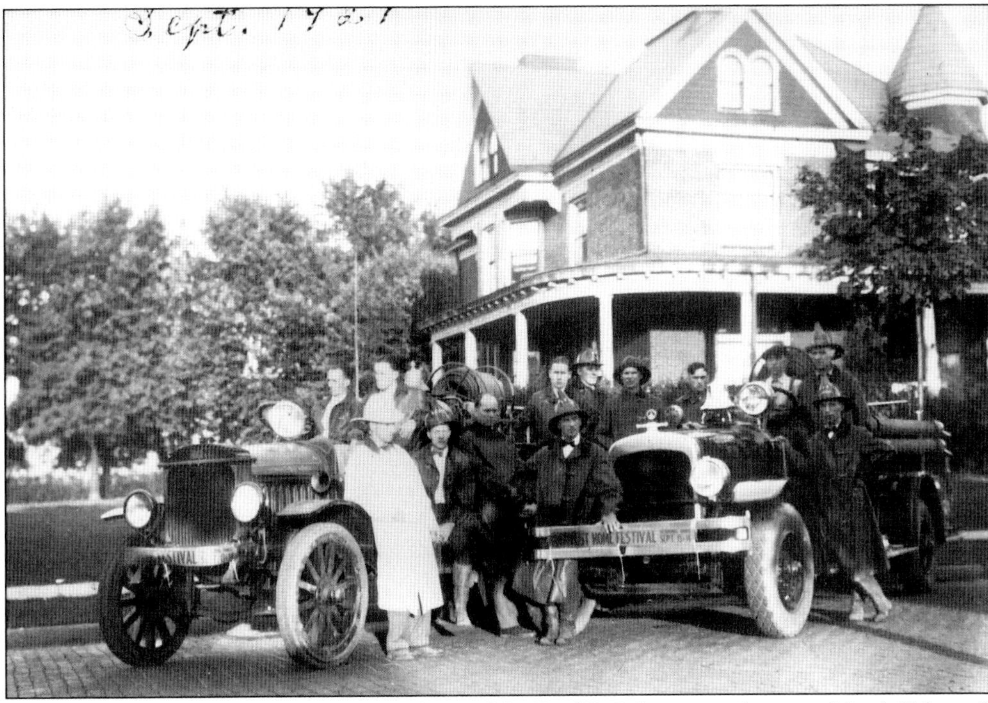

Members of the fire department pose in front of the Fred E. Sebring residence on North Fifteenth Street and East Maryland Avenue in September 1929. The fenders of the fire trucks advertise the upcoming Harvest Home Festival.

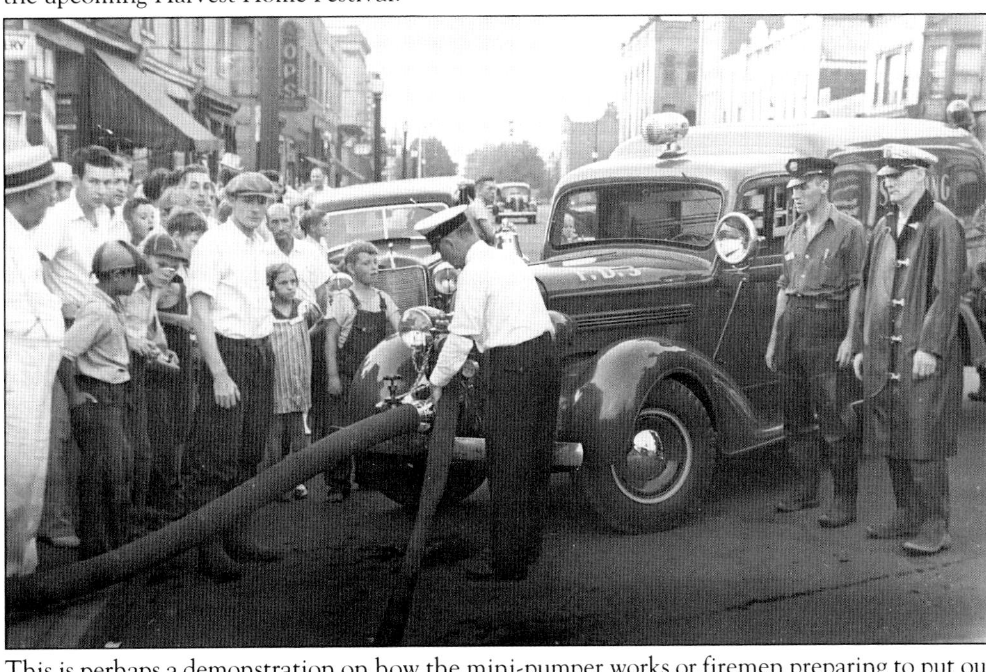

This is perhaps a demonstration on how the mini-pumper works or firemen preparing to put out a fire. Sal Trainer (standing on the right), who was "bones trimmer" of the department, stands here in the late 1930s with adults and children alike, along the edge of the sidewalk on North Fifteenth Street as the hoses are attached.

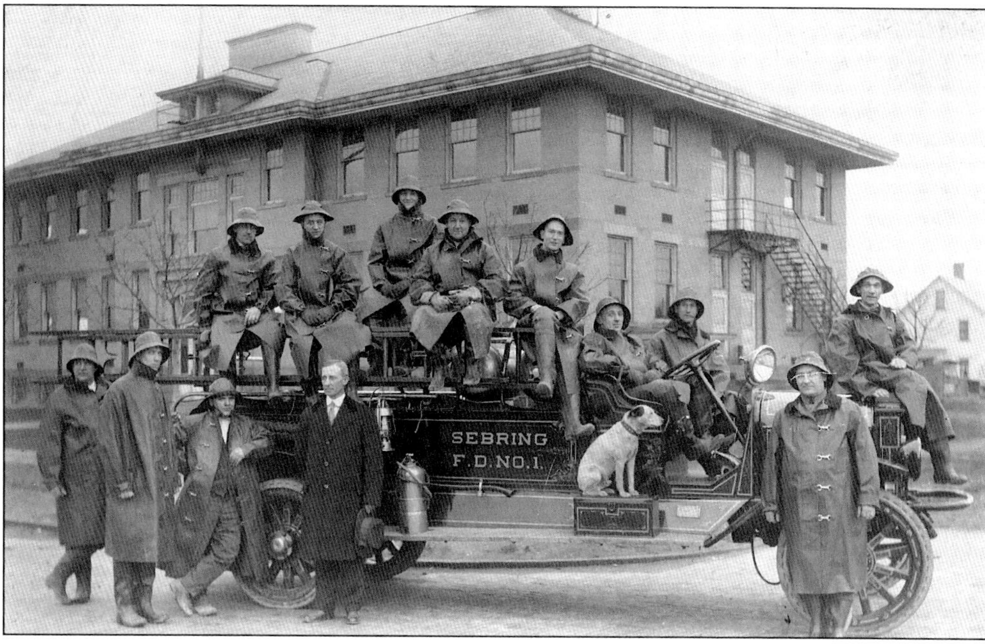

The Lincoln School Building is the backdrop for this 1920s photograph of the firemen in their coats and hats. Note the dog sitting statue-like on the truck. He is one well-trained animal.

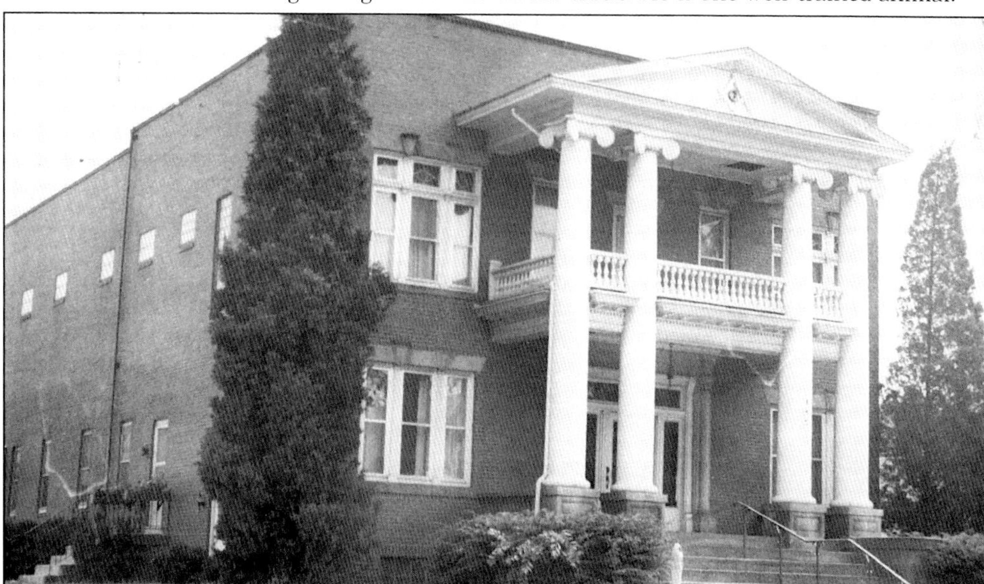

Sebring Lodge No. 626, F. & A.M. held their first meeting on April 22, 1913, on the second floor of the Citizens Banking Company. A charter was granted to the Sebring lodge on October 22, 1914, at which time F.O. Brooks was named grand master. They built their temple in 1914, and it was severely damaged by fire in 1941. In May of the same year, the building was moved from the corner to the center of the property, and a basement was added for a central heating system. The building was remodeled inside and renovated outside. A brick veneer was put on the outside, and the pillars from the old E.H. Sebring residence were placed in front. The home was rededicated in June 1942.

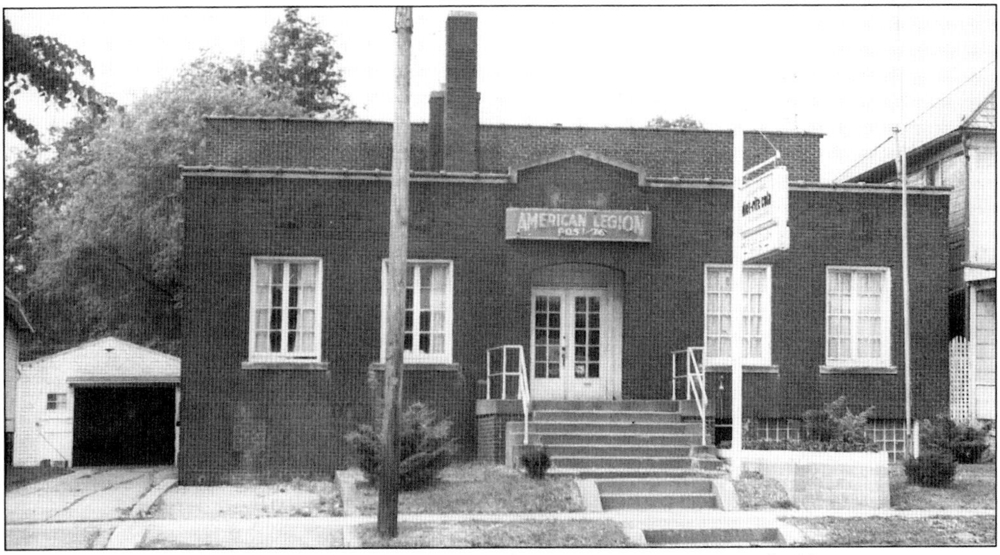

The American Legion in Sebring was organized on August 8, 1919, with 30 veterans signing on as charter members. On September 9, 1919, the post was instituted and the officers were elected. The officers elected were James Eardley, commander; Hal Surls, vice commander; Emmett Barrett, secretary; and Harold Weaver, treasurer. In 1924, ground was broken for the construction of this Memorial Hall. The American Legion has made many contributions to the community, including assisting the fire department with the Harvest Festival, providing baskets of food to the needy during the Depression, and sponsoring basketball and softball games. On August 16,1998, Post 76 dedicated a new building at 395 West California Avenue.

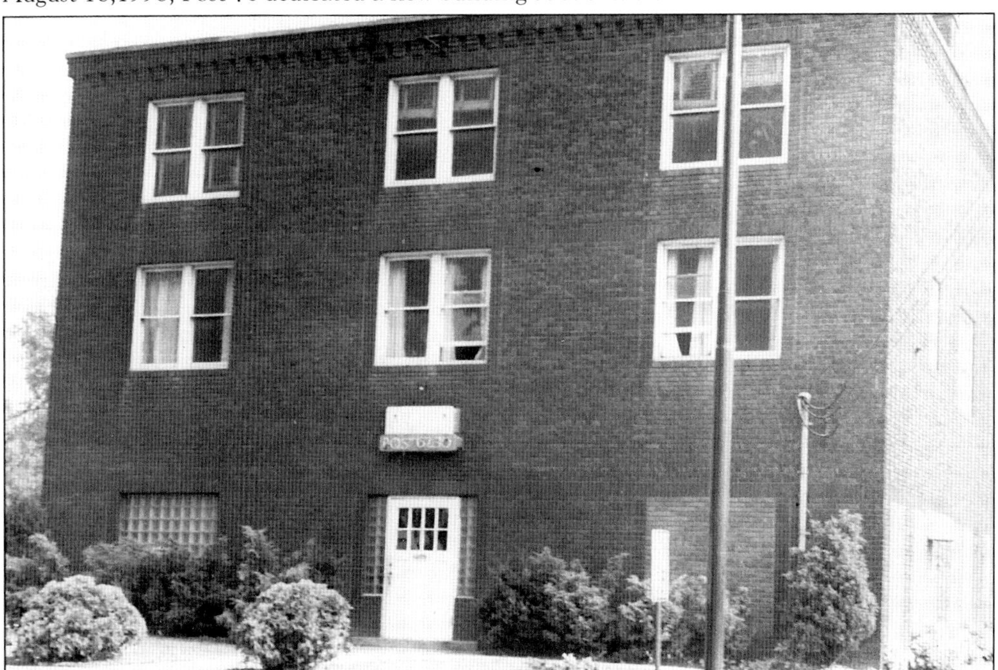

Veterans of Foreign Wars, Cross of Malta Post No. 6730, was formed in 1945. They purchased the Pythian Temple at 206 East Ohio Avenue in the late 1940s.

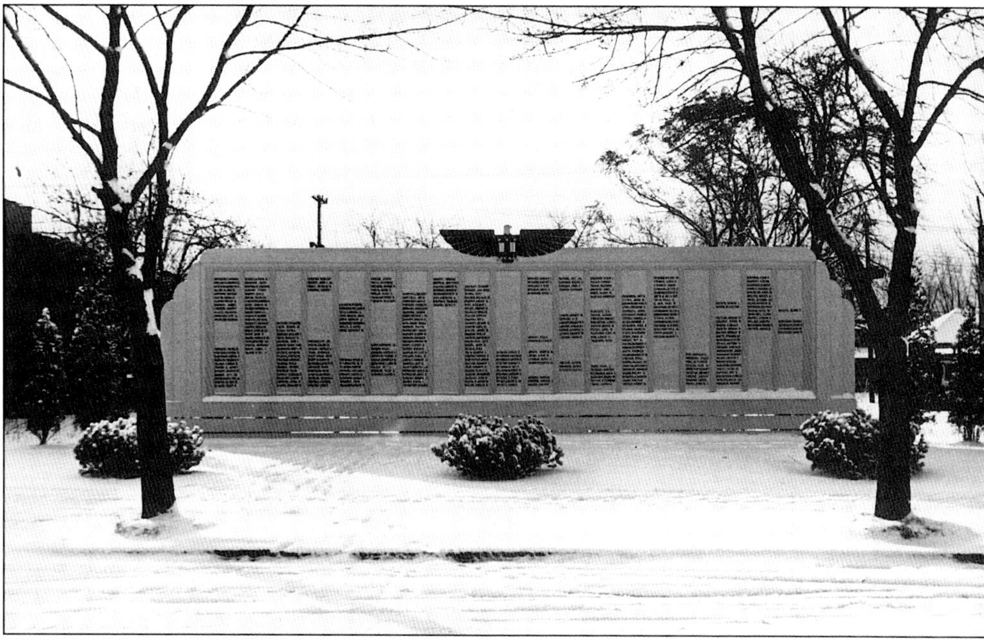

The honor roll was dedicated on June 30, 1943. The *Sebring Times* best captured the sentiment of this photograph, taken by Bob Deemer, in saying: "Boys in the service of Uncle Sam, scattered in the far flung battlefronts of the world, ready to do their utmost for their country, on land, in the air and on the sea, are held in most respectful and appreciative memory by the folks back home. While the fondest memories are recorded indelibly only in the hearts of their friends and loved ones, this dignified panel containing the names of all the Sebring and Smith Township boys stands out as the most respected and honored spot in Sebring."

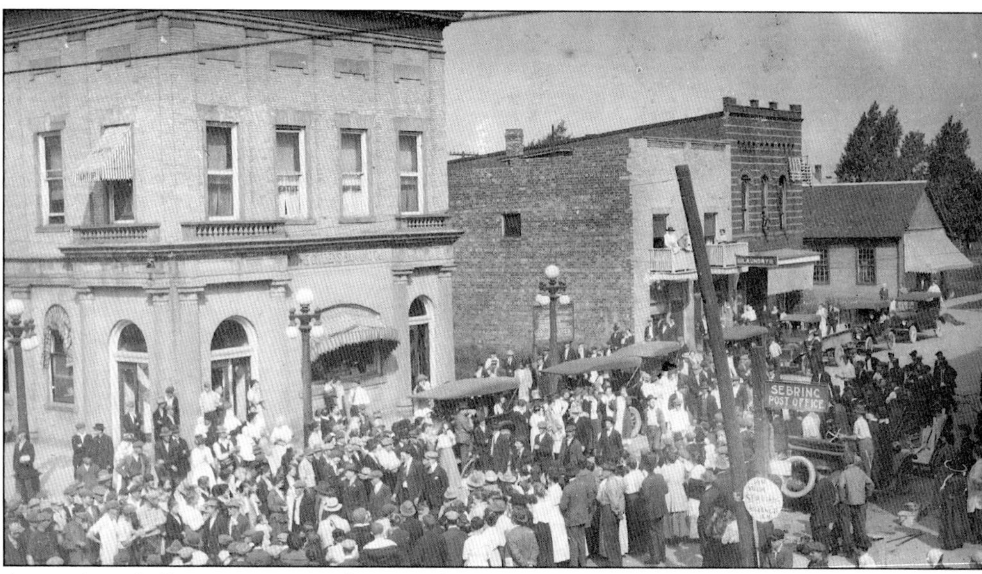

A grand sendoff to an uncertain future is shown in this photograph. On September 19, 1917, a contingency of Sebring men were honored in front of the Citizens Banking Company by their community as they prepare to leave for boot camp. In the small community of Sebring, a total of 244 men served in WW I, and six died as a result of injuries or sickness.

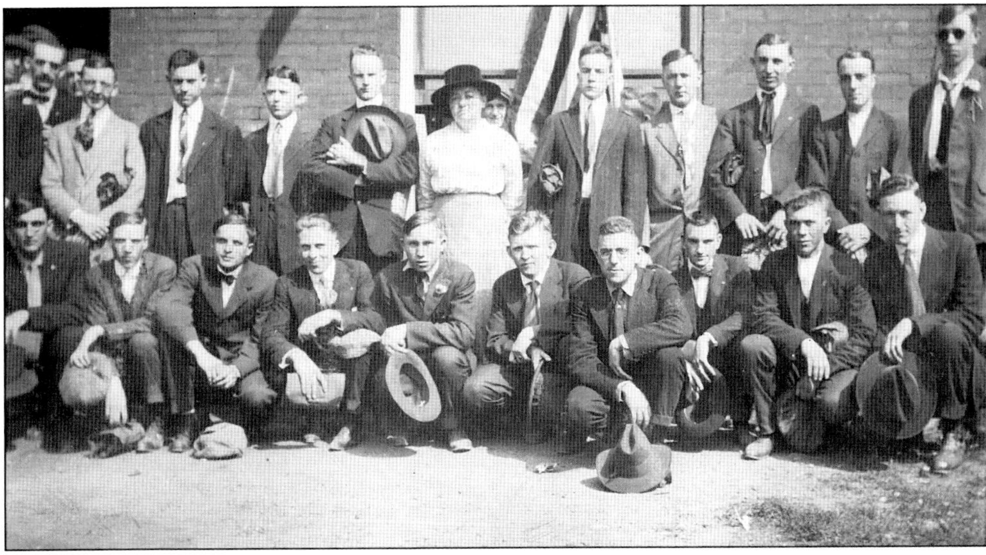

This group of 26 young men pose with a woman, perhaps someone's mother, outside the mayor's office on September 19, 1917. Their potential involvement in Europe's trench warfare awaited them, and for many, it would leave an indelible mark for the rest of their lives.

A train awaits these men at the Sebring depot for the long trip to camp. For many, this was the first time they left the comfortable boundary of their community. The climax of a day, filled with mixed emotions, was when the men paraded down North Fifteenth Street on September 19, 1917, to the train station.

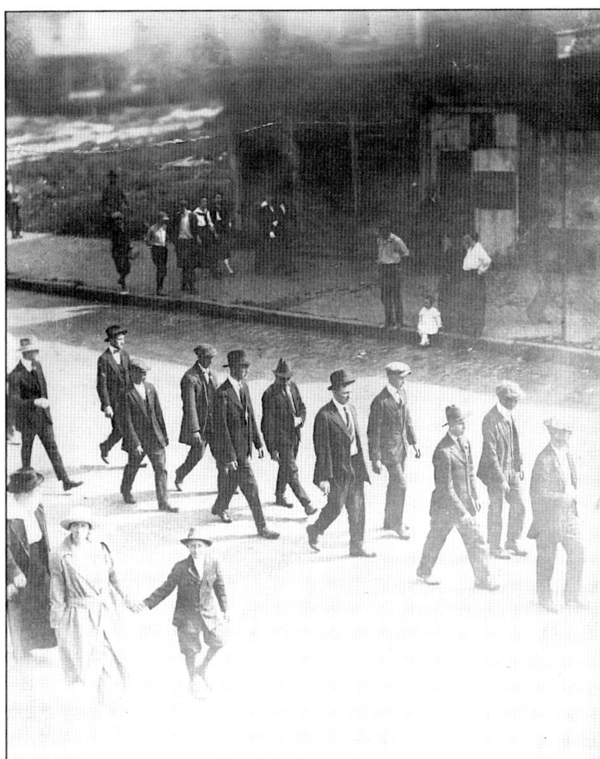

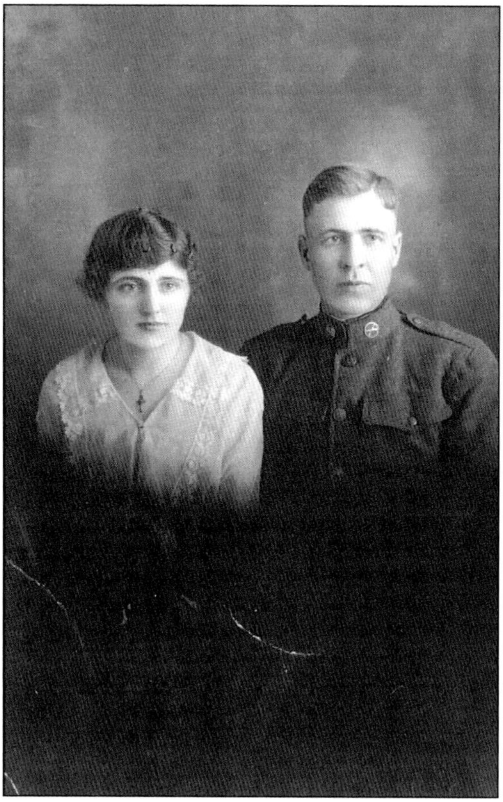

Mr. and Mrs. (Carmen Laughlin) Ernest Workman posed for this picture during WW I. The Workmans were the parents of Dale and William Workman, and Mrs. Kenny (Thelma) Doyle. At a time of war, it was common for couples to have their pictures taken because it was a comforting keepsake until they could be together again.

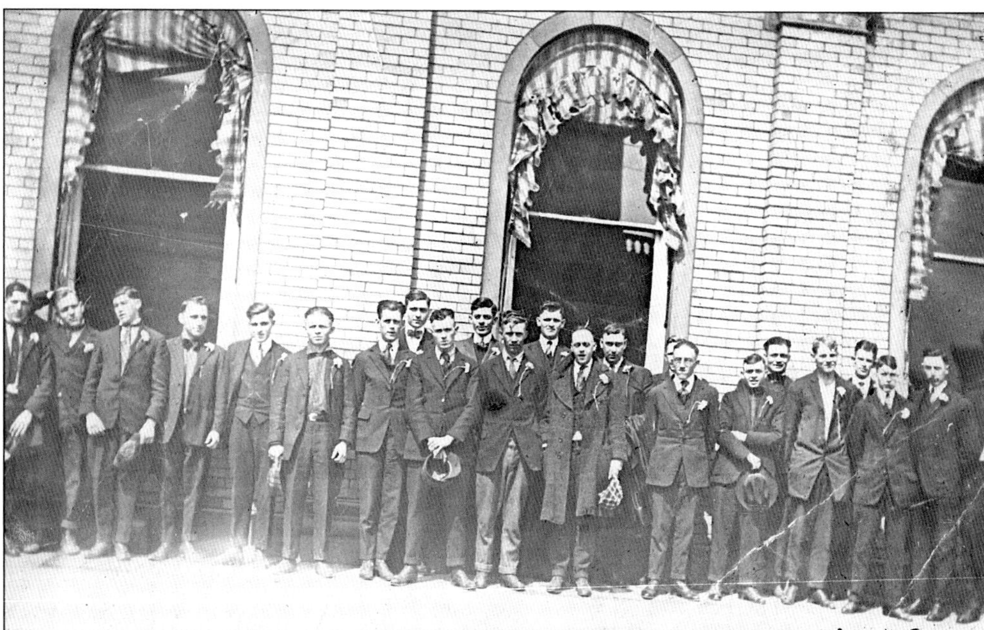

A contingency of men posed in front of the Citizens Banking Company building prior to leaving for duty during WW I.

Seven

VARIATIONS

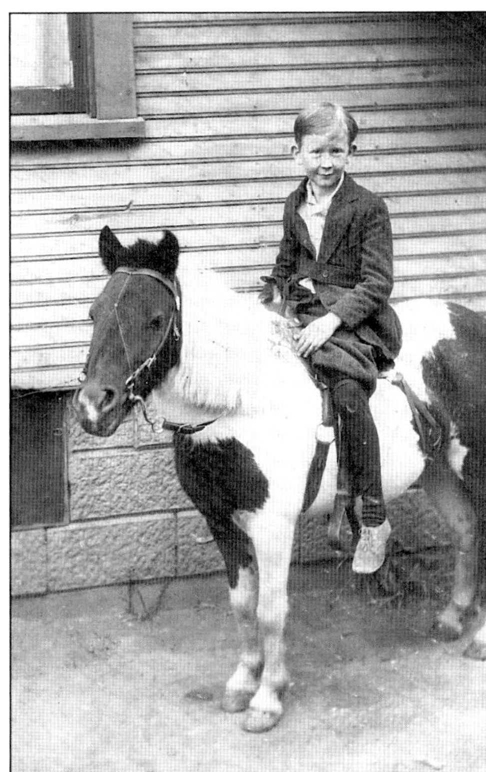

A pony ride was the highlight of the day for Orville "Red" Beaton in 1920. During the early years of this century, men traveled around to various communities offering to take children's pictures on a pony, or in a goat cart, and in return they asked for a free meal, a place to sleep, or a small amount of money.

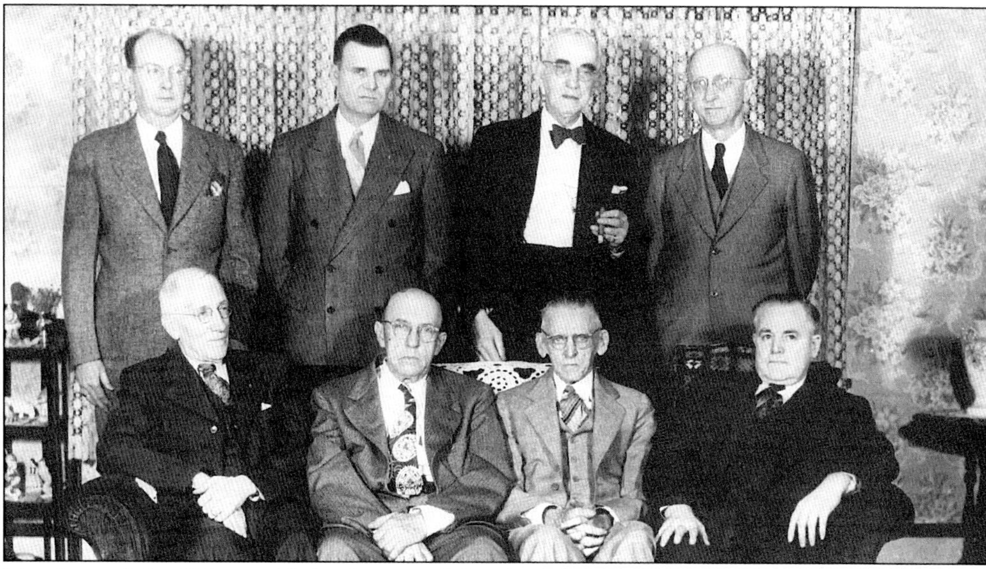

Members of the Kibitzer Club who posed for this photograph at the home of member Ron Wilson in 1945 are, from left to right, as follows: (standing) Ron Wilson; Clyde Eastham, owner of Eastham's Grocery; Ernest Hundley; and Sumner Oesch, owner of Leonard Hardware; (seated) Frank L. Herman, owner of Herman's Dry Goods; J.E. Torbert, owner of The *Sebring Times*; M.A. Sutherin, retired agent with the Pennsylvania Railroad; and Maurice Coffman, owner of Coffman Furniture Store on West Ohio Avenue. The Kibitzer Club was a men's bridge club that met on Tuesday evenings.

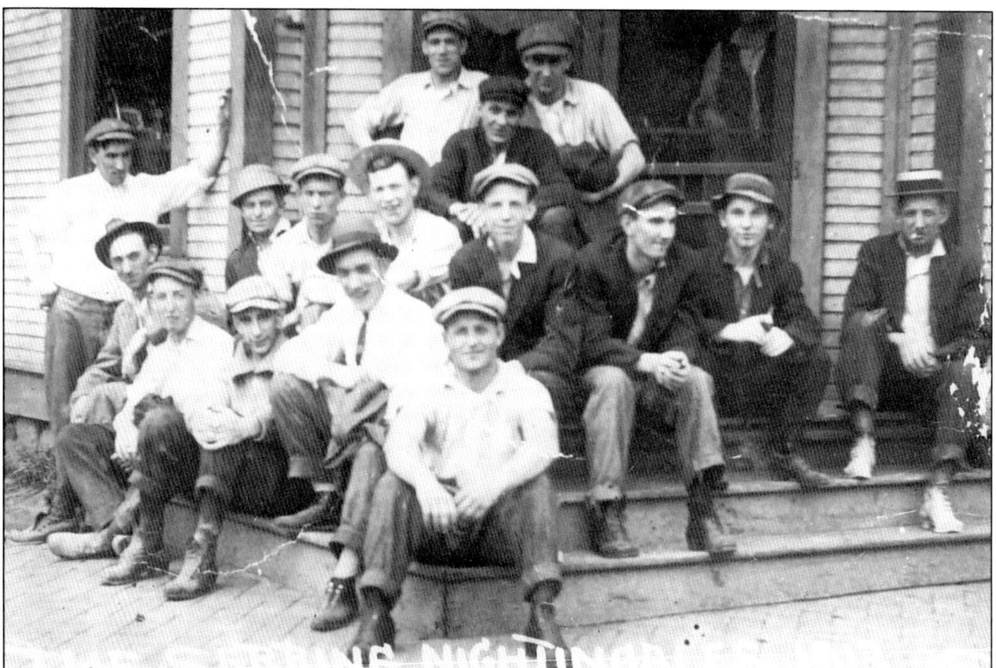

The Sebring Nightingales relax on the steps of the Hotel Sebring in 1913. The only identification on the photograph are the names of Howard Pinkerton, Ray Pinkerton, and Sharpnecks.

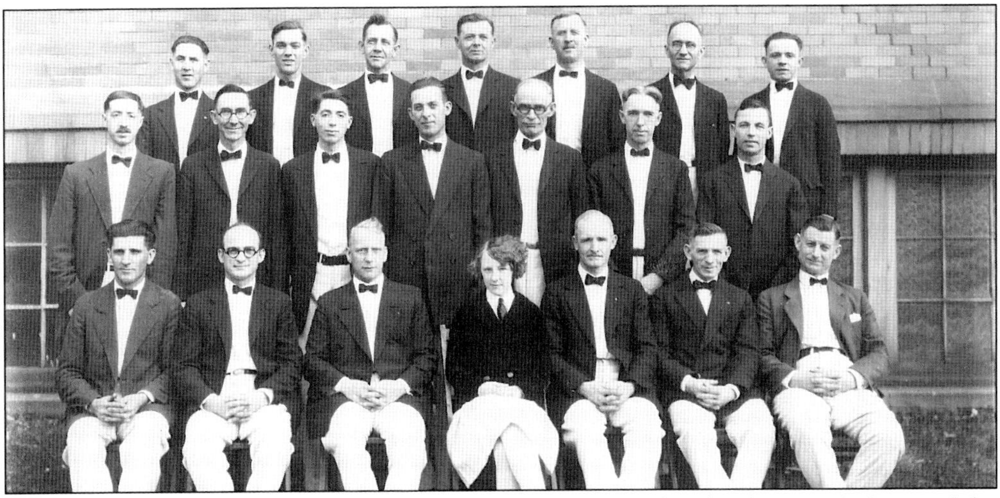

Members of the Sebring Glee Club pose in front of the high school in 1925. Some of the members have been identified, from left to right, as follows: (seated) John Hoffmeyer, Elmer Shaffer, Arthur Grindley Sr., Thelma (Grindley) Iddings, Will Davies (director), and Colin Anderson; (middle row) Joseph Yates, Carl Hamilton, James Yates, ?, James Earley, Larry Maley, and Timothy Desmond; (top row) Jess Green, ?, Allen West, George Wilcoxon, John Foden, and two unidentified people.

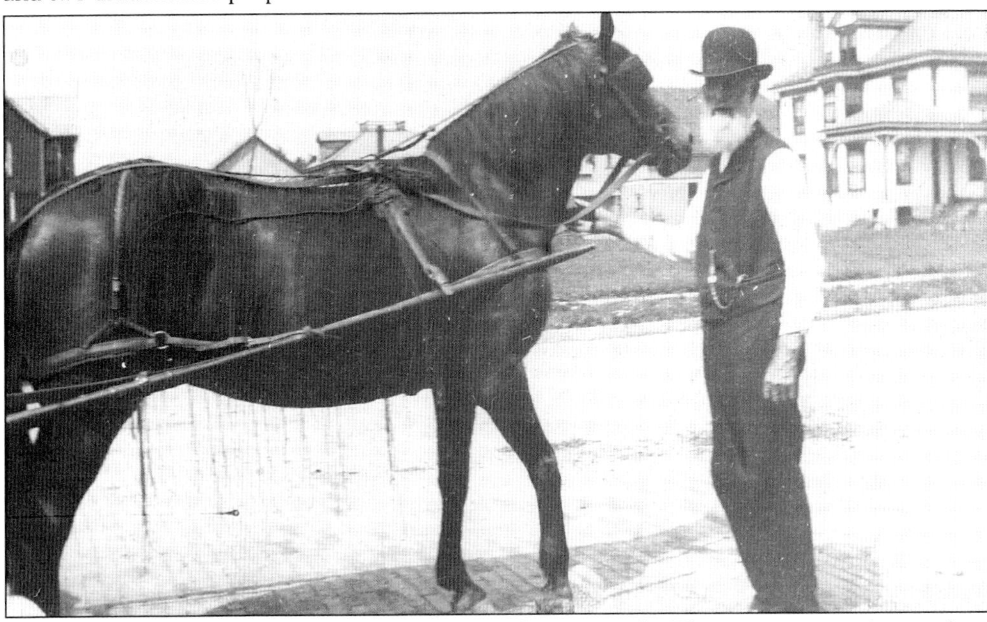

George Sebring Sr. hitches up his horse for an afternoon ride. The picture was taken in front of his home on the southeast corner of West Ohio Avenue and North Sixteenth Street around 1905. The home in the background is the Frank Sebring residence, and the empty lot next to the residence is where the post office stands today. Mr. and Mrs. Sebring followed their sons and daughters to the new community from East Liverpool. For a short time, he operated a grocery store on Ohio Avenue. His family made repeated attempts to get him to retire, though he always resisted. According to his obituary, he once said "would rather wear out than rust out in idleness." He eventually settled down and enjoyed his remaining years greeting people along the streets. He always preferred to be called "Uncle George."

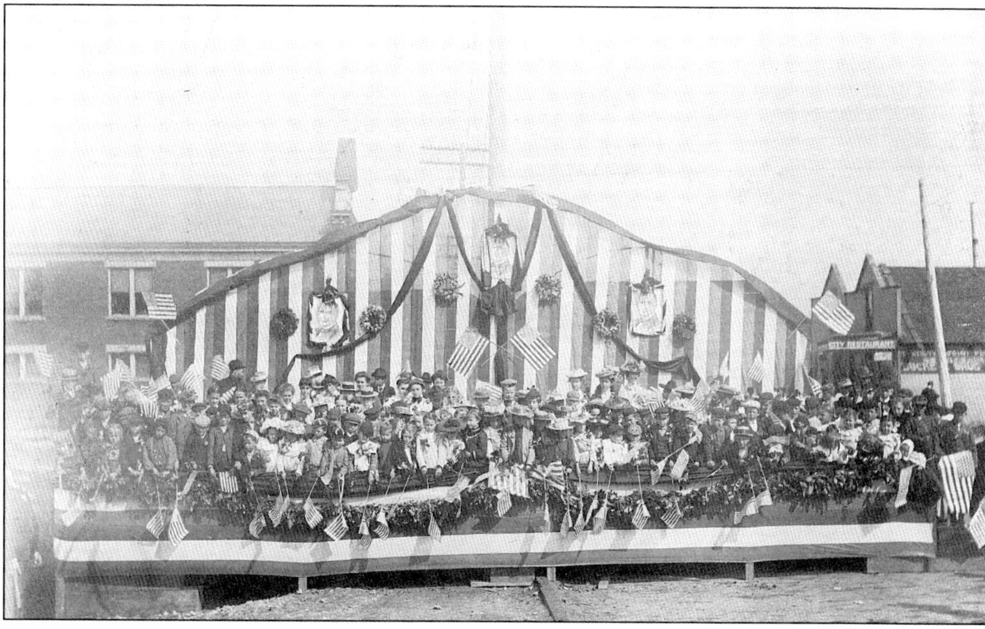

Because Sebring was situated along a major railroad line, it had the opportunity to take part in numerous historic events. One such event was the return of the body of the late President William McKinley to Canton, Ohio. Pictured is the School Children Arch, built out of wood, paper streamers, floral arrangements, and photographs of the martyred president. The children of the community hold flags while waiting for the funeral train to pass by.

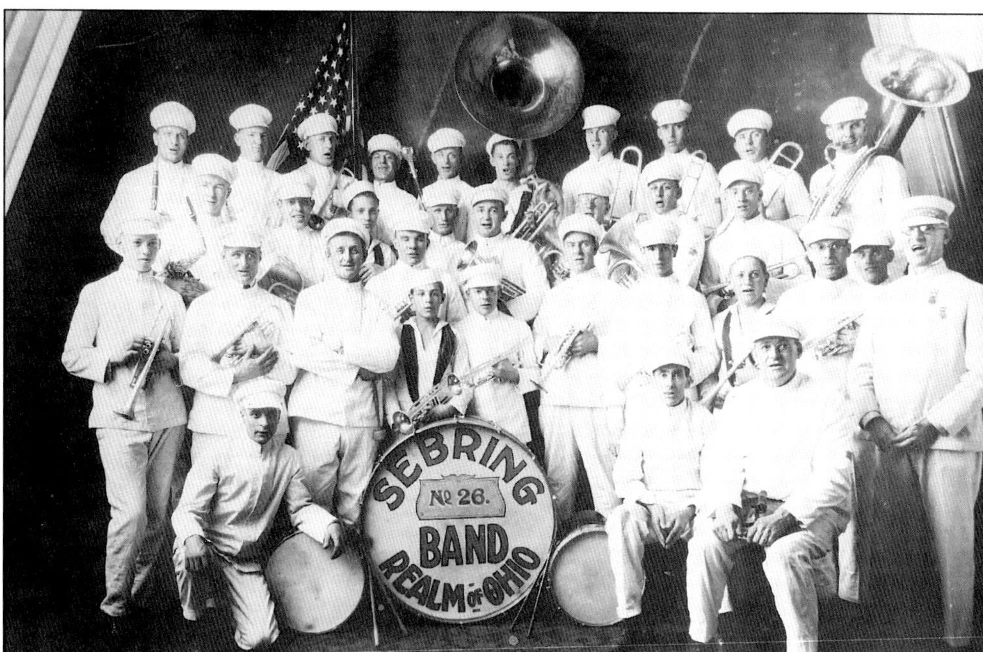

The members of the Sebring Band, No. 26 Realm of Ohio, sing out a tune for the cameraman at Schoch Studio of Alliance in 1923. The gentleman in the top row with the baton is identified as Clem Smith. There is no other identification.

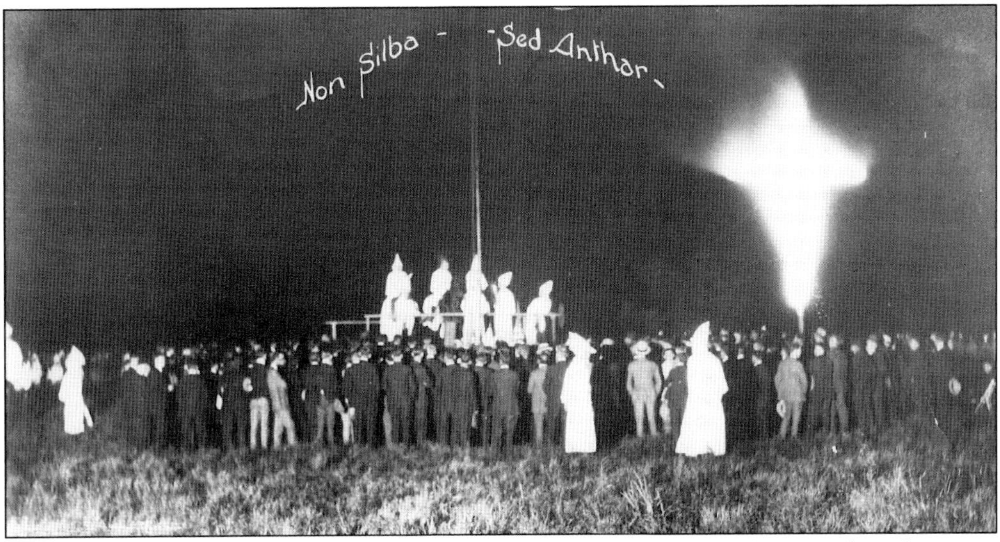

Every community has a dark side to its history that many would rather forget or deny; however, it can not be ignored. The Ku Klux Klan was a well-established and organized group in many villages and towns throughout the Midwest in the 1920s. Sebring was no exception. Here we see the Klan, and many curious bystanders, watch as a cross is burned and the flag is raised during one of their numerous meetings in a field just outside of town. It is not necessary to know who was directly involved or their reasons for involvement. The papers and oral histories note that this "secret society or fraternal group" was active in numerous events in the community. They included the Harvest Home Festivals, Sebring's 25th Anniversary Celebration, and the dedication of Maple Ridge School in 1925.

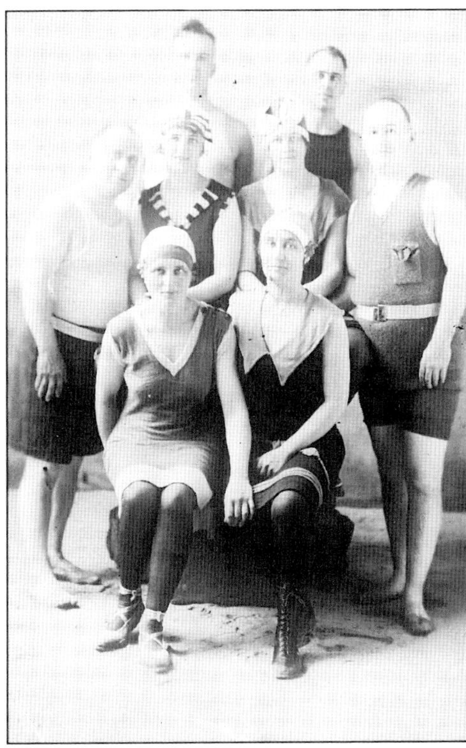

"The Bunch," as they were often referred to, prepare to take a dip in the ocean at Atlantic City in 1918. The wool outfits were not always so comfortable. Before the "Roaring Twenties," a lady never exposed her knees in public, as seen in this picture. The couples were residents of Sebring and Alliance, and their friendship evolved through various business and social events. They are pictured here, from left to right, as follows: (seated) Blanch Morris and Connie Sebring; (middle row) Dr. Willis Sanford, Jessie Sanford, Margaret Lamborn Zang, and Arthur Morris; (top row) Charles Leigh Sebring and Fred J. Zang.

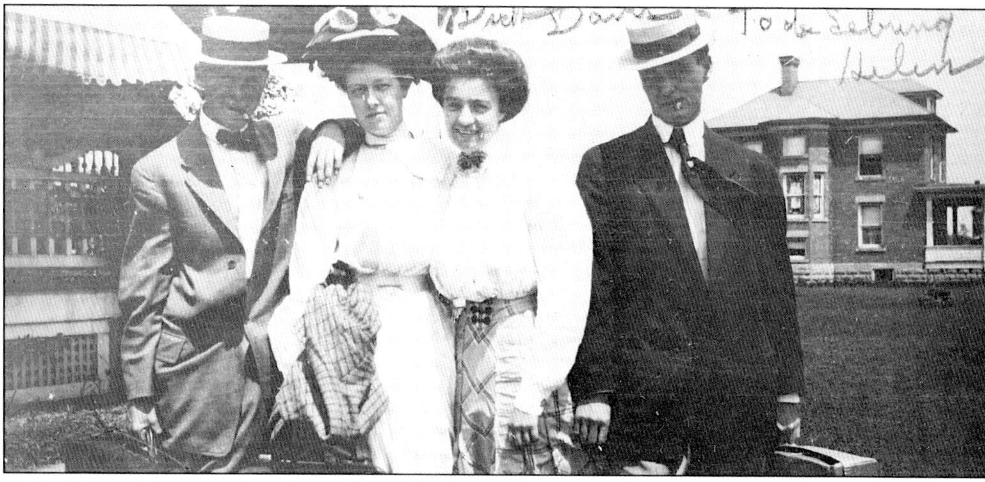

Dick Davis, Margaret Lamborn Zang, Helen Sebring Gahris, and Frank H. (Tode) Sebring prepare for an outing in the early 1900s. They are standing in front of the home of Charles L. Sebring (Helen and Tode's brother). Frank Harbison (Tode) Sebring was a graduate of Yale University and, at the time of his death, at age 45, in 1934, was head of the Salem Pottery Company and director of the Limoges China Company. He was married to Margaret Ramsey, the daughter of Willis H. Ramsey of Alliance. Mr. Ramsey was an executive with Morgan Engineering Company, which was owned by his brother-in-law, Colonel William H. Morgan. Mr. and Mrs. Frank Harbison Sebring had two children, Frank and Shirley.

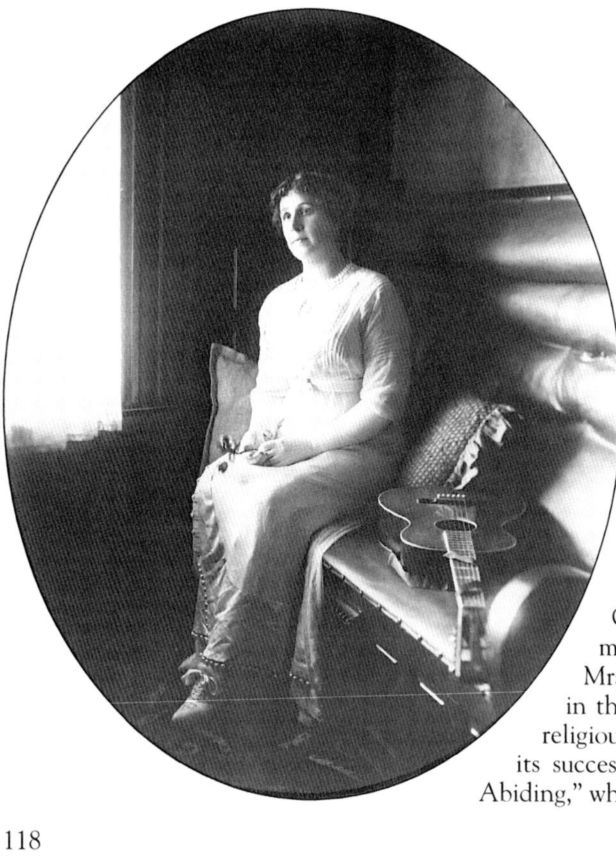

Anna Sebring Murphy was the daughter of Oliver Howard and Matilda Jane Hume Sebring. She was born in East Liverpool, Ohio, on November 11, 1878. As mentioned in a previous chapter, Mrs. Murphy's primary interest was in the Sebring Camp Grounds, and her religious convictions were the reason for its success. She wrote a hymn "Constantly Abiding," which reflected her faith in God.

In much of Sebring's historical material, there is a great amount of information on the Sebring brothers and how they were instrumental in the development of the community. There is an adage that says, "behind every successful man is a good woman," and it has also been said that behind every successful brother is a loyal sister. In 1899, Eva and Emma came with their husbands and families to help their brothers' dream of building a community come true. They tramped through the muddy streets, suffered from the heat of summer, and endured the bugs from the surrounding swamps. Here, we see Emma Barclay and Eva Norris in Sebring, Florida, on March 2, 1936. The picture was taken by R.L. McClure, Emma's grandson.

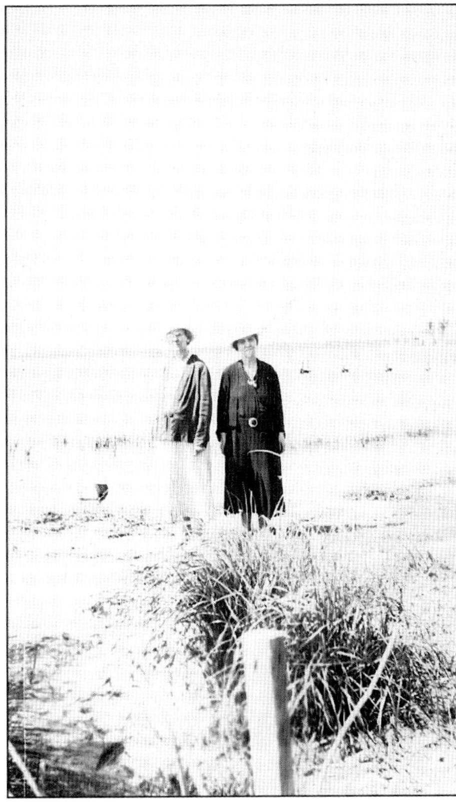

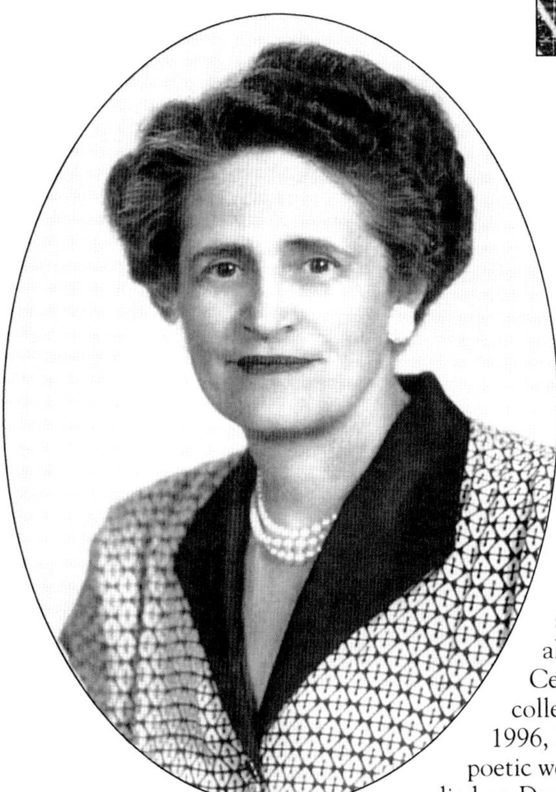

Miss Margaret Kadisch was born in Copenhagen, Denmark, in 1904 and was raised in England. During WW II, she and her family endured the German bombing raids. In the 1940s, she moved to Plainfield, New Jersey. Before coming to Sebring, she created medical drawings, served as a governess, and worked for Gort Pottery. In 1948, she moved to Sebring and was appointed art director of the Spalding China Company. After a fire closed the plant in 1957, Miss Kadisch served as librarian at the Sebring Public Library. She was also an active member of the Alliance Art Center. Many of her portrait paintings are in collections throughout the United States. In 1996, Miss Kadisch published a volume of her poetic works, titled *Verse-A-Tile*. Margaret Kadisch died on December 6, 1998.

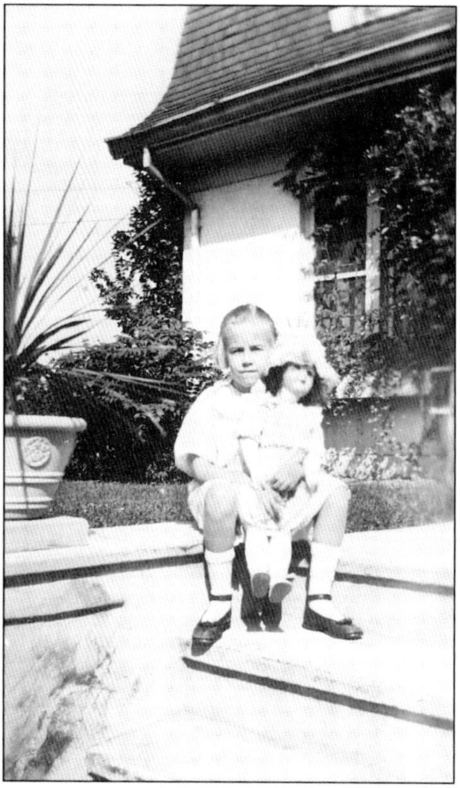

Celebrating her seventh birthday on September 13, 1920, Gretchen Gahris poses with her new German bisque doll on the front steps of her West Ohio Avenue home. She was the daughter of Willard I. and Helen Sebring Gahris. Gretchen was a graduate of Dana Hall School in Wellesley, Massachusetts, and of Smith College in Northampton, Massachusetts. After her marriage to J. Harrison Keller, they remained in this home until the mid-1960s. Gretchen Keller was active in many organizations throughout her life, which included the Alliance Flower Garden Club, Coterie, president and volunteer for the Alliance Chapter of the Red Cross, 35-year member of the Alliance Hospital Auxiliary, YWCA, and the Alliance Woman's Club. She died in July 1986.

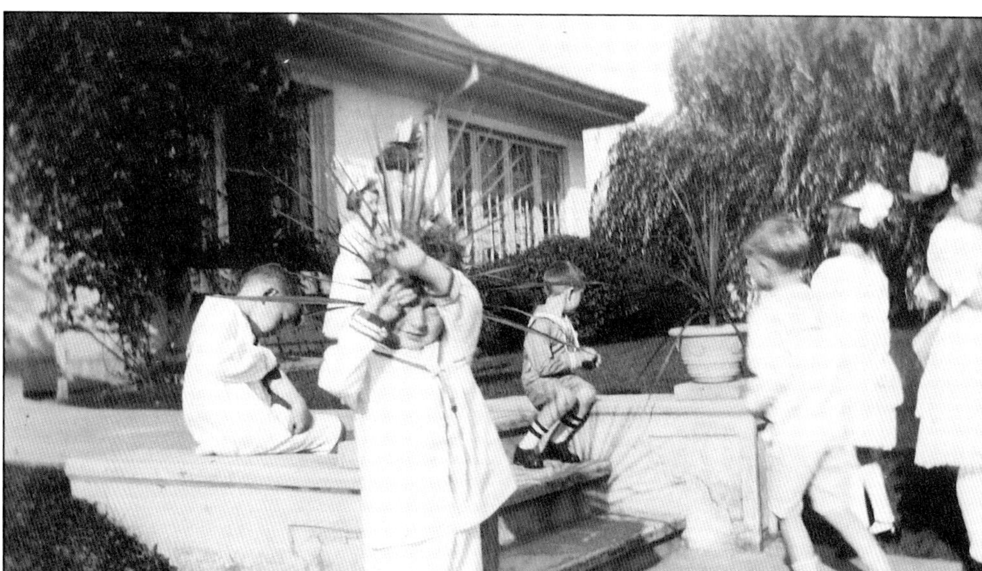

Friends and family, including the Cliff children and Leroy Lamborn Zang, celebrate Gretchen's seventh birthday in the front yard of the Gahris residence. Gretchen's mother passed away in August 1919, and her father died in August 1924. She lived with her grandparents Frank and Emma Harbison Sebring until their deaths.

Women from the French Saxon China Company enjoy the company's annual picnic at Idora Park. A few of these women are pictured, from left to right, as follows: Mildred Zeppernick, Emma Crum, Dorothy Strain, and Florence Eckley.

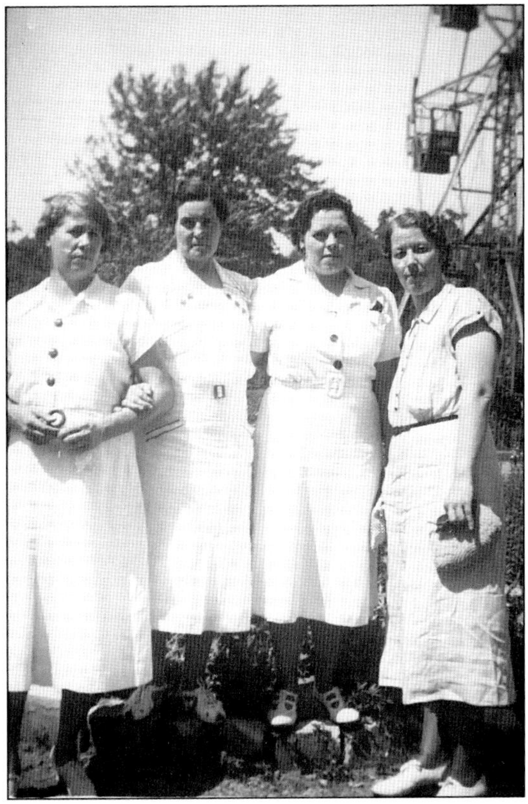

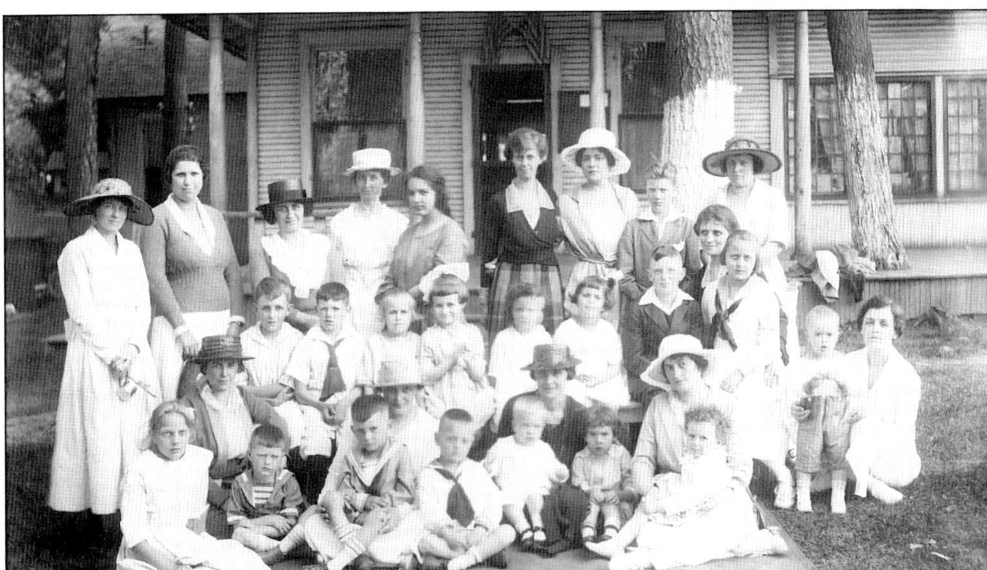

The Sewing Club was comprised of prominent women in the Alliance and Sebring area. They included Mrs. Charles L. (Conradine) Sebring and Evelyn Sebring; Ada Cassaday Turkle and her children, Rebecca (Betty), Barbara, and Brinton; Katherine Stamp and her children, Jane and Lewis; a young Gretchen Gahris; Milicent Weybrecht; Grace Reeves; Blanche Morris; and Hazel Shidler.

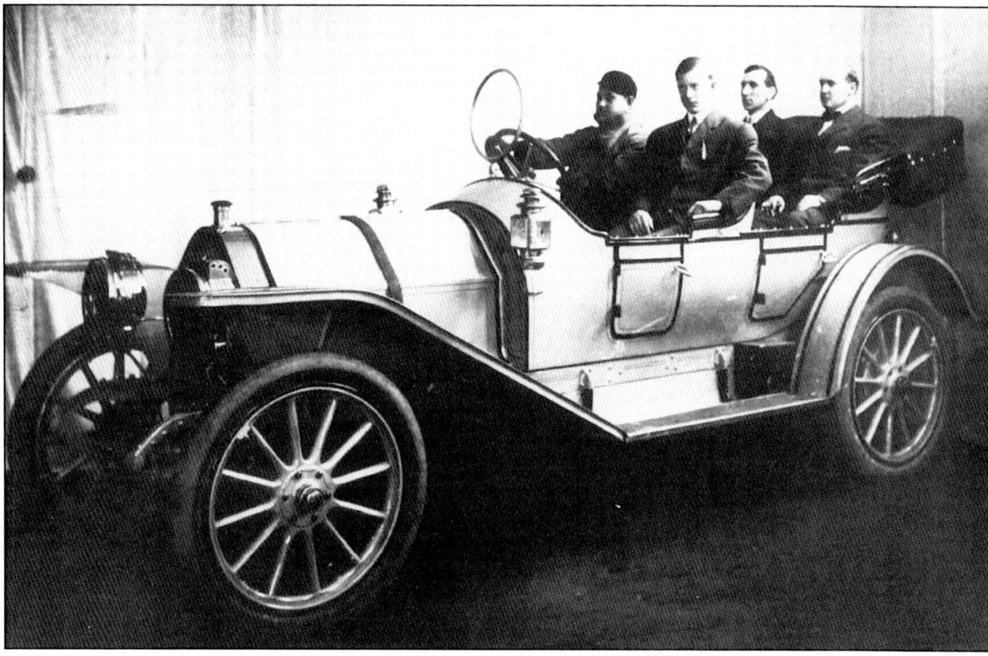

A pictorial history book on Sebring would not be complete without photographs of the "Sebring Six." The car was designed by Jim Gwin and Bob Allen. They brought their idea to Oliver H. Sebring, who along with his son Bert, backed it financially. Posing in the very first "Sebring Six" are, from left to right, as follows: Louis Peoz, driver; Bob Allen, passenger side; Mr. Campbell (engineer), in the back; and James Gwin (president of the Sebring Six Company), on the left. The company was organized in the later part of 1909. A prototype was completed in January 1910, and was given a test run from Sebring to East Liverpool and back, the entire trip being made in high gear.

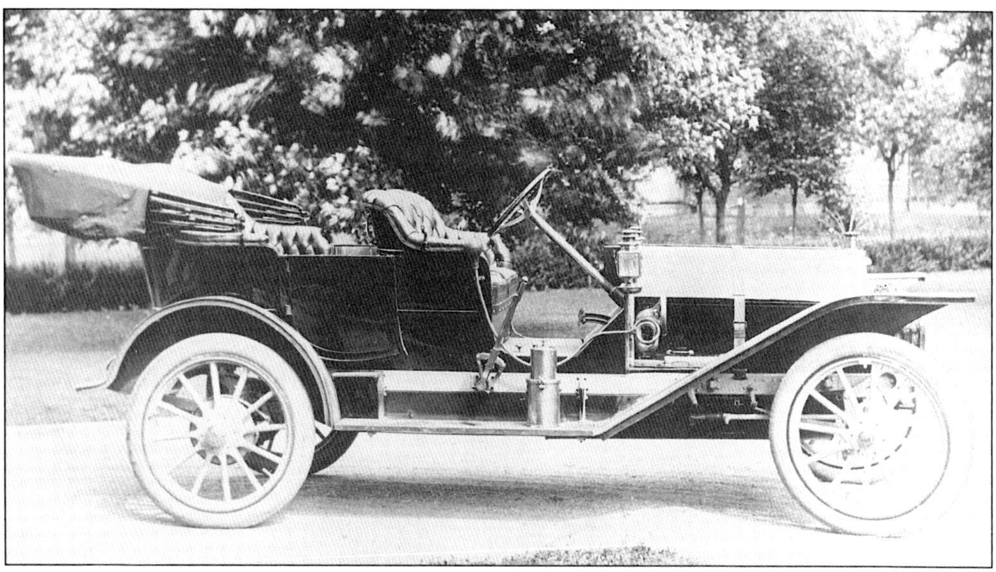

The Sebring Six "Thoroughbred Car" made its debut at the Cleveland Automobile Show in March 1910. The National Association of Historic Cars said there was a sporting flair to the "Thoroughbred Car." After the manufacture of 25 cars, production was discontinued in 1912.

Shown here is an advertisement for the "Thoroughbred Car."

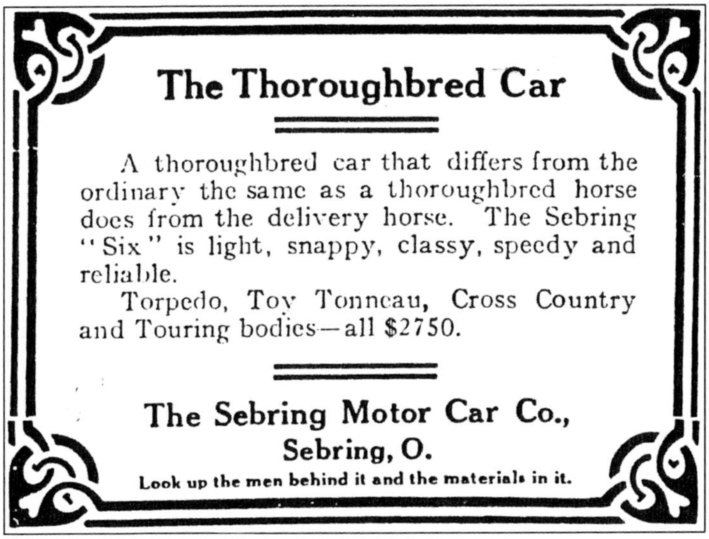

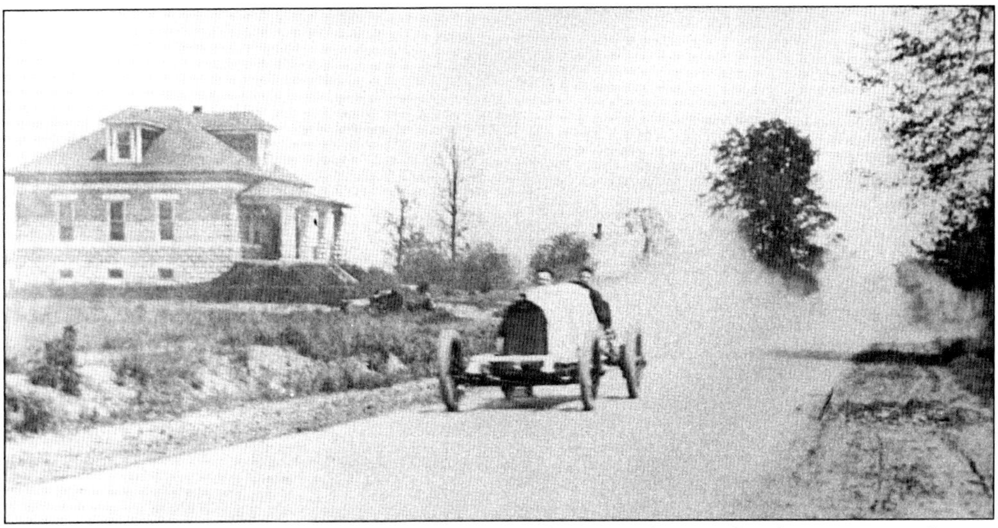

The modified Sebring Six, driven by Joe Cooper, leaves Beloit in the dust as it travels at a high rate of speed down what is now East Ohio Avenue in front of Bailey Ford, Inc. The stone block house in the background still stands today. Joe Cooper and the "Sebring" participated in numerous dirt track meets in northeast Ohio. In 1915, Cooper and his car gained national fame in the 500-mile races at Indianapolis Speedway and Chicago Racetrack. The August 1915 issue of "Motor Age" discussed the tragic end of Joe Cooper's life at the inaugural race at Hawkeye Speedway in Des Moines, Iowa, in stating: "Joe Cooper was killed near the end of his thirty-ninth mile. He was in second place and close on de Palma's Stutz. Both cars were going better than 90 miles an hour, when at the end of the turn into the home stretch the Sebring's left rear tire blew out. The treads on this tire had been worn off two laps earlier. When the tire blew, the rear end of the machine swerved and skidded toward the inside of the oval. The car was almost at right angles with the track. Cooper fought desperately to hold it to the course and did succeed in keeping it from the inside of the saucer, only to have it skid a distance of 30 feet directly into the outer rail. This crumpled like tissue paper as car and riders went through it." Apparently, Cooper wanted to avoid hitting people in the inner circle of the racetrack and steered into the wall instead.

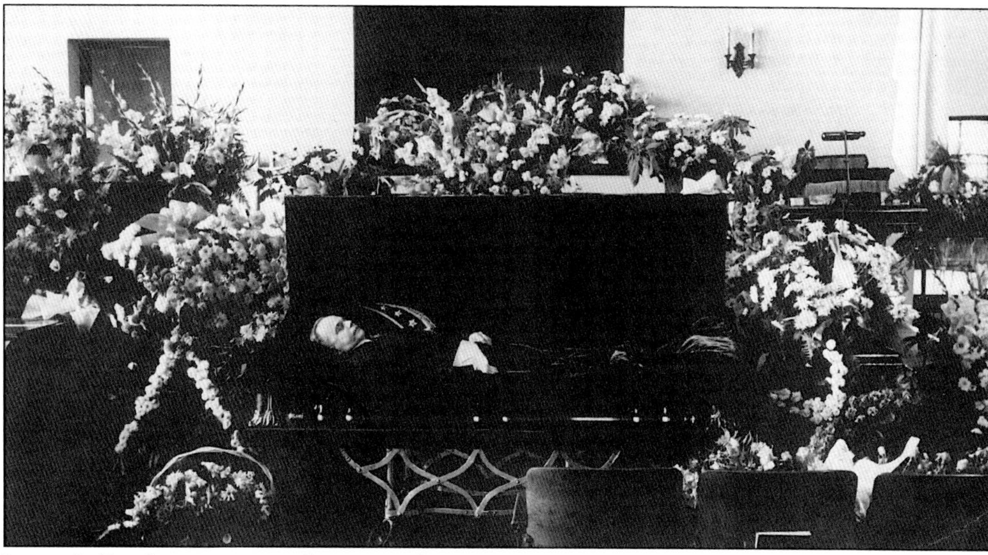

Lewis A. Bandy, prominent pharmacist for many years and mayor of Sebring from 1940 to 1942, lies in state at the Church of Christ. Bandy was serving his second term when he was stricken with a heart ailment and died December 1942. The Alliance and Sebring newspapers gave the following tribute to him, "As Mayor, "Lew" Bandy was making just the kind of official people expected him to be. He had his own ideas of what was right and wrong, what was possible and practical and what was not, and while he would always listen to reason, he never swerved by any motive of expediency or favoritism. And because he was true to his own ideals, yet not flaunting his virtues in the faces of others, he was loved and respected by his fellow citizens in all walks of life." On the day of his death, a new flag was raised at the village hall at half-staff. The flag was draped over the casket during the funeral procession and was placed in the coffin, as shown in this picture.

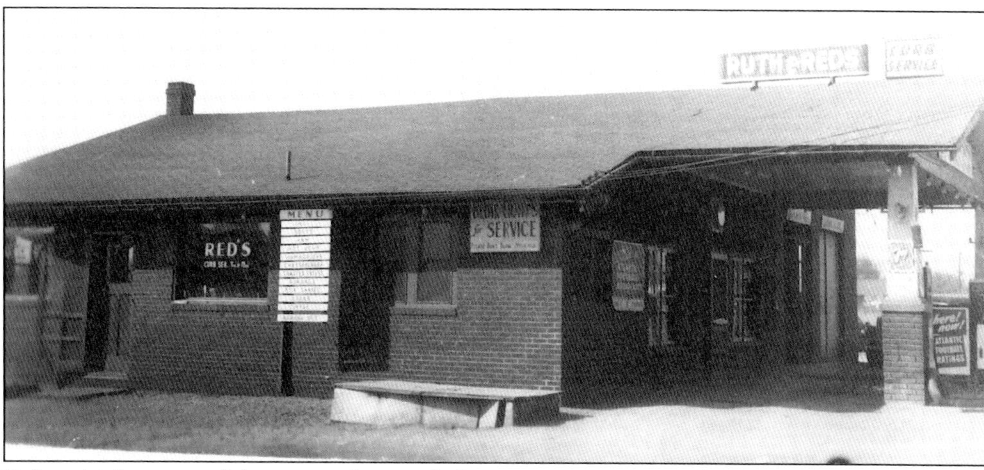

Before highways and bypasses, the roadside service station, with its small restaurant, was commonplace. During the 1930s and 1940s, Ruth and Red Tuel rented this building on the Alliance-Sebring Road from John Malmsberry. Ruth and Red's offered the first curbside service in the area. According to Ruth Tuel, "hamburgers with all the toppings was the big hit. When the bridge was out on Lake Park Boulevard our business flourished." They were in operation for approximately 17 years. In the 1920s, this place was called the "Tea Pot Dome," named for the scandal during President Harding's Administration.

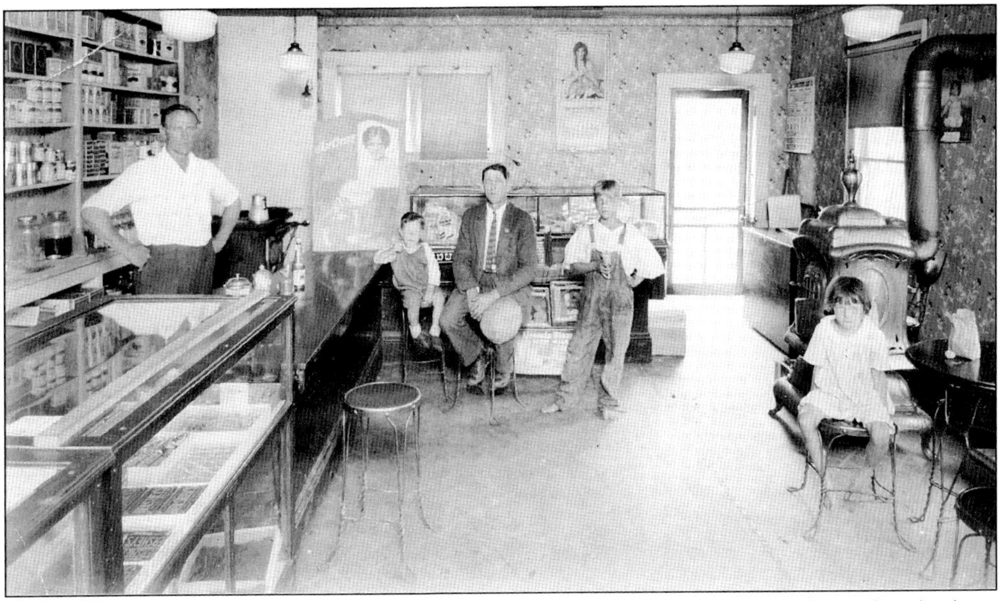

Herbert A. Tetlow's store was built around 1926. According to Vera Tetlow Chamberlain, the store sold tickets for the streetcar, pop, ice cream, tobacco, while Sadie Tetlow sold ham sandwiches after basketball games. Pictured with Mr. Tetlow are, from left to right, as follows: Dean Mercer, Bill Mercer, Charles Mercer, and Lavern.

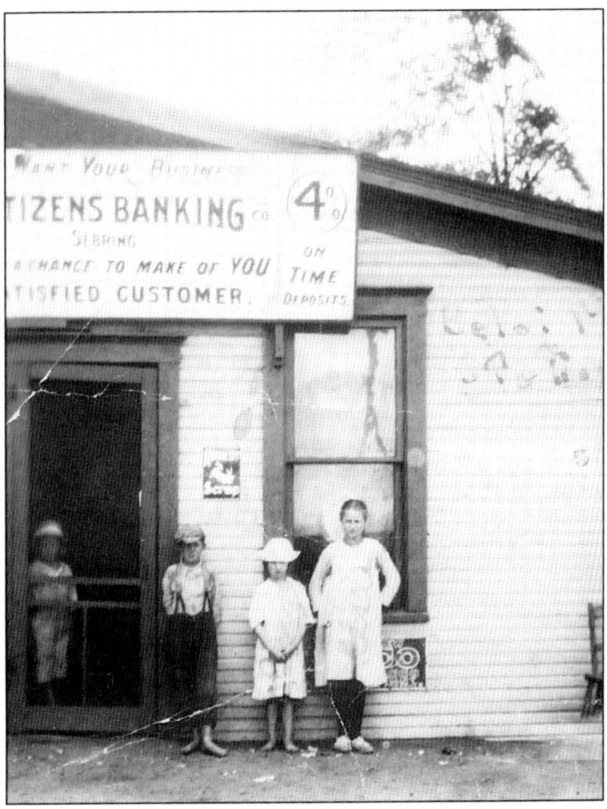

Margaret and Elsie Tetlow and the Cameron boy stand in front the Stark Electric streetcar station in Beloit. The small-frame structure was located just south of the railroad tracks.

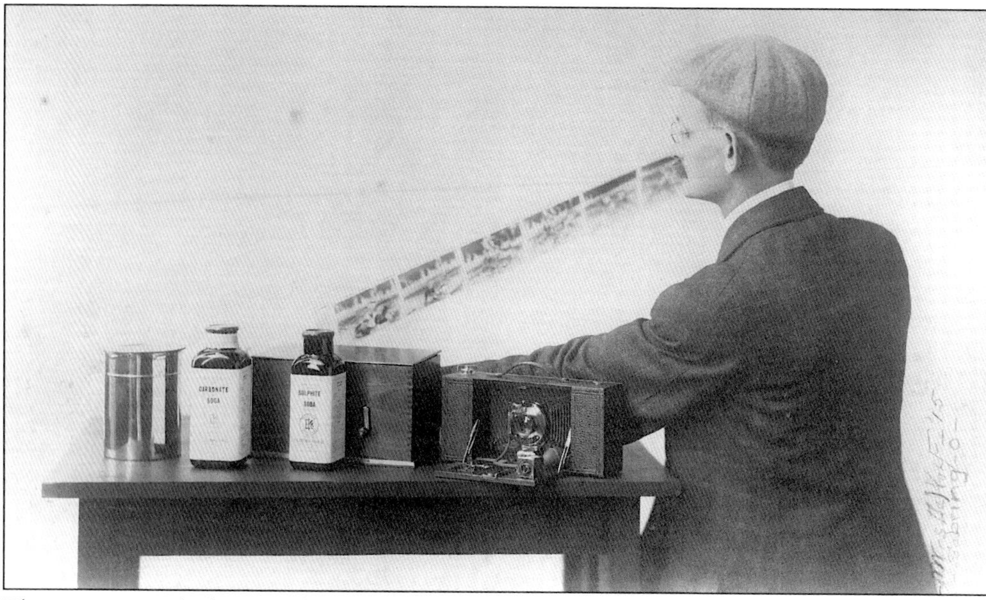

There are several photographers we can thank for preserving the events of our community's past. While the Dimit Brothers and Schoch Studio are two very important names, one of Sebring's most recognized is James W. DeWolf. Here we see him with his camera, chemicals, and negatives. How did he take this picture? Well, his wife snapped this shot. She signed it Mrs. DeWolf -'15 Sebring - O -.

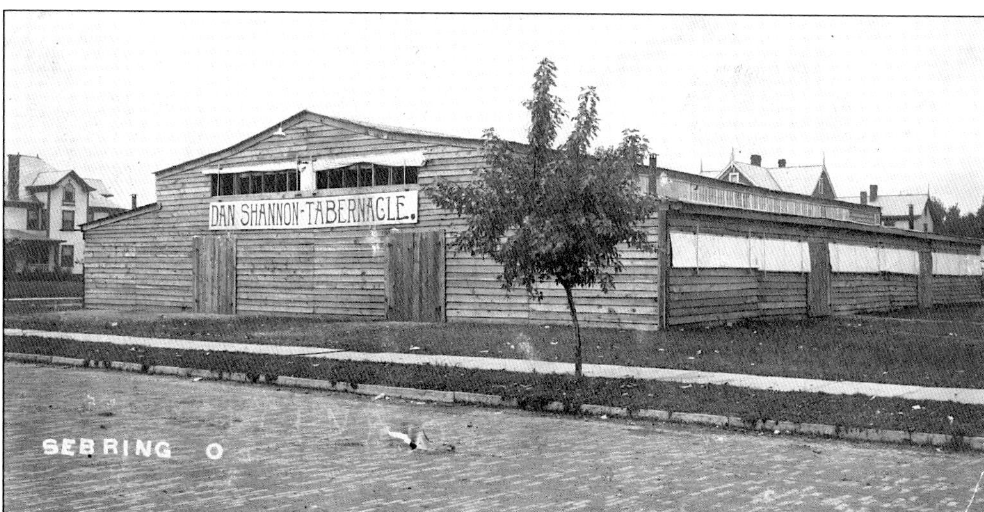

As mentioned in a previous chapter, religion played an important part in the development of Sebring, and between 1910 and 1930, evangelism was at its peak. At that time, Ammie Semple McPherson and Billy Sunday were household names. The Dan Shannon Tabernacle was located on the northeast corner of West Ohio Avenue and North Fifteenth Street. Hundreds of people from all over the area frequently gathered here for salvation.

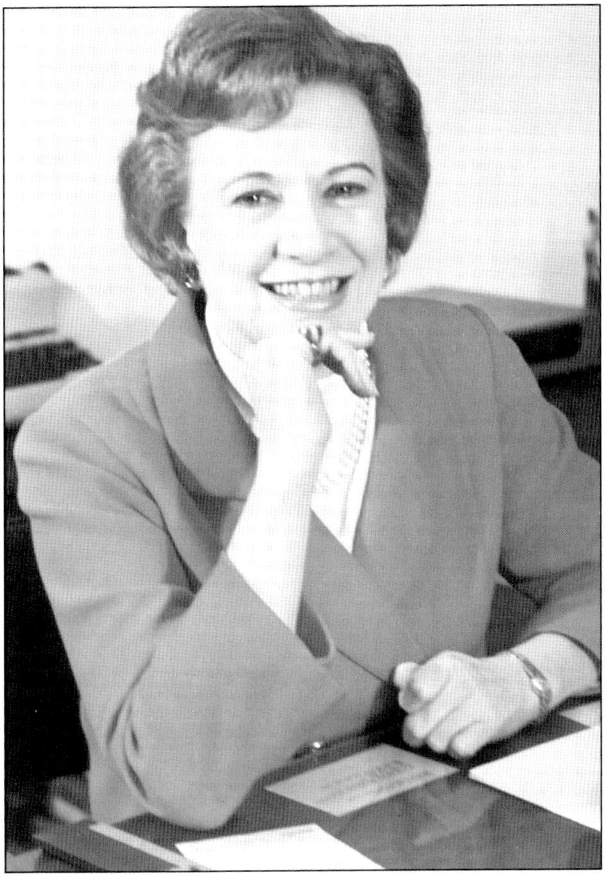

Devotion is the word connected to the name Rose Mary Woods. Born in Sebring on December 26, 1917, Miss Woods graduated from Sebring McKinley High School in 1935. Her first job was as a secretary at the Royal China Company. In 1943, she went to Washington, D.C., to take a position with the Office of Censorship. She worked for the International Trading Administration from 1945 to 1947, when she joined the Christian A. Herter's Committee on Foreign Aid, which was studying the Marshall Plan. Richard Nixon was a young Congressman on Herter's committee, and Miss Woods was impressed with Nixon's honesty and frugality as he was impressed with her competence and efficiency. In 1951, after working as a secretary with the Foreign Service Educational Foundation, she began her 23-year career as Richard Nixon's secretary. The late President Nixon wrote in his book *Six Crisis*: "that rare and unique characteristic that marks the difference between a good secretary and a great one—she is always at her best when the pressures are greatest." A 1973 *New York Times* article "Women in the News" profiled Miss Woods's career and dedication to Richard Nixon; however, she was more than a great secretary. In a sense, Rose Woods was Richard Nixon's link to the past, a person who has been with him through good times and bad. In the White House, where Mr. Nixon's principal advisors, Henry Kissinger and Alexander Haig Jr., were relatively recent acquaintances, she was the exception. She was a staff member who lived privately with the Nixon family and was someone who knew the Nixon daughters since they were children. She officially retired after Nixon left the White House, but she flew to California to help Nixon with his memoirs. She was named one of the 75 "Most Important Women in America" by *Ladies Home Journal* in 1971, while other distinguished women included Jacqueline Kennedy Onassis, Betty Friedan, and Barbra Streisand. The *Los Angeles Times* named her one of the ten "Women of the Year" in 1961.

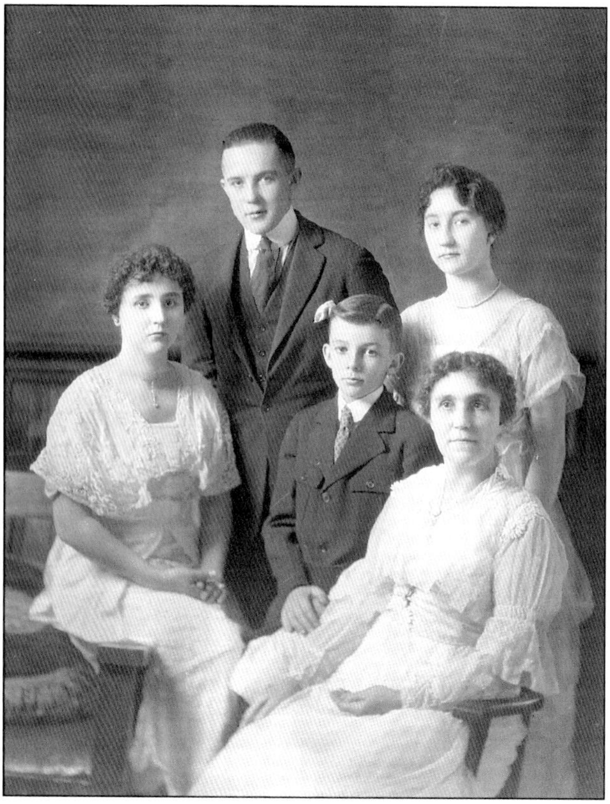

The family of the late Charles Albright posed for William Louis Koehne of Chicago in the 1920s. Mrs. Emma Albright was the daughter of George E. and Elizabeth Sebring Sr. and was a founder of Sebring, Ohio. Members of the Albright family are represented, from left to right, as follows: (seated) Mildred Albright Lindsey and Emma Sebring Albright Barcley; (standing) Donald Albright, Charles Albright Jr., and Lucille Albright McClure.

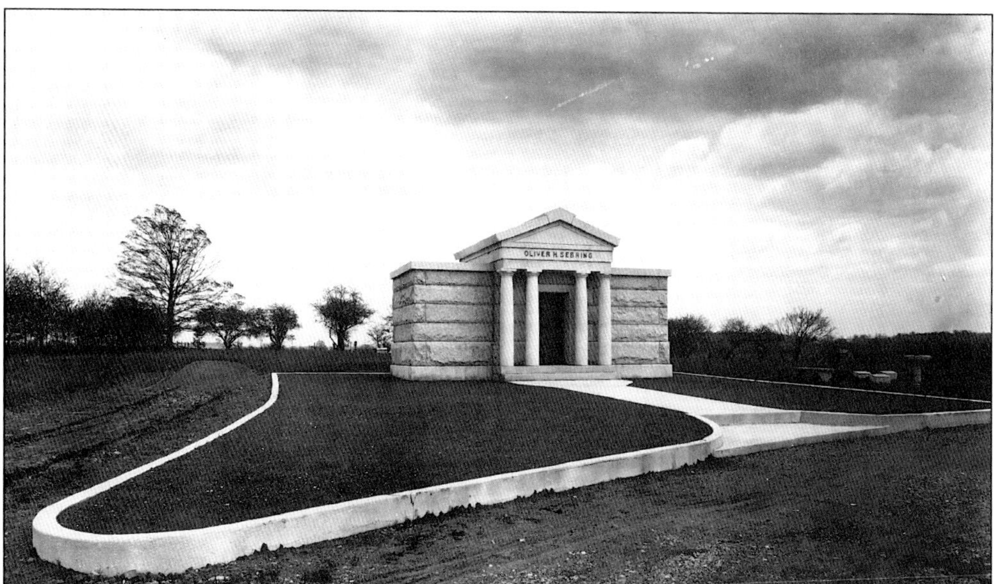

This photograph depicts the Oliver H. Sebring mausoleum shortly after its construction at Grandview Cemetery. The immediate family of Oliver Sebring are interred in this tomb, including his wife, Matilda Hume Sebring, son-in-law and daughter (Will and Annie Murphy).